DANCING
with the
WHEEL

DANCING
with the
WHEEL

....

The
Medicine
Wheel
Workbook

Sun Bear, Wabun Wind,
and Crysalis Mulligan

PRENTICE
HALL
PRESS

New York   London   Toronto   Sydney   Tokyo   Singapore

The authors wish to thank the following artists for their lovely work contained
within *Dancing with the Wheel:*

Thunderbird Woman (Erika Malitzky) for the art on pages xx, 4,15, 24, 31, 42, 48, 122, 146, 172, 174–192,
198 copyright © 1991 by Thunderbird Woman (Erika Malitzky)
Gwyn George for the art on pages 27–30, 82, 96, 100–102, 104, 108, 148–162, copyright © 1991
by Gwynn George
George Monacelli for the art on pages 8, 22, 40, 58, and 124–139 copyright © 1991 by George Monacelli
Mary Fallahay for the art on page 12, copyright © 1991 by Mary Fallahay
Pru See for the art on pages 70 and 92, copyright © 1991 by Pru See

PRENTICE HALL PRESS
15 Columbus Circle
New York, New York 10023

Library of Congress Cataloging-in-Publication Data

Sun Bear (Chippewa Indian)
    Dancing with the wheel: the medicine wheel workbook / Sun Bear.
    Wabun Wind, Crysalis Mulligan.
        p.   cm.
    Includes bibliographical references and indexes.
    ISBN 0-13-572843-6
    1. Indians of North America—Religion and mythology.
    2. Astrology. I. Wind, Wabun.   II. Mulligan, Crysalis.
    III. Title.
    E98.R3S924   1991
    299'.7—dc20
                                                                                                                    91-8169
                                                                                                                    CIP

Designed by Richard Oriolo

Printed on recycled paper.

Manufactured in the United States of America

10 9 8 7 6 5 4 3 2 1

First Edition

To Kyla Anna Eve Wind,
Yarrow Goding, Winona LaDuke Kapasheit,
Waseyabin, Aajuawak, Autumn Garry
—our next generation—and to
all generations to come.

Acknowledgments

The vision of the Medicine Wheel is an unfolding vision. Although it originally came to me, many people have added to it over the years. Wabun, my medicine helper and coauthor, has been instrumental in bringing this vision to the people. She has helped each step of the way, both by writing about my vision and by organizing the original Medicine Wheel Gatherings. Nimimosha and Thunderbird Woman did the art for the original Medicine Wheel circle and *Medicine Wheel Book,* and in that way added their artistic interpretations to the vision. All the people who have helped organize Medicine Wheel Gatherings and all those who have participated in them have also added their essential part to the sacred whole that is the Medicine Wheel. I would like to particularly acknowledge Wabun, Shawnodese, Glenn Schiffman, Donna Singing Pipe Woman, Jaya Bear, Randy North Star Ducharme, Jude Davis, Casey DuPree, Lou and Mary Kay DeSabla, Dawn Songfeather and all the individual Medicine Wheel Gathering organizers for their parts in arranging the first gatherings and in helping them to continue over the years. I also want to thank all the teachers and participants at the gatherings.

Shawnodese and Wabun, Elisabeth Turtle Heart, Nimimosha, Sandra Pathweaver, and all the Medicine Wheel consultants have helped the vision to grow by finding ways to help people locate their current positions on the wheel through Medicine Wheel consultations. With the help of Jaya Bear, Page Bryant, Scott Guynup, Nimimosha, Wabun, and Shawnodese we have developed the Earthstones, which are another way to allow people to understand themselves better by working with the Medicine Wheel. Elisabeth Turtle Heart is head of the Earthstone Institute, the organization that arranges for Medicine Wheel consultations for people who wish to know where they currently stand on the Medicine Wheel of their own life.

Wabun brings her knowledge of Medicine Wheel consultations, the Earthstones, and the Medicine Wheel Gatherings to this book, and thus makes it a much richer work because it is based on the true life experience of the many people with whom she's worked. Wabun thanks all those who have taken the Medicine Wheel consultation course and thus helped her in defining how the Medicine Wheel affects people in their daily lives.

Crysalis, our coauthor, has danced with the wheel in other ways. Through her love for the mineral and color kingdoms, she has found ways of building wheels that can help people heal on all levels of being. Through her understanding of the sensory and artistic aspect of life, she has devised ceremonies, to help people experience the wheel in a more complete manner, and ceremonial medicine tools, to allow them to bring their understanding into the physical realm. Crysalis brings her expertise in these areas to *Dancing with the Wheel.*

When we let people in the Medicine Wheel network know we were looking for art based on the original vision, we were overwhelmed with the response. Quite a number of people have been inspired to interpret my original vision artistically in all media: oils, acrylics, ink, beadwork, featherwork, wood, clay. Some of these artistic interpretations are found within this book.

We would like to specifically acknowledge and thank for their help with this book the following artists: Gwyn George, Thunderbird Woman, George Monacelli, Pru See, and Mary Fallahay. We would also like to thank Richard Oriolo, who did the overall design for the book, and Pru See for the cover work. Special thanks go to Kim Lawrence, for her help in preparing the manuscript and designing all the charts throughout the book. Thanks to Anderson Reed for her help with the mineral chapter and for her help to Wabun throughout the project. Thanks too to Rosemary Gladstar for sharing her immense knowledge of herbalism for the plant chapter. Thanks to Blue Camas and Helen Hogue for helping type the manuscript.

As always, I wish to thank those who are at the Bear Tribe for helping all of my visions unfold on a daily basis. I also want to acknowledge and thank all those who have read the original *Medicine Wheel Book,* and made the vision come alive as part of their daily lives. Each of you has been an important dancer in this vision.

Wabun would like to personally thank Shawnodese and Kyla for their love, support, and patience. And I would like to thank all of the people who are at the tribe and especially Jaya Bear.

A special acknowledgment to all of our relations in all of the kingdoms for their help with this book. The trees have been particularly inspirational and so we thank these stately members of the plant kingdom for being with us in this project and for being with us on the Earth Mother. We honor them by printing this book on recycled paper. May you tree beings long remain. To all of you who have participated and will participate in the Medicine Wheel vision, we give our acknowledgment and thanks. You are an important part of this vision, as you are an important part of what is happening on the Earth Mother right now. Always remember that, and be as gentle with yourself as you are with the rest of the creation.

—SUN BEAR
1990

I give acknowledgment and appreciation to Sun Bear and Wabun for their love, support, and confidence as well as special thanks to Shawnodese, Kyla, Kim Lawrence, Robyn, Andy and Peter Dunau, Blue Camas, Gary and Aurora Graham, Helen Hogue, John McKenna, Hilary, John and Raven Leal, the Wednesday night L.A. and Spokane pipe group, Annu, Pearl and Eric, Ed Averett, Marsha O'Neil, Melody and Will McNally, the Calloways, the Nufers, the Piestrups, the Culkys, the L.A. Moon Lodge, Maureen Mulligan, Jay, Ricky, Cori, Matt, Jill, Joshua, and those Mulligans who have been supportive.

I would like to express complete appreciation and warmth to Peter Nufer for his unfailing love and support in all that I do.

Deep-felt is my thanks to Spirit and all the mineral, plant, animal, and nature kingdoms for the opportunity to live each day to the fullest in contact with the beauty and life resonating all around us.

—CRYSALIS
1990

Contents

Part I
The Steps to the Dance

Part II
The Wheels

List of Visualizations, Exercises, and Ceremonies

Part I

The Steps to the Dance

Preface: Create the World You Like

The Medicine Wheel dance has had a strong beginning. In the late 1970s, Spirit gave me a powerful vision. In this vision I saw a hilltop bare of trees. A soft breeze was blowing, gently moving the prairie grass. I saw a circle of rocks that came out like the spokes of a wheel. Inside this large circle was another circle of rocks, nearer to the center. As I was looking at this vision I knew this was the Sacred Circle, the hoop of my people. Inside of the Center Circle was the buffalo skull, the skull of the Grandmother. I looked around me and saw coming up through ravines, from the four directions, what at first looked like animals. As they came closer, I saw that they were not animals but people wearing headdresses and costumes to honor the animal kingdom. They moved to the circle, entered it sunwise, and made a complete circle before they settled onto their proper place on the wheel.

First people settled in the place of the North, the place of the winter, the time of rest for ourselves and for the Earth Mother. The North represents the time when we have white hairs of snow upon our heads. This is the time when we prepare to change both worlds and forms. Other people went to the East, the place of awakening, of dawn, and of spring. The East is the place that represents mankind's birth and beginning. Next people settled in the South. The South is the time of summer, of the years of our fruitfulness, and of our most rapid growth. Still others continued until they came to the West. The West is the time of autumn, the time when we reap our harvest, when we have found the knowledge needed to center ourselves. The West is the home of the West Wind, Father of All the Winds.

The people I saw were singing the songs of their seasons, the songs of their minerals, their plants, their totem animals. Most important, they were singing songs for the healing of the Earth Mother. A leader among them was saying, "Let the Medicine of the sacred circle prevail. Let many people across the land come to this circle and make prayers for the healing of the Earth Mother. Let the circles of the Medicine Wheel come back."

I saw in this vision people from all the clans, from all the directions; people representing all the totems. I saw that in their hearts they carried peace.

That is my original vision, a vision that I knew had to be fulfilled.

I shared what I had seen with Wabun and with other members of the Bear Tribe. I knew this was a vision that had to become reality on the physical plane. The world being as it is today, I needed the printed word to bring this vision to the people. First Wabun and I wrote the words for the Medicine Wheel Circle, which contains the essence of my vision. We had it printed and started making it available to people. One of the people with the tribe sent a copy of the Medicine Wheel Circle to Oscar Collier, Wabun's literary agent who was then working as an editor at Prentice Hall. The Medicine Wheel Circle arrived on his birthday. He felt that the information contained in the circle gave him a whole new understanding of life, one that he thought should be shared with other people. He contacted us and asked whether we would be willing to write a book based on my Medicine Wheel vision. We agreed. In 1980, that book was first published.

By the time I write this in 1990, it is probable that close to 1 million people in the world have danced with the Medicine Wheel of my original vision.

The power of the vision I was originally given continues to grow. People are building wheels all over the world. Untold thousands of wheels now exist because of this vision. The *Medicine Wheel Book* is published in English, German, French, Spanish, Dutch, Greek, Hebrew, Danish, Japanese, and Turkish. In Europe, people are dancing around the Medicine Wheels. Isn't it amazing that the vision of one Native American has spread across the Great Water to affect so greatly the descendants of those who once crossed that water to take Turtle Island from its Earthkeepers? Doesn't this in itself teach something about the power of this great wheel?

The Medicine Wheel is a springboard of power that will allow you to link up with all the energies of the universe. It is a place where the great teachers of knowledge will gather to share with each other and the people. The Medicine Wheel is a place where we can speak of medicine to heal our sick, of ways to produce food to feed the hungry, of methods to house the homeless, and of means to teach people to find a balance in their lives and harmony with the earth.

The Medicine Wheel is the sacred hoop of the nations. For the world to come back into real balance the nations must be healed. For this healing to occur there can no longer be war between nations because one nation covets the wealth or territory of another. There can no longer be hate over religion or race.

If we want to have a better world, people must be in balance and harmony. The world is made up of people along with the rest of the creation. It is the people on the earth who are out of balance and who need to right their relationship with the rest of creation. The sacred Medicine Wheel can teach proper balance.

In this book we give you a deeper understanding of how to connect with the powers of creation. The Medicine Wheel has always been an earth teaching. It does not take you out to the stars. Rather it brings you down to earth. In the

Native teachings we acknowledge that all parts of the creation are our relations because we all live on the same Earth Mother and get water, air, food, fuel, and shelter from her. So we are all related.

The native people think of minerals, plants, and animals as all having certain powers. We refer to these other beings as our relations and as our totems. We know each species has a protector spirit. When we need help we pray for that protector spirit to help us. We see the universe as having both a visible and invisible world. The visible world is all we see around us and the invisible world is that of the spirit beings who are placed here to oversee everything on the planet. These spirits work with the Creator and they are available to help humanity.

By doing ceremonies—like those having to do with the Medicine Wheel—you get in touch with these spirits. A ceremony is a way for humans to center their energy and connect with these spirit powers who can help heal both humans and the earth.

Many powerful things have happened to let me know the spirits are reaching out and saying that now is definitively the time to return to the Medicine Wheel. In Europe and England many "mysterious" circles have appeared in the middle of the fields. Now these circles are appearing in the United States. These are spirit circles created by powers beyond our understanding to tell us that now is the time to return to the way of the Medicine Wheel.

So many people have danced with the wheel. For some this has been a brief whirl; for others a dance that has profoundly changed their whole lives. As with all dances, the steps change a little with each dancer. Some people have danced with the wheel so powerfully that their steps have added richness and variety to the original vision. That is all good.

But times are changing. The earth changes are becoming more intense. The earth needs more of her children to take their rightful positions as her keepers. To do this we must have an ever-increasing commitment to the earth and an ever-growing understanding of her needs. As the earth changes, so must we.

The Medicine Wheel is an important tool for these times. By learning about the wheel, we learn about the universe. Through traveling around the wheel, we bring life-giving changes into our own lives and into the world.

Dancing with the Wheel does more than bring you up to date with how my original vision has unfolded. This book gives you important new information that will help you to use the Medicine Wheel as a life tool, whether you are an old hand at earth dancing or someone who is just beginning to hear the earth's song.

Often as I've traveled and taught about the Medicine Wheel, people have asked me for more ways in which to make the wheel part of their daily lives. *Dancing with the Wheel* answers that request.

I hope that through this book you can better understand the Medicine Wheel and the sacred law of relationship. As each of us learns how to live in a sacred manner, how to walk in a way harmonious with all the creation, we put our steps on the path of love and harmony. When enough people on the planet are walking on that path, then we will have a better world.

This I have spoken.

—SUN BEAR
1990

Part I

THE STEPS
TO THE
DANCE

The Medicine Wheel—by Thunderbird Woman

1

The Dance Begins

To enjoy dancing with the wheel you must first learn the steps to the dance. Like most earth-based ceremonies and tools, the Medicine Wheel appears to be simple. After all, it is merely a structure of thirty-six stones. Yet there are untold levels of meaning to this simple circle and the lines within the circle. *Dancing with the Wheel* is a step-by-step guide to these levels.

To understand the Medicine Wheel dance you must first know that the Medicine Wheel of this vision is similar to the 20,000 Medicine Wheels that existed on this continent before the European people immigrated here. These Medicine Wheels served many purposes for the Native people of the Americas. They were the ceremonial centers of culture, astronomical laboratories, and places people would come to mark the times and changes in their own lives as well as the life of the earth. They were places to pray, meditate, contemplate, strengthen your connection with nature, and come to a higher degree of understanding of yourself and your relationship with all the creation. Medicine Wheels were usually placed on areas where the energy of the earth could be strongly felt, and their use in ceremony made this energy get even stronger. Consequently, Medicine Wheel areas became what people now call vortexes: places of intense earth energy and healing. The new areas where Medicine Wheels have been built are serving the same function.

The Medicine Wheel

1. Creator
2. Earth Mother
3. Father Sun
4. Grandmother Moon
5. Turtle
6. Frog
7. Thunderbird
8. Butterfly
9. Waboose
10. Wabun
11. Shawnodese
12. Mudjekeewis
13. Snow Goose
14. Otter
15. Cougar
16. Red Hawk
17. Beaver
18. Deer
19. Flicker
20. Sturgeon
21. Brown Bear
22. Raven
23. Snake
24. Elk
25. Cleansing
26. Renewal
27. Purity
28. Clarity
29. Wisdom
30. Illumination
31. Growth
32. Trust
33. Love
34. Experience
35. Introspection
36. Strength

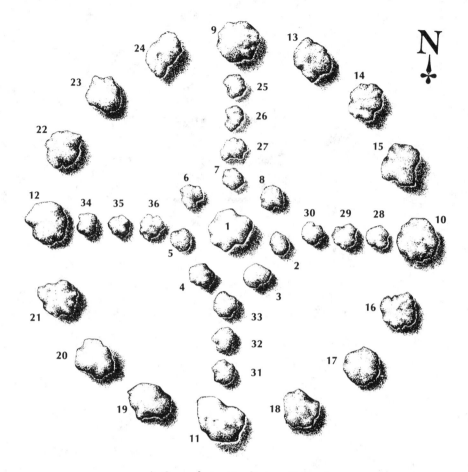

A Complete Medicine Wheel

Forms of the Medicine Wheel exist all around the globe from the great stone circles of Europe to the mandalas of India. All of these are reminders of our past when the world was guided by the law of right relationship, and humans respected themselves and all their relations—mineral, plant, animal, spirit—on the Earth Mother. Learning about the Medicine Wheel can help you remember your connection with all these aspects of the universe. Each stone in the Medicine Wheel is a tool to help you understand your ties with the ancient past that molds both personal and planetary present and future. Each position in the Medicine Wheel will directly affect you at some point in your life.

The Creator stone, or symbol, is the center of the Medicine Wheel as the Creator is the center of all life, always creating without beginning or ending, always moving, always continuing. From this center radiates the energy that creates all the rest of the wheel. The seven stones that surround the Creator form the Center Circle of the wheel and represent the foundation of all life. Slightly to the south of East is the stone that represents the Earth Mother, the being who gives us our home and our lives. Continuing in a sunwise (clockwise) direction—as we almost always do in building and using the Medicine Wheel— is the stone honoring Father Sun who warms and quickens life. Next comes the stone for Grandmother Moon who guides our dreams and visions, followed by the Turtle clan stone, representing the element of earth; the Frog clan, representing the element of water; the Thunderbird clan, representing the element of fire; and the Butterfly clan representing the element of air. These seven stones teach about the basic building blocks of all life.

The anchor stones for the outer circle of the Medicine Wheel are the four stones honoring the Spirit Keepers: Waboose in the North; Wabun in the East; Shawnodese in the South; Mudjekeewis in the West. These Spirit Keeper stones divide the circle into the quadrants that set the boundaries for the twelve moon stones in the outer circle. These stones represent the moons that divide the year. From them we learn more about each season; each time of day and time of life; and each mineral, plant, animal, elemental clan, Spirit Keeper, and human associated with that moon.

Completing the Medicine Wheel are four Spirit Paths, each consisting of three stones. These paths go from the Spirit Keeper stones toward the Center Circle. They represent qualities that take us from daily life into the sacred space of the Creator.

That simple physical description of the Medicine Wheel provides you with the first basic steps for dancing with the wheel. But to really understand the wheel, your comprehension must surpass the physical and the intellectual. You can never dance well if you are always thinking about where to place your feet. To dance you need to listen to the music and allow that music to be a part of your body and being. That takes time and practice. When you are ready to begin, use the following simple technique, the first of many that will help you dance with the wheel.

Throughout the book, these techniques are called visualizations or an exercise. These provide ways for you to mentally see, feel, and imagine yourself and your life as something different from what it is now. All visualizations and exercises, if treated with respect, can be done as ceremonies that are ways for you to connect your energy with the energy of the universe and to thank the universe, and all of its parts, for the gift of life.

HEARING THE EARTH'S SONG

What you need. A quiet space and, if desired, notebook and pen or tape recorder.

Estimated time. Ten minutes at first, five when you have done this visualization a few times.

1. Sit comfortably in a chair, or on the floor, or lie down. Take a few really deep breaths, allowing your breath to go through as much of your body as it can.
2. Close your eyes. Relax your jaw and stomach.
3. Be aware that the earth is beneath you even if you are on the fiftieth floor of a skyscraper. Feel your energy connecting with the energy of the earth.
4. When you are relaxed and feel connected, just listen.
5. Do you hear something? Faintly at first then louder you will hear a beat that sounds like a drum.
6. What is it? Listen closer. *Tum, tum, tum, tum.* The drumbeat you hear first is the beat of your own heart. Listen longer.
7. *Tum . . . tum . . . tum . . . tum . . .* goes a slower drumbeat. You feel your heart slow to beat with this new music and you feel yourself deeply relaxed, deeply connected to the source of this music: the Earth Mother.
8. Enjoy the music, enjoy the few moments in sacred space.
9. When you are ready, come back to your normal reality.
10. Take a moment to feel any differences in your body, to sense changes in your perception.
11. If you wish, write down or record your reactions.

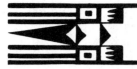 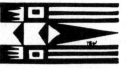

Medicine Wheel
Reference Chart

The Center

Stone Number	Name of Stone	Element	Mineral	Plant
1	Creator	All or Any	All or Any	All or Any
2	Earth Mother	Earth	Clay	Corn, Beans, Squash
3	Father Sun	Fire & Air	Geode	Sunflower
4	Grandmother Moon	Water	Moonstone	Mugwort
5	Turtle Clan	Earth	Petrified Wood	Cattails
6	Frog Clan	Water	River Rock	Algae
7	Thunderbird Clan	Fire	Lava Rock	Fireweed
8	Butterfly Clan	Air	Azurite	Butterfly Weed

The Spirit

Stone Number	Name of Stone	Element	Mineral	Plant
9	Waboose (North)	Earth	Alabaster	Sweetgrass
10	Wabun (East)	Air	Pipestone	Tobacco
11	Shawnodese (South)	Water	Serpentine	Sagebrush
12	Mudjekeewis (West)	Fire	Soapstone	Cedar

The Moons

	Stone Number	Dates	Name of Moon	Mineral	Plant
North	13	Dec. 22-Jan.19	Earth Renewal	Quartz	Birch
North	14	Jan. 20-Feb. 18	Rest & Cleansing	Silver	Quaking Aspen
North	15	Feb.19-March 20	Big Winds	Turquoise	Plantain
East	16	March 21-April 19	Budding Trees	Fire Opal	Dandelion
East	17	April 20-May 20	Frogs Return	Chrysocolla	Blue Camas
East	18	May 21-June 20	Cornplanting	Moss Agate	Yarrow
South	19	June 21-July 22	Strong Sun	Carnelian Agate	Wild Rose
South	20	July 23-Aug. 22	Ripe Berries	Garnet & Iron	Raspberry
South	21	Aug. 23-Sept. 22	Harvest	Amethyst	Violet
West	22	Sept. 23-Oct. 23	Ducks Fly	Jasper	Mullein
West	23	Oct. 24-Nov. 21	Freeze Up	Copper & Malachite	Thistle
West	24	Nov. 22-Dec. 21	Long Snows	Obsidian	Black Spruce

The Spirit

Stone Number	Name of Quality	Position	Mineral	Plant
25	Cleansing	Outer North	Sodalite	Echinacea
26	Renewal	Middle North	Peridoto	Red Clover
27	Purity	Inner North	Herkimer Diamond	Trillium
28	Clarity	Outer East	Mica	Rosemary
29	Wisdom	Middle East	Jade	Sage
30	Illumination	Inner East	Calcite	Wild American Ginseng
31	Growth	Outer South	Fluorite	Comfrey
32	Trust	Middle South	Lapidilite	Borage
33	Love	Inner South	Rose Quartz	Hawthorne
34	Experience	Outer West	Hematite	Olive
35	Introspection	Middle West	Lapis Lazuli	Chamomile
36	Strength	Inner West	Amber	Nettle

N

E

S

W

Medicine Wheel
Reference Chart

Circle

Animal	Color
All or Any	All or Any
Tortoise	Forest Green
Lizard	Sky Blue
Loon	Silver/White
Turtle	Green/Brown
Frog	Blue/Green
Thunderbird	Red
Butterfly	Translucent w/Blue

G
B
R

Keepers

	Animal	Color	Season	Time of Day	Time of Life
N	White Buffalo	White	Winter	Midnight	Elder & Newborn
E	Golden Eagle	Gold & Red	Spring	Dawn	Child
S	Coyote	Yellow & Green	Summer	Midday	Adolescent & Young Adult
W	Grizzly Bear	Blue & Black	Autumn	Twilight	Adult

and Totems

Animal	Color	Spirit Keeper	Complement	Elemental Clan
Snow Goose	White	Waboose	Flicker	Turtle
Otter	Silver	Waboose	Sturgeon	Butterfly
Cougar	Turquoise	Waboose	Brown Bear	Frog

Animal	Color	Spirit Keeper	Complement	Elemental Clan
Red Hawk	Yellow	Wabun	Raven	Thunderbird
Beaver	Blue	Wabun	Snake	Turtle
Deer	White & Green	Wabun	Elk	Butterfly

Animal	Color	Spirit Keeper	Complement	Elemental Clan
Flicker	Pink	Shawnodese	Snow Goose	Frog
Sturgeon	Red	Shawnodese	Otter	Thunderbird
Brown Bear	Purple	Shawnodese	Cougar	Turtle

Animal	Color	Spirit Keeper	Complement	Elemental Clan
Raven	Brown	Mudjekeewis	Red Hawk	Butterfly
Snake	Orange	Mudjekeewis	Beaver	Frog
Elk	Black	Mudjekeewis	Deer	Thunderbird

Paths

	Animal	Color
N	Raccoon	Pale Green
	Earthworm	Dark Green
	Dolphin	Translucent White
	Hummingbird	Clear
E	Owl	Jade Green
	Firefly	Fluorescent Blue
	Rabbit	Violet
	Salmon	Lavender
S	Wolf	Rose
	Whale	Steel Grey
W	Mouse	Royal Blue
	Ant	Golden Yellow

Hearing the Earth's song can give you a whole new understanding of the Medicine Wheel because when you become aware of this music you begin to understand the law of relationship: Each of us is deeply connected to everything that exists, each of us is a critical part of the sacred Medicine Wheel of life.

The law of relationship is a natural law, a real law that is absolutely critical to these times when we have lost our sense of balance, our sense of connectedness with all that is life. The Medicine Wheel can help you regain some of what you have lost.

The Medicine Wheel will help you understand your real relationship with all of the beings on the earth: the elements, the plants, the animals, the humans, the spirits. These beings can teach you about many other layers of the wheel. In *The Medicine Wheel* book we introduced you to the mineral, plant, and animal totems for the twelve stones representing the times of the year. In *Dancing with the Wheel* we introduce you to the totems for all the positions of the wheel and tell you what each totem has to teach you about life and about relationship.

As you learn the steps of this dance and hear the music more clearly, you may desire ways to honor your new relationship with life. Through respect for the correct use of ceremony you will find them. Ceremony that brings you into a deeper relationship with the earth is an important part of the Medicine Wheel. So are exercises and visualizations to help you gain a personal understanding of all the elements of the wheel. You will find such exercises throughout the book.

After you have learned about ceremony and the different individual aspects of the wheel it is likely some of you will want to build a wheel so you can experience its energy. In *The Medicine Wheel* we gave basic instructions for building a wheel; in this book we will give more detailed instructions for building a basic Medicine Wheel, and we will tell you how to build various kinds of Medicine Wheels: ones to experience specific mineral energies, to honor trees, to honor the element of fire, and one you can use when traveling.

When you have explored these aspects of the Medicine Wheel you will be ready to experience how the wheel can teach you about your own life. Although you have a basic position upon the wheel determined by your time of birth, you do not remain in that one position for your entire life. Everyone travels around the Medicine Wheel, experiencing life from as many of the positions as possible. This means it is likely that at various times you will act, think, and feel like a person born under one or all of the other eleven moon positions. Being able to discern your movement, to know which positions are influencing you at a given time, will help you understand yourself and another layer of the wheel.

Experiencing other positions on the Medicine Wheel is not strictly a matter of chance. It is possible for you to move purposely to another position when you need to understand the life lessons that position represents. Throughout the book we encourage you to seek a certain stone if you are striving to balance yourself in a particular way. This is because each stone represents many layers of life. Being near a particular Medicine Wheel stone, either physically or in imagination, can help bring balance to different aspects of your being.

In your movement around the wheel you are likely to experience times when the element of change affects you more than anything else. These are times when you are under the influence of the thirteenth moon, the invisible moon missing from our calendar-oriented world. Understanding the thirteenth moon and how it influences your life will shift your world view, adding a new dimension to your feelings about life and vastly increasing your self-understanding.

When you understand the physical and ceremonial aspects of the Medicine

Wheel and how this simple circle affects your life, you will be almost ready to do some powerful dancing. Before you begin you might wish to create some new tools to help you in your dance: pouches, jewelry, rattles, wands, staffs, shields, and masks. The ceremonies of creating these are another level of the wheel.

With your new tools you are ready to dive from the springboard of the Medicine Wheel into the water of healing, both of yourself and of the earth. From healing ceremonies connected with the Medicine Wheel you will understand even more of the sacred circle of life and the power of the wheel.

When we help people prepare to go to the earth to cry for their vision we always remind them that the vision is not just for themselves. A true vision is one that will benefit all of your relations on the Earth Mother, not just humans but all the beings in all the kingdoms.

When you have experienced enough of the Medicine Wheel to truly understand your power for healing you are ready to go to the second section of *Dancing with the Wheel.* In this section we turn our attention to each of the kingdoms with which we share the earth. Because so many of us live in environments where we spend most of our time with people we need to familiarize ourselves with the representatives of the mineral, plant, animal, and color beings honored as part of the Medicine Wheel. From knowledge about these beings and how they connect with the wheel you will learn how to gain respect for all of our relations on the earth and learn both how to heal and be healed by these other children of the earth.

The Mineral Wheel, the Plant Wheel, the Animal Wheel, and the Color Wheel are all critical layers of the Medicine Wheel. By looking at each one separately you will gain a naturalist's appreciation and a healer's understanding of your relations in each of these kingdoms.

To make the healing energies of the wheel readily accessible during times of distress *Dancing with the Wheel* concludes with quick reference charts for the mineral, plant, animal, and color wheels; a listing of different states of human imbalance; and the proper place on the wheel to go to seek balance.

Most chapters of the book contain exercises to help your understanding of the wheel surpass the intellectual. Although a mental knowing will increase your ability to dance with the wheel, true mastery will only come when you can *feel* this knowledge, not just think it. Each exercise begins with a list of items you will need and an estimation of the minimum time required. Because it is impossible to read and do the exercise at the same time, you might wish to record the exercise and then follow from the recording. Tapes are also available to guide you through the exercises. More information about these is included at the end of the book.

Dancing with the Wheel is a comprehensive guide to the Medicine Wheel and to ways in which you can personally help to create a beautiful, balanced world. You will gain the most benefit from this book if you read it in its entirety first, then return to the beginning and reread the chapters and do the exercises in the order in which they appear. Remember the reference charts in part II if you need help quickly.

Let the dance begin.

**Waboose—Spirit Keeper of the North
—by George Monacelli**

2

Ceremonies and Respect

If you live life in a harmonious way, always respecting the sacred circle and all other beings in it, every step you take can be a ceremony that celebrates your connection with the Creator. If you live in this way you realize you, like the Medicine Wheel, are a tool of life guided by the Creator that is within you and around you.

Most people must learn this way of life because so much of what they have been taught has separated them from the sacredness that surrounds them. The Medicine Wheel can be an important teacher of this life view.

Throughout this book are exercises and ceremonies to help you find your connection with the Creator and all of earth's children. For these to be as helpful as possible, you must approach them with respect. Sometimes people new to ceremony and to the circle of life feel unsure about how to show their respect. Earth ceremonies seem alien to them. They want to participate fully, but they don't know how to begin.

The most important thing to remember about ceremony is that it is a way for humans to give back to the creation some of the energy that they are always receiving. The Earth Mother constantly gives us two-leggeds a surface on which to place our feet; Father Sun warms us; and Grandmother Moon brings dreams. The element of earth gives us a place to grow food and the ability to make homes and tools. The water keeps us alive. The fire warms our homes and cooks our food. The air gives us the sacred breath of life. Each part of the Medicine Wheel, each part of life, is constantly giving gifts to us humans.

Through ceremony, we learn how to give back. When we sing, we give energy through our voice; when we drum, we allow the earth's heartbeat to join with our own; when we dance, we bring the energy of earth and sky together in our bodies and give it out; when we pray, we give energy through our hearts; when we look upon our relations, we give blessings through our eyes. When we put all these activities together, we have a ceremony, one of the most powerful forms of gift-giving we humans possess.

Ancient peoples knew the importance of ceremony. Throughout the year they would celebrate different parts of the earth through this vehicle. They would have seasonal ceremonies, deer dances, strawberry festivals, corn festivals, bear dances, full moon ceremonies, and thanksgiving celebrations. These were not arbitrary events, rather they were well-planned ways of keeping the balance of the sacred circle.

When humans participate in ceremony they enter a sacred space. Everything outside of that space shrivels in importance. Time takes on a different dimension. Emotions flow more freely. The bodies of participants become filled with the energy of life, and this energy reaches out and blesses the creation around them. All is made new; everything becomes sacred.

This giveaway and rebirth is the core of all ceremonies, whether a school graduation or a Medicine Wheel Gathering.

To get to the core you must approach ceremony with understanding, respect, and gentleness toward yourself and all the creation. All of the Medicine Wheel ceremonies we share are ones designed to help you improve your relationship with the creation, to give you the healing and help you need. They are all ceremonies and exercises to help promote the highest good of all those involved with them.

The ceremonies in this book are ones that are self-generated: ones that have come to us in our own visions, dreams, or meditations. Self-generated ceremonies seem most appropriate for people learning about ceremony and their relationship with the earth. This type of ceremony allows one to have a good framework to which he can add components that come to him in his own intuitive work.

Self-generated ceremonies are very different from traditional ceremonies. Traditional ceremonies, like the pipe ceremony or the sweat lodge, have been handed down through generations of Native peoples. In traditional ceremony it is imperative that the ceremony is done in an exact way. Many traditional ceremonies can call some very powerful spirit helpers. These helpers must be treated in the appropriate manner.

The only way to learn traditional ceremonies is to study with a medicine person who knows them. The only time to perform traditional ceremonies is when that medicine person has given you specific permission to do so. Traditional ceremonies should never be changed on the whim of a person doing them or combined with other ceremony or vision. Doing so is not for the highest good of anyone. It is critical that people interested in the traditional ways of Earth People show respect for them and for their traditions. Lack of respect for these ceremonies can cause serious problems for all concerned. If you are not sure whether a ceremony is traditional or self-generated, ask the person doing it. If you feel drawn to that ceremony ask if you can learn it and what is required in this learning. Some traditional ceremonies require a long and arduous apprenticeship.

When you first become involved in ceremonies you might be tempted to try to speed your learning so that you can provide healing to people and the earth as quickly as possible. That is not a good idea. Part of being gentle with yourself in ceremony is going slowly.

Ceremony is a wonderful teacher of patience. In some ceremonies contained in this book you might find yourself standing or sitting for hours with very little happening on the physical plane. You might be hearing repetitive drumming or chanting. At first you will probably become restless or impatient, hoping that the ceremonial leader will get on with it. But if you allow yourself to relax into the music or the movement you might find that it is this very repetition that carries you into the sacred space. It is when you still your restless mind that the powers of the Medicine Wheel can come to you.

Other than the restlessness—and some possible physical discomfort from standing, sitting, or dancing—none of the ceremonies contained in this book should make you feel uncomfortable. If you are doing a ceremony and you feel a churning in your stomach or a tightening of your solar plexus, be wary. If this ever happens it is best to stop, cleanse yourself, and cease whatever it was you were doing. There are a lot of spirit helpers in the ethers and some of them can be more mischievous or harmful than helpful. If you feel in doubt about the energies of a place or of a ceremony, stop and tell the spirits that you don't want anything to do with them. If you just say no firmly, they won't bother you.

If you are working with a teacher, ask them what occurred. If you are working on your own, contemplate the experience until understanding comes. Usually you will find that you have become careless in your methods or that you were pushing to go too quickly. The slower you approach ceremony, the better you will become at doing it. Wait until you understand one step in a ceremony before you proceed to another. Wait until you are proficient at doing one ceremony before you learn or generate more.

When you are doing ceremonies, keep reminding yourself that you are not the one bringing healing or help. You are the tool of the Creator who is sending health and help through you to some of your relations on the earth. Remembering this will give you the proper perspective for any ceremonies you might do.

Like most events in life, ceremony has a beginning, a middle, and an end. However, the end is the beginning of another ceremony. The circle continues, just as it does with all things.

Most ceremonies begin with some form of cleansing. Smudging is the form most often used in earth ceremonies and is often used in ceremonies of other religions, from the incensing of the Orient to the frankincensing of the Catholic church. Smudging uses the smoke from burning herbs to cleanse the energy field of a person, place, or thing. Smoke is an etheric substance that penetrates between the realms of creation from the dense to the more subtle.

The herbs most often used for smudging are the plants of the Spirit Keepers: sweet grass of the North; tobacco of the East; sagebrush of the South; and cedar of the West. Sweet grass calls in the positive energies, tobacco absorbs either positive or negative, sagebrush drives out negativity, and cedar cleanses. You may also add many of the other Medicine Wheel plants to your smudge mixture. Using the plant will help to call in the power it represents.

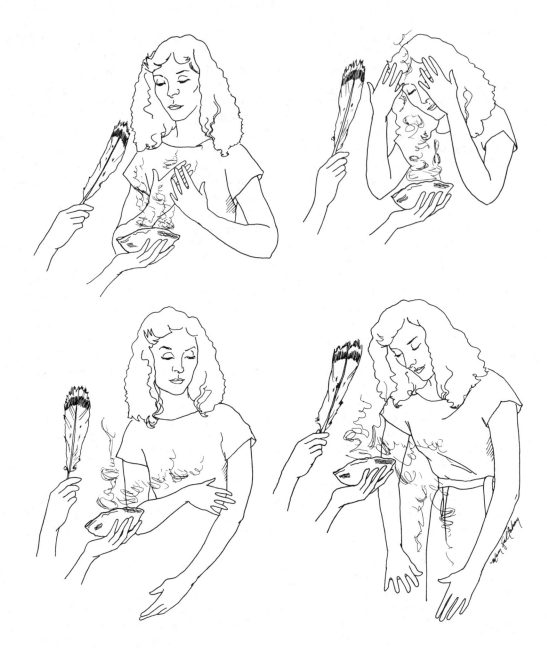

THE SMUDGING CEREMONY

What you need. Sage, sweet grass, cedar, or tobacco, singly or in combination, or other Medicine Wheel herbs; a shell or bowl; a fan or feather; and matches.

Estimated Time. Five minutes alone, more time if with a group.

1. Mix together the plants you will be using, place them in a shell or sturdy bowl, and light them.
2. When they are burning, use a fan or feather from a domestically raised bird (chicken, turkey, pheasant, or duck) to put out the flame. Throughout the ceremony you will need to intermittently fan the herbs to keep them smoldering.

3. Once the herbs are smoldering draw the smoke (not the bowl, just the smoke) to your heart, then over your head, down your arms, and down the front of your body then the back of your body toward the ground. If you need special balancing or healing in some part of your body you can emphasize by pulling the smoke there.

4. It is your responsibility to cleanse your own energy field. The plants help. They do not do it for you.

5. Next offer smoke to the six directions: up to the Creator, down to the Earth Mother, North to Waboose, East to Wabun, South to Shawnodese, and West to Mudjekeewis.

6. After you have smudged yourself and offered the smudge you can hold the bowl while other people present smudge.

7. You may then walk around the area you will be using, wafting smoke. If you are inside, smudge around the walls of the room paying particular attention to the corners.

8. Smudge any medicine tools you will be using in the ceremony.

Other Methods of Cleansing

Although smudging is most often used as a cleansing method in Medicine Wheel ceremonies, there are occasions when another way of cleansing is appropriate. If you are doing a fire ceremony you may offer herbs to the fire and then smudge yourself with the smoke from the fire.

If you are doing a ceremony related to water, Grandmother Moon, or the Frog clan—and circumstances permit—you can cleanse yourself by submerging in water to the point where the water covers the crown of your head. Duck yourself once briefly to cleanse yourself, once to cleanse for your family, and once to cleanse your relationship with the Creator.

You can also cleanse yourself with sound. Use a rattle or drum and smudge yourself with the sound beginning at your head and going to your feet. Afterward flick off any energy clinging to the instrument and ground this energy in the earth.

CENTERING YOURSELF
■■■■■

There are many ways to center yourself in a ceremony. Using one of them is critical because the more centered you are the more powerful the ceremony will be. Basically any centering technique helps to bring all your energy together, allowing you to let go of the everyday world and thus enter the sacred space.

Some of the ways we often use to center energy is to drum, rattle, and/or chant.

CENTERING YOURSELF THROUGH DRUMMING

What you need. A drum and drumstick and, if desired, chanting or drumming tapes and a tape recorder.

Estimated Time. Fifteen minutes minimum.

Drumming is most effective when you know your drum well. This means that you should set aside time to practice drumming as often as possible.

1. To begin drumming you should quiet yourself and listen to your own heartbeat.
2. Begin to drum your heartbeat on the drum.
3. As your heartbeat shifts, allow your drumming to change.
4. Do not try to change the drumbeat rapidly. A slow, repetitive beat is most effective for centering.
5. If your drumming is accompanying a chant, listen to the chant first. Make the drumbeat complement the chant, not compete with it. Under no circumstances should you drown out the chant with the drum.
6. You can become more proficient at drumming by listening to chanting or drumming tapes and drumming along with them.
7. At the end of a chant you make several rapid beats, which serve the purpose of sending the song out to spirit and announcing the song is completed.

CENTERING YOURSELF THROUGH RATTLING

What you need. A rattle.

Estimated time. Fifteen minutes minimum.

To learn to rattle, follow the same instructions given for drumming. It is more difficult to get a heartbeat sound with many rattles, so go even more slowly in your learning process.

CENTERING YOURSELF THROUGH CHANTING

What you need. Your voice, knowledge of the chant, and, if desired, chanting or drumming tape and tape recorder, rattle, or drum.

Estimated time. Fifteen minutes minimum.

When you chant properly you take the energy of the earth in through your body, magnify it, and send it out to all of your relations on the planet. This means that you should feel the chant throughout your body, not just in your throat. It should cause a vibration that touches all your energy centers. It does not matter if you do not think you can sing. Chanting is a way of centering and sending energy, not a way of proving your vocal ability. However, if you are going to sing a chant you should show respect for it by learning it before you sing. Listen to the person leading it until you are sure you know the words and the tune. Some chants change words or tune unexpectedly so don't be too quick to join in. When you are sure of the chant, sing it with gusto. Following are the words to some simple chants we use to honor parts of the Medicine Wheel. If you haven't heard them sung, we have music tapes available that contain these chants. With a tape, you can sing along until you are sure you have learned the song. Most chants are repeated in sets of four, with the person who began the chant determining when to end it and signifying this by saying, "Ho!"

 **Medicine Wheel Chants**

Hey Ya Hey

This is a welcoming centering song, which was given to Wabun.

> Hey ya hey
>
> Hey ya hey
>
> Hey ya hey
>
> Hey ya hey
>
> yo hey
>
> yo hey
>
> yo hey
>
> yo hey

The Earth Is Our Mother

This is a song to honor the earth, and the direction North. It is attributed to several sources. What we present here is called the "healed" version of the chant, because it affirms that we are taking care of the earth.

> The Earth is our Mother
>
> We're taking care of her
>
> The Earth is our Mother
>
> We're taking care of her
>
> Hey younga, ho younga, hey young young
>
> Hey younga, ho younga, hey young young
>
> Her sacred ground we walk upon
>
> With every step we take
>
> Her sacred ground we walk upon
>
> With every step we take
>
> Hey younga, ho younga, hey young young
>
> Hey younga, ho younga, hey young young

Fly Like an Eagle

This chant is also attributed to many sources. It is to honor the East, the eagle, and all winged ones as well as the air in which they fly. There are several versions of the chant. This is the one we most often use. This can be sung as an echo chant with the leader singing one line and participants singing the same line back.

> Fly like an eagle
>
> Flying so high
>
> Circling the Universe

On wings of pure light

Ho witchi tai tai

Witchi tai o

Ho witchi tai tai

Witchi tai o

We all fly like eagles

Flying so high

Circling the Universe

On Wings of pure love

Ho witchi tai tai

Witchi tai o

Ho witchi tai tai

Witchi tai o

The He and She Wolf Chant

This song was taught to us by Brooke Medicine Eagle. It celebrates the
union of the male and female energy. It honors the South, the wolf,
and all four-leggeds.

Women sing the part in parentheses; men sing the part in brackets.
If you do not have both men and women present, get in touch with
both energies within you and sing both parts.

(Wowo wowo wowo wowo

[Wo yaa) yaayaa yaayaa yaayaa

(Yaa wo] wowo wowo wowo

[Wo yaa) yaayaa yaayaa yaayaa]

Evening Breeze

This is a song to honor the West, the wind, and the ocean. It is also
attributed to a variety of sources.

Evening breeze, spirit song

Comes to me when day is done

Mother Earth awaken me

To the heartbeat of the sea

The Dawning

This is a good closing chant that honors the people and the time we
now live in. It is a song from Thunderbird Woman.

The dawning of a new time is coming

The dawning of a new time is coming

Golden light is flowing all over the Earth

Golden light is flowing all over the Earth

CENTERING YOURSELF THROUGH YOUR BREATH

What you need. A comfortable quiet place.

Estimated time. Fifteen minutes when beginning; five minutes when proficient.

1. Many traditions throughout the world use breathing as a method of centering. To begin, relax your body. If this is not easy for you to do, begin with your toes, tighten the muscles as tight as possible, then release them. Tighten the muscles of your feet, then release them. Tighten the muscles of your calves, release them. Tighten your thigh muscles, release them; tighten your genitals, release them; tighten your buttocks, release; tighten your stomach, release; tighten your diaphragm, release it; tighten your chest, release it; tighten your lower back, release it; tighten your midback, release it; tighten your upper back, release it; tighten your shoulders, release them; tighten your neck, release it; finally tighten your scalp, release it. Scrunch up the muscles of your face, then release them.
2. Allow your breath to go through as much of your body as possible.
3. Take long, slow, deep breaths.
4. Pay attention as you breathe.
5. Feel your breath fill you and connect you with the earth, the sky, and all that is around you.

CENTERING YOURSELF THROUGH NATURE

What you need. A safe, comfortable place in nature.

Estimated time. Fifteen minutes when beginning; five minutes when proficient.

1. Find a place in nature that feels safe and comfortable.
2. As you stand there, be aware of the earth under your feet and the sun touching your head. Feel the breeze on your skin.
3. Hear the sounds of nature. Allow them to pass through you, increasing your ability to center.
4. Relax your body as much as you can, paying particular attention to your knees, your stomach muscles, and your jaw.
5. Follow your breathing.
6. Feel your breath coming up the rear of your body, connecting you with the sun overhead, going down the front of your body and connecting you with the earth beneath your feet.

This exercise can also be done sitting.

CENTERING YOURSELF IN A CIRCLE

Drumming, rattling, chanting, breathing, or nature centering exercises all work very well to center and focus the energy of a group of people as well as an individual. The breathing or nature centering should be done with people joining hands. The energy flows better in a circle if people place their left palm up and their right palm down.

OFFERINGS
.....

Making an offering is a good way to give your thanks to nature or to some element of nature that is helping you. The most usual offerings are tobacco and cornmeal, although many other substances can be used. For example, we suggest birdseed as a good offering to honor both spirits and the winged ones. Some people make offerings of feathers, sometimes tying them in a bush or a tree. If you don't have anything with you and wish to make an offering, you can use a strand of your hair. You can also make an offering of a prayer or a chant.

Whenever you take something from nature, it is good to leave an offering to honor the gift you are being given.

There are many ways to make offerings. They are all fine, as long as your thanks goes along with the offering.

AN OFFERING TO THE SIX DIRECTIONS

What you will need. Tobacco, cornmeal, a strand of hair, or some other offering meaningful to you.

Estimated time. One minute.

1. Take a pinch of tobacco, cornmeal, a strand of your hair, or whatever else you have been guided to offer.
2. Raise the offering to the sky while making a prayer of thanks to Creator. This can be as simple as saying, "Thank you Creator for life and for the earth." It could also include special items for which you are grateful.
3. Touch the offering to the Earth Mother, thanking her.
4. Face North and raise the offering to Waboose, thanking this Spirit Keeper; face East and thank Wabun; face South and thank Shawnodese; face West and thank Mudjekeewis.
5. Place the offering on the earth making another prayer of thanks.

OFFERING YOUR ENERGY

What you need. Tobacco, cornmeal, a strand of hair, or some other offering meaningful to you.

Estimated time. One minute.

1. Take a pinch of tobacco, cornmeal, or whatever you choose to offer.
2. Lower the offering to the earth, giving a prayer of thanks to the Earth Mother. Slowly bring the offering up the front of your body, about one foot away from yourself. As you raise the offering up allow some of the energy from all your energy centers to go into it. Bring the offering to the crown of your head, then bring it in front of your mouth and breath on it.
3. Gently place your offering on the earth or on the object you are thanking.

CEREMONIAL ENDINGS
#####

One of the most difficult parts of ceremony for many people is the ending. Because of all the energy that has been generated, whether individually or in a group, and because of the ecstatic feeling of being in the sacred space, many people just don't want the experience to end. However, a good ending provides the proper beginning for the next part of the ceremony of your life. The ending of a ceremony is also the crucial time in which all the good energy that has been generated is disbursed out to the universe. Consequently the ending insures the success of that for which you have been working.

If you are doing a ceremony alone, you must decide when you have reached completion and then end the ceremony promptly but without hurry. If you are working with a group, the ceremonial leader should explain the importance of the ending to participants. He or she should instruct them that after the ceremony concludes they should quietly and gently leave the area. It is better if people go away from the ceremonial area to say their farewells, give hugs, have a feast, or otherwise enjoy human company. Doing this shows respect both for the ceremony and for the location in which it has been held.

It is also important that participants ground themselves at the conclusion of a ceremony so that they are totally back into normal consciousness. Following are some methods for grounding and concluding a ceremony.

GROUNDING WITH THE EARTH

What you need. People who have completed a ceremony, and the earth.

Estimated time. Five minutes.

1. At the conclusion of the ceremony you or the group leader, if you are working with a group, should instruct people who do not feel totally back in normal consciousness to get on their hands and knees and place their forehead on the earth.
2. Smell the earth and be aware of her solidity under you.
3. Feel the earth energy coming into your body, grounding you.
4. As you feel ready, slowly rise up.
5. When you are standing be sure your energy is back solidly in your body. If it is not, repeat this exercise.

GROUNDING THROUGH THE EYES

What you need. People who have completed a ceremony, and the earth.

Estimated time. Five minutes.

1. As the ceremony concludes you or the group leader, if you are working in group, should ask people to close their eyes for a moment and think about the ceremony and the new beginning it has provided.
2. When you open your eyes you should first look up at the sky. See if it looks different.

3. Next look at the tops of any trees in the area.
4. Look at the grass or ground.
5. As you feel your energy solidly grounded in your body, look slowly around the circle of people or other beings who have shared this experience with you.

SENDING THE ENERGY OUT FROM CEREMONY

Estimated time. Five minutes.

1. If you are doing a ceremony alone, when you feel grounded in your body think about the ceremony and the energy it has generated.
2. Feel that energy within your body.
3. Reach down and send this energy into the earth.
4. Reach your hands up and send this energy to the Creator.
5. If you are working in a group, wait until people are grounded in their bodies, then ask them to take a moment to think about the ceremony and the energy it has generated. Have them follow the same procedures you would if you were working alone.

**Wabun—Spirit Keeper of the East
—by George Monacelli**

3

The Center Circle
and Spirit Keeper Stones

To live, humans, both individually and as a species, need the help of every power represented on the Medicine Wheel. However, there are some powers that do not need humans. They existed long before human beings. These are the powers honored in the center of the wheel and in the four cardinal directions.

The stones of the Center Circle and of the Spirit Keepers represent the powers, the energies from which all other life is formed. They are the first beings, the building blocks for everything else. These forces surpass human understanding. It is only by experiencing them that true comprehension comes. In the past it was solely the shamans, the medicine people, who would reach out to these powers. These forces were perceived as too mysterious and dangerous for other people to seek.

At this time on the earth when man questions the existence of the Creator; when man threatens the continued existence of Earth Mother; when man has truly tried to steal fire from Father Sun, in the form of nuclear power; when man has walked on Grandmother Moon and torn off parts of her surface; when man both creates and destroys the elements, convincing himself he can achieve a new balance; when man forgets the Spirit Keepers and all they represent, it is necessary for as many humans as possible to seek these spirit powers bravely.

The Medicine Wheel provides you with tools for this exploration: tools that will help you understand the mystery and avoid the dangers.

By reaching for knowledge of these powers you help to bring balance to yourself and the earth. You can begin your quest by learning how these forces affect you, and you can continue by going to each of these stones, either physically or in visualization, and feeling the power of the associated force. These are such intense powers that while humans can choose to experience them for short periods of time, they do not remain in these positions for prolonged periods. To do so would show dishonor to these powerful spirits and risk their displeasure. These twelve stones, these twelve forces both directly and indirectly affect the other twenty-four positions of the Medicine Wheel.

The Center Circle and Spirit Keeper stones each have different and unique gifts to give you as you travel around the Medicine Wheel. The Creator, Earth Mother, Father Sun, and Grandmother Moon give life and vision. The Spirit Keepers each give the power of the direction they represent; the power of a particular time of day, year, and human life; of a wind, an element, mineral, plant, animal, and color. The Spirit Keepers each directly affect the three moon signs within their quadrant of the wheel.

The elemental clans—the clans representing the elements of earth, water, fire, and air—give humans tools to use the powers they have, and tools to deepen their connection with the universe. These clans each directly affect the three moon signs governed by the element they represent.

The Spirit Keeper and elemental clans paint the large picture of your current positions on the Medicine Wheel. The moon signs fill in the details. The Spirit Keepers can help you understand the major lessons you are striving to learn at any one time, whereas the elemental clans can show you the tools nature provides for your education. Together the Spirit Keepers and elemental clans affecting you at any time teach a great deal about your life lessons, challenges, and opportunities.

The understand further these forces you need to learn about each individual position.

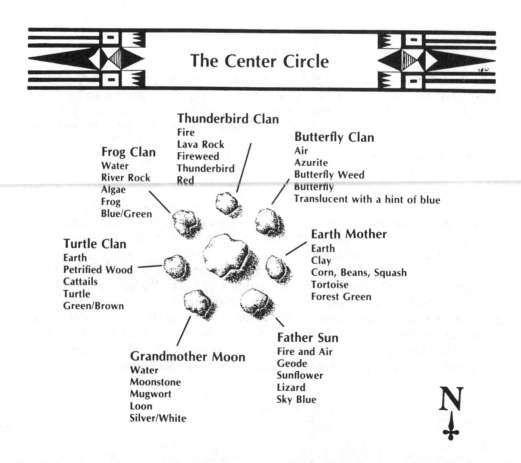

The Center Circle

Thunderbird Clan
Fire
Lava Rock
Fireweed
Thunderbird
Red

Butterfly Clan
Air
Azurite
Butterfly Weed
Butterfly
Translucent with a hint of blue

Frog Clan
Water
River Rock
Algae
Frog
Blue/Green

Earth Mother
Earth
Clay
Corn, Beans, Squash
Tortoise
Forest Green

Turtle Clan
Earth
Petrified Wood
Cattails
Turtle
Green/Brown

Father Sun
Fire and Air
Geode
Sunflower
Lizard
Sky Blue

Grandmother Moon
Water
Moonstone
Mugwort
Loon
Silver/White

N

THE CENTER CIRCLE

·····

The Foundation

THE CREATOR

The center of the Medicine Wheel, the Creator, stands alone. The object depicting the Creator force can be a stone of any sort, a buffalo skull, or an object of deep significance to the people building the wheel. Once at a gathering near the Pacific Ocean someone brought a whale's skull from a museum to represent the Creator. Other people have used crystal clusters, cow skulls, trees, and contained fires. The Creator is all of these and none of these. The Creator is the beginning of life and its ending, the great mystery within all things and around all things, the universal energy, that which many people address as God. In many Native languages the word for the Creator was not a noun. The word was a verb, indicating the movement, the activity, the motion, the pulsation of this sacred, never-ending force.

Because the Creator is within everything there are no totems associated with this position. All minerals, all plants, all animals, all colors, all humans, all spirits are part of the Creator.

The Creator stone is the place on the Medicine Wheel that teaches you about your own ability to create, about your faith, about your own sacredness, and about your ability to develop to your fullest.

When you are afraid, when you do not have enough energy, when you either fear that you can create things with your mind or that you cannot create things with your mind, when you feel that you do not really have a deep knowledge of the universe, you should go to the center of the Medicine Wheel and ask for the help that you need. When you are not quite sure what your spiritual values are or you feel the need for change or when you desire an initiation into a different way of seeing life, at all of these times you should go to the center of the Medicine Wheel, to the Creator.

THE EARTH MOTHER

The Earth Mother stone is the first one placed in the Center Circle of the Medicine Wheel. This stone goes slightly to the south of East, representing the love and new beginnings the Earth Mother always gives her children. In many of our Medicine Wheels we put a potted tree and a green prayer robe by the Earth Mother stone. The tree represents the tree of life and the green represents the fecundity of the earth. The prayer robe, which is a sacred object to many Native people, should only be made if you have been instructed how to do so correctly by someone familiar with this tradition. Otherwise you could garland your tree with a green cloth or ribbon. If you are building a large permanent Medicine Wheel you could plant a small tree by this stone.

The totems associated with the Earth Mother position are clay in the mineral kingdom; corn, beans, and squash in the plant kingdom; and the great tortoise in the animal kingdom. The color is forest green, and the element is earth. This is the place on the Medicine Wheel that teaches about the nurturing female energy within you and about the earth herself. The Earth Mother stone is the place to help you feel the earth energy more strongly. It is here you can find solace when you are feeling a deep sadness or anguish about the condition the earth is in now. The Earth Mother stone can help when you feel that things are not likely to change and that the condition of life on the earth approaches hopelessness.

This is the stone to seek when the ideas of pollution, overpopulation, or earth changes overwhelm you and when you are looking for positive solutions to all of the problems now besetting our planet.

The Earth Mother position can also help if you are experiencing problems with infertility, if you are preparing to become a parent, or if you are already a parent and want to become as loving a parent as you possibly can be.

FATHER SUN

Moving in a clockwise direction in the Center Circle you would next place the stone honoring Father Sun, slightly to the east of South, representing the growth and clarity the sun brings to earth. In Medicine Wheel Gatherings we usually use another potted tree to honor this stone. With this tree is a prayer robe made with blue cloth to honor both Father Sun and the sky in which he dwells.

The totems associated with Father Sun are the geode, the sunflower, and the lizard. The color is sky blue, and the elements are both air and fire. This stone teaches about the core masculine energy and about the active principle of the universe. This is the place to go if you need more energy, if you need warmth and expansion in your life. You would seek the sun stone to gain knowledge about the masculine principle or if you feel a block of the masculine energy in your own life. The sun stone can help your understanding if you find yourself hating men or the things they have done. In this position you can learn to accomplish things and find courage. The sun stone can also teach about discrimination: the healthy ability to set limits, to say no when that is what you want to say. Such discrimination is a much-needed lesson for many people today, particularly for some women who consistently give too much. Because of the connection between the sun and nuclear energy, this is also the place to pray if you are feeling concerned about the presence of nuclear weapons or fear the threat of nuclear war.

GRANDMOTHER MOON

The next stone in the Center Circle is that honoring Grandmother Moon. This stone is placed slightly to the west of South, honoring the trust that comes from the introspective energies of the moon. In many Native traditions the moon was considered the leader of feminine life, in part because women, like the moon, experience different phases, different cycles. Grandmother Moon teaches about a different aspect of the feminine than the Earth Mother does. This aspect of the feminine is the one strong enough to be receptive, the one strong enough to surrender to life. This aspect of the feminine is the one wild enough to seduce the active forces, visionary enough to conceive of new life coming from the old. Grandmother Moon dreams the children Earth Mother nurtures.

The totems associated with Grandmother Moon are the moonstone, mugwort, and the loon. The color is silver-white, and the element is water.

The stone representing Grandmother Moon is the place to go when you want to examine the lesser-known aspects of your being. This position can offer you help with your dreams and with your visions. Grandmother Moon can aid you in increasing your intuitive and psychic abilities. When you go to the place of Grandmother Moon, you can learn more about your own sensuality as well as your sexuality. You can learn about the emotional side of your being and the parts of you that defy logic. This is the stone to seek when you find yourself fearing your own deepest emotions or when you need help in understanding them.

Grandmother Moon's soft, gentle light allows you to examine the shadow side of your being, the parts of yourself buried so deep you fear looking at them in the full light of day.

The Elemental Clans

As the elements provide the building blocks for all life on the earth, so the elemental clans provide you with the building blocks that allow you to take the powers that are given to you by Spirit and put them to use in service for all people. As each element has its own way of building, so do each of the elemental clans. The gifts of these clans are as different from each other as the element of fire is from the element of water, as the element of air is from the element of earth. From each elemental clan position you visit, you gain more tools, more abilities, and more ways to discover your true talents and the joy that comes from putting them in service to the Earth Mother and to all of her children.

THE TURTLE CLAN—THE CLAN OF THE EARTH

The Turtle clan represents the earth. The stone is placed slightly south of West in the Center Circle. The mineral associated with the Turtle clan stone is petrified wood, the plant is cattails, and the color is green-brown. The Earth Renewal Moon (December 22 to January 19; Snow Goose), the Frogs Return Moon (April 20 to May 20; Beaver), and the Harvest Moon (August 23 to September 22; Brown Bear) are all directly associated with the Turtle clan and governed by the element of earth. When you are in a Turtle clan position you learn about the solid, creating, strengthening powers of this most dense element. From the earth, which grain by grain appears delicate, both mountains and skyscrapers are formed.

Because of its association with the element of earth, the Turtle clan is the most dense, stable, and slow-moving of the elemental clans. People who are influenced by a Turtle clan position are stable, solid, practical, grounded, persevering, steady, deliberate in their actions, and discerning in their views. Turtle clan people are extremely well organized and can provide the foundation for any undertaking. They are cautious in expressing themselves, except about viewpoints in which they believe strongly. They are very good at defending whatever it is they are helping you to build. These are people who are very practical and security conscious and expert at taking care of the earth, minerals, plants, animals, and other human beings.

Turtle clan people feel a great attraction to the element of earth as well as to the Earth Mother. They often like to go outside and feel the earth energy, either by running their hands over the earth or by sitting on her.

Because the element earth is slow moving, people who enter Turtle clan positions often have the tendency to want to remain in this position even when it is time for them to leave it and change and grow. If people become too rooted in a Turtle clan position, they can become cool—verging on frigid—blocked, unfeeling, closed, inflexible, and narrow minded in the way they perceive life around them. They also can be crafty, manipulative, and exceptionally stubborn. Turtle clan people who get stuck have a tendency to martyr themselves for whatever it is they have built.

If you find yourself expressing any of the tendencies described above, whether positive or negative, it is good to look at whether you are rooting yourself to the point that you have become root-bound. If that is the case, it is time for you to move to a different position on the wheel under the influence of another elemental clan.

If, on the other hand, you find that you are feeling very spacey and ungrounded, it is a good time to move yourself to a Turtle clan position where you can learn about solid growth and a good sense of connection with the energy of the earth. This is the stone to seek when you yearn to be more oriented toward the earth, more able to help her in every way that you can. This is the place in which you can learn the true meaning of loyalty to the earth and to all of your relations on her.

People under the influence of a Turtle clan position can be among the most supportive, encouraging, friendly, and affirming individuals that you would ever want to meet. They are truly compassionate and have a gift for giving and for teaching their love of the earth.

THE FROG CLAN—THE CLAN OF THE WATERS

The Frog clan is the clan associated with the waters. The Frog clan stone is placed midway between West and North in the Center Circle. The mineral associated with the Frog clan is river rock. The plant associated with this clan is algae, and the color associated with the Frog clan is blue-green. The Big Winds Moon (February 19 to March 20; Cougar), the Strong Sun Moon (June 21 to July 22; Flicker), and the Freeze Up Moon (October 24 to November 21; Snake) are all directly associated with the Frog clan and governed by the element of water. When you are in a Frog clan position, you can learn about your own agility on all levels of being. You can learn about the transformative, rejuvenating, and regenerating powers of this most liquid of the elements. Water appears to be formless, but it in fact creates many forms. Water is very life giving. Without the gift of water, most life as we know it on the earth could not survive.

When you experience a Frog clan position, you can learn about the life-giving aspects of yourself; about your own fluidity, your own ability to constantly change, your own ability to be bubbling and refreshing, and to let your heart guide your head. You can also find out about the reflective parts of your being, the parts that can mirror both your internal nature and the internal aspects of other people. The Frog clan can teach you about the cleansing aspects of your being, such as those aspects that allow you to purge yourself of past hurts through the gift of tears. It also teaches about the earth cleansing.

Frog clan people are able to go easily between different levels of reality. They are very empathetic. They have a natural gift for touching the emotions within others and for feeling their own emotions. However, the depth and strength of their emotions is sometimes so intense that it frightens them. When frightened, Frog clan people have a tendency to dam themselves up. The longer they keep themselves dammed up, the more afraid they become of letting go of the strong emotions they are feeling. This can create a difficult cycle until the person either decides to let go or moves to another position on the wheel that better allows him to express his feelings.

People who are in a Frog clan position feel a special closeness to Grandmother Moon as well as to the water. Frog clan people like to participate in moon ceremonies. They also find great pleasure in being near the waters of the earth. Sometimes just having a drink of water can rejuvenate them. Actually sitting by a river or stream can become an almost religious experience.

When you are passing through Frog clan positions, you need to be careful to allow expression to the feelings that are inside you. In the Frog clan position people sometimes have a tendency literally to hold too much water within their bodies. When this is the case, it is an indication they are damming themselves up or fixating on one thing to the extent that it is blocking the flow of every-thing else around them.

Going to a Frog clan position is a good thing to do if you are having a difficult time feeling your own emotions or becoming aware of the reflective, still aspects of your being. A Frog clan position will help you to become aware of the life that bubbles through you and of your own psychic and intuitive abilities. The powers of the Frog clan positions are the powers of slow-but-steady change, the powers of cleansing, the powers of transformation. The gift of the Frog clan position is the gift of feeling deeply and of becoming aware of your connection with the moon. When people are in a Frog clan position, any latent gifts for healing that they have, particularly gifts of healing emotional blocks, may be brought out.

THE THUNDERBIRD CLAN—THE CLAN OF THE FIRE

The Thunderbird clan is the clan of fire. The Thunderbird clan stone is placed in the North in the Center Circle. The mineral associated with this clan is lava rock, the plant is fireweed, and the color is red. The Budding Trees Moon (March 21 to April 19; Red Hawk), the Ripe Berries Moon (July 23 to August 22; Sturgeon), and the Long Snows Moon (November 22 to December 21; Elk) are directly associated with the Thunderbird clan and governed by the element of fire.

The Thunderbird clan is a clan of vitality and a clan of transformation. Fire can help humans or destroy them. Fire changes whatever it touches by reduction to base components. In a similar manner, people under the influence of the Thunderbird clan have the tendency to be very fast moving and intense. Thunderbird clan positions are volatile ones. They are ones where people learn about the power of penetration and of compete transformation. These are very innovative positions on the Medicine Wheel, ones that have the tendency to be as eruptive as the volcano from whence comes the lava rock.

People who are in Thunderbird clan positions can often seem like people of paradox. At one moment they are radiant, robust, attractive, warm, and vital. But in the next moment they seem hyperactive, voracious, consuming, over-powering, and domineering. Both sides of this picture are equally true for the Thunderbird clan positions. The gifts of fire are definitely two-edged ones.

The Thunderbird can bring the life-giving rain or the lightning that destroys a forest or a home with one bolt. The fire can bring life-giving warmth or de-struction. The volcano can build new parts onto the earth, or it can destroy things that already exist.

When people are under the influence of the Thunderbird clan, they become aware of this duality within their own nature. Thunderbird clan people are very good at doing things, beginning things, exploring, pioneering, and inventing. They are not as good at following through. The Thunderbird clan position is one that brings the gift of magnetism, charisma, courage, and optimism. When people are in these positions, they do have a way of mesmerizing and captivat-ing those around them. This very charm allows them to control and deceive others, if that is their goal.

When people are in a Thunderbird clan position, they can use their intense energy for the good of the Earth Mother and all those around them, or they can use it for their own gain. Making this choice is one of the lessons that comes from the Thunderbird clan positions. Thunderbird people need to be very clear about where their power comes from and how they use it.

They also must learn to temper their own intensity, or they will get illnesses that will force them to slow down.

The power of the Thunderbird clan position is the power of innovation, the power of passion, and the power of transmutation. When people are under the influence of the Thunderbird clan positions, they can learn some of their strongest lessons about what reality is on all levels of their being. Thunderbird clan people can be among the most charming, witty, clear-sighted, and forthright people that you will ever meet or they can be among the most deceptive. Sometimes they can be both at the same time. It is at those points that they have come to their time of greatest challenge.

THE BUTTERFLY CLAN—THE CLAN OF THE AIR

The Butterfly clan is the clan associated with the element of air. The mineral associated with the Butterfly clan is azurite, the plant is butterfly weed, and the color is translucent tinged with blue. The Rest and Cleansing Moon (January 20 to February 28; Otter), the Cornplanting Moon (May 21 to June 20; Deer), and the Ducks Fly Moon (September 23 to October 23; Raven) are all directly associated with the Butterfly clan and governed by the element of air. The Butterfly clan is the clan associated with sudden change. It is the clan of the element that is always in motion—the wind. The energy of the air is transforming and active whether it is a gentle breeze or a typhoon. Air contains the breath of life. The wind seems to be free and brings out that yearning in humans. The wind can go wherever it will, do whatever it wants, and affects all that it touches.

People who are in positions influenced by the Butterfly clan seem as nimble and quick as the element of the air. They are often graceful and almost always energetic, flamboyant, exotic, and buoyant. People under the influence of the Butterfly clan tend to be lighthearted, idealistic, and visionary. They are people who seek evolution for themselves, for the species, for the entire planet. They are extremely adaptable and adjustable people. They like the act of emerging and the feeling of being unbounded.

As the wind touches many, so Butterfly clan people like to communicate widely in a way they think will serve many people. These are people who love the idea of service. Yet they have to beware that they are not being self-serving when they think they are serving others. Butterfly clan people can be open-minded to a point that infuriates all others. Sometimes their open-mindedness closely resembles total indecisiveness.

When people are under the influence of the Butterfly clan, they have to bound their energy occasionally and check a tendency toward unpredictability that verges on the chaotic. They need to be careful that they do not let themselves move so quickly that their very movement causes them pain or disease. One of the main lessons of the Butterfly clan position is that of discrimination. This is a position in which you must learn what it is that truly needs changing. Then you must learn whether you are capable of making that change.

The Butterfly clan position is one in which you can learn about your own grace, your own energy levels, and your own ability to change trends. The Butterfly clan positions are the places to go if you feel that you need to become more articulate, more ethereal, more creative, or more innovative. It can also aid you in teaching, in understanding philosophy, and in having a much broader perspective. It can also show you ways to synthesize the knowledge you already have. People can seek the Butterfly clan stone when they wish to learn more about their own intellect and when they want to bring metamorphosis into their life.

The gift of the Butterfly clan is the gift of quick change, of sudden transformation, of breath—of life itself. People who are passing through a Butterfly clan position have the ability to move quickly, to cover a lot of territory, to find out whether they are truly doing what they want to do and, if not, to explore quickly what their true goal is. Butterfly clan people are very good at bridging between the different realms of life, at communicating among different groups of people, and at bringing people together. Although they are not organized, their high energy often compensates for this lack. It is the Butterfly clan people who most like to play games, make jokes, and bring the gift of humor to others who tend to take their journey around the Medicine Wheel a bit too seriously.

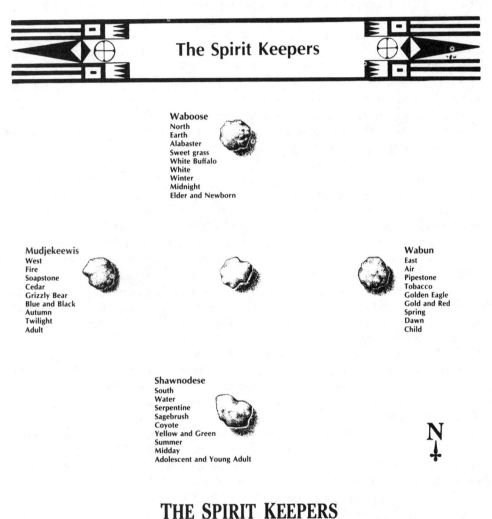

The Spirit Keepers

Waboose
North
Earth
Alabaster
Sweet grass
White Buffalo
White
Winter
Midnight
Elder and Newborn

Mudjekeewis
West
Fire
Soapstone
Cedar
Grizzly Bear
Blue and Black
Autumn
Twilight
Adult

Wabun
East
Air
Pipestone
Tobacco
Golden Eagle
Gold and Red
Spring
Dawn
Child

Shawnodese
South
Water
Serpentine
Sagebrush
Coyote
Yellow and Green
Summer
Midday
Adolescent and Young Adult

N

THE SPIRIT KEEPERS

• • • • •

The vision of the Medicine Wheel showed us that each of the cardinal directions (North, East, South, West) has a particular Spirit Keeper. As you make your journey around the wheel, it is important to be aware of the Spirit Keeper who is helping you at any time. This Spirit Keeper is the spirit being responsible for teaching earth's children about the power of the direction, the times, the season, the aspect of humans that they represent. The lessons of the Spirit Keepers are those of power in all its forms, and of the ethereal realms.

As the elemental clans help you discover the tools that uncover your true talents, the Spirit Keepers give you the power to work with these talents in a way that can bring more balance to you and the earth.

WABOOSE, SPIRIT KEEPER OF THE NORTH

Waboose, the Spirit Keeper of the North, is represented by the element of earth. Its mineral is alabaster. Its plant is the sweet grass. Its animal is the white buffalo. The color associated with Waboose is white. The season is winter. The time of day is midnight. The time of life is both the time when we are elders with the snow upon our heads and the time of life when we are newborns coming back into the world. Waboose directly influences all the moons in the northern quadrant: the Earth Renewal Moon (December 22 to January 19; Snow Goose), the Rest and Cleansing Moon (January 20 to February 18; Otter), and the Big Winds Moon (February 19 to March 20; Cougar).

The North is the most paradoxical time of the Medicine Wheel. It is the time when things seem to be sleeping. Yet within this apparent dormancy some of the deepest growth is occurring. It is in the winter when seeds lie frozen within the earth that they take into themselves all of the earth's energy that allows them to grow in the seasons that follow. It is in the North that our bodies cannot move as easily as they have in the past or will in the future, that we seem forced to take into ourselves the wisdom of the Spirit we will use as we continue our journey around the wheel.

The time of Waboose is a time of slowing down, of apparent restriction, when outward activity definitely diminishes. It is a time of darkness, quiet, and dreams. It is a time when humans are fragile, when their skin is wrinkled and resembles the soil and the face of the Earth Mother herself. It is a time when people tend to reminisce and from their reminiscences share the wisdom they have gained. It is a time of assessing accomplishments and aims and of preparing for the major giveaway of death and of birth. It is a time when many people come to an understanding of their own life, an acceptance of what they have or have not achieved. It can be a time of peace, a time of power, a time of forgiveness and compassion for all around you. It is a time to give up old patterns, to surrender to the small changes of body and mind in preparation for the major changes that will come.

Waboose is a time of both ending and beginning, of life and death, of new life cloaked in apparent death. In the winter the earth appears dead, but there is much happening within. The same is true in human life. Even when we shed our human envelopes, our spirit, our energy goes to a place that prepares us for the new beginning that will come.

The major lesson of Waboose is that of the giveaway. When we are elders, it is our responsibility to give away to the people all of the knowledge that we have gained. It is our responsibility to impart to our relations what we have learned as we have journeyed around the Medicine Wheel of life. It is our responsibility, ultimately, to give away our body to the Earth Mother who has fed us during all the time we have walked on her. When we are infants we readily give away all of the love we have gained in the world between, knowing then that the more we give the more we have available.

One of the gifts of Waboose is an intuitive understanding of this giveaway. Coming with this understanding are increased psychic abilities and a great acumen in attuning to dreams or visions, both your own and those of other people.

The white buffalo, the animal associated with Waboose, is an animal who gave up everything for the people: meat, hide, bones, and spirit. It is the White Buffalo Woman who gave the pipe to the people.

When you are experiencing a moon influenced by Waboose, it is a good time to contemplate your life, to contemplate the paradoxes of life. It is a good time to think about questions of life and death and to examine your attitudes toward both. It is a time to learn patience. It is a time when your psychic and mystical abilities will be far above average. It is a time to see how you feel about giving away all the many gifts that life has given to you. It is a time to practice the small giveaways that prepare you for the larger ones.

During times of Waboose, you will need to make a point of grounding yourself, of remembering that you are a being of the earth as well as the sky. One of the paradoxes of Waboose is that while this is a time of intuition and mystical abilities, Waboose is also the direction that governs the physical level of life, both how we relate to our bodies and how we relate to the world around us. While your mind wanders through the skies, you must also learn that you need to take care of your body here on earth.

Waboose is the place of physical healing, the place we come to give thanks for healing that has occurred and to ask for healing that is needed both for ourselves and for others. This can be healing of the body or healing of the way in which we relate to the world around us. The power of Waboose is the power of spirituality grounded on earth; the power of patience that allows all things to grow in their proper way. The power of Waboose is acceptance of life, acceptance of death, and acceptance of the necessity of sharing all that has been given you.

WABUN, SPIRIT KEEPER OF THE EAST

The element associated with Wabun, the Spirit Keeper of the East, is air. The mineral associated with Wabun is catlinite, or pipestone. The plant of Wabun is tobacco, the animal is the golden eagle, the colors are gold and red, the season is the spring, the time of day is dawn, and the time of human life is that of infancy and early childhood. Wabun directly influences all the moons in the eastern quadrant; the Budding Trees Moon (March 21 to April 19; Red Hawk), the Frogs Return Moon (April 20 to May 20; Beaver), and the Cornplanting Moon (May 21 to June 20; Deer).

The power of Wabun is a very straightforward power: It is that of new beginnings. Wabun brings the time of new growth to all of earth's children. The time of Wabun is the time of freshness, newness, enthusiasm, and creativity. It is the time of bursting through, of the light that comes after each darkness, of the brightness that you see after you have come out of the void. The East is truly a time of rebirth, a time when all things are possible. It is a time of innocence and a time of awakening.

Wabun brings the eternal promise of spring, the eternal promise of dawn. Wabun helps us to know that each moment can be a new beginning. The gifts of Wabun are the gifts of spontaneity, playfulness, wonder, inquisitiveness, and truth saying. Wabun brings the abilities to explore, to feel high energy, to be full of curiosity, to question everything, and to have the determination to see what is around the corner.

People under the influence of Wabun feel that they are the messengers of truth and, in reality, they do have the ability to see farther and more clearly than people who are under the influence of other Spirit Keepers. In part, this comes about because of their connection with the golden eagle, the animal associated with Wabun. Like all eagles, the golden eagle has the ability to fly high, to soar to the Creator. From this height, the eagle can see what is happening on earth. Like the eagle, people who are experiencing Wabun also have this ability to soar and to see from a broad perspective.

When the earth enters the time of Wabun, all of life seems to be bursting forth with new energy. The seeds that were frozen in the breast of the Earth Mother poke their tiny heads up through her soil and begin to greet and dance with the energy of Father Sun. In the time of Wabun many of the animal people bear their young and begin to teach them the lessons that they need to prosper on the earth.

When humans are in the time of Wabun, they are like the rest of nature. They're bursting with enthusiasm, energy, and the willingness to try as many new things as they can. The time of Wabun is a magical time both for the earth and for all of her children. It is a time when everything seems to be possible, when each breath, each moment is a new beginning, when incredible energy is available for growth on all levels.

When you are experiencing a position influenced by Wabun, it is a good time to explore life on all levels of your being. It is a good time to contemplate doing those things you only dreamed about when you were in other positions on the Medicine Wheel. It is a good time to soar and to see and to learn how to say the truth you have been shown.

During such times it is important that you do not volunteer truth to people who have not asked to have your help in seeing the world. It is very easy for people who are under this influence to lose whatever sense of discrimination they have and to lose their knowledge of limits, and boundaries. When you are under the influence of Wabun, you also need to learn to control your energy. Otherwise, it can be difficult for you to work with others or to sustain either a project or yourself.

Some of the important lessons you can learn in the East are how to turn the knowledge of the Spirit outward and how to find a way to take this knowledge into the world. Wabun provides a good time to take advantage of your clear-sightedness, your ability to work with things of the earth while still remembering the lessons you have learned from other realms.

The time of Wabun is the time of healing of the mind. This is the place we seek if we need to find the truth of life and get rid of any lies that might be binding us to old places that keep us from new beginnings.

Wabun is the place to come if you wish to have healing on the mental level. The Wabun position can help if you wish to make a new beginning in any aspect of your life or in any of your relationships. It bestows abundant energy, intensity, and persistence. It is the place to come if you want to look at the world with new eyes, if you wish to open up untapped sources of creativity, if you want to become more optimistic, observant, passionate, or determined. Wabun can help you know what truth really means to you and how you can communicate that to others. This is the stone to seek to understand that although the mind is very important to life, it is not the only part of you that has importance.

The powers of Wabun are those of truth, of openness, of illumination. Exploring Wabun will help you to know how to let the sacred energy that is the Creator flow freely and vitally throughout your whole being.

SHAWNODESE, SPIRIT KEEPER OF THE SOUTH

The element associated with Shawnodese, the Spirit Keeper of the South, is water. The mineral is serpentine. The plant is the sagebrush. The animal is the coyote, the colors are yellow and green, the season is summer, the time of day is midday. The time of life is that of our older childhood, adolescence, and young adulthood. Shawnodese directly influences all the moons in the southern quadrant: the Strong Sun Moon (June 21 to July 22; Flicker), the Ripe Berries Moon (July 23 to August 22; Sturgeon), and the Harvest Moon (August 23 to September 22; Brown Bear).

Like the power of Waboose, the power of Shawnodese is a paradoxical one. Shawnodese brings the time of rapid growth, a time when every being has to reach out for fulfillment so quickly it does not have time to question the path laid down for it by the Creator.

The plant that poked its head through the soil and began to grow during the time of Wabun now needs to leaf out fully, flower, fruit, bear its seed, and prepare for the time of harvest. So it is with all life influenced by this quadrant.

Humans are no exception. In the time of Wabun, we explore everything with little discrimination trying to find what makes us feel good, what seems to fit with us. In the time of Shawnodese, we begin a more directed form of exploration. The South is the place where many people seek their visions and ask the Creator to point them in the direction they should go. Often after the Creator has made this direction known, people have to follow it so rapidly that they must learn to trust the Creator and not question their path. To aid in following the new path, Shawnodese gives the gifts of energy, adaptability, maturity, playfulness, and humor.

For many humans the time of Shawnodese is one of self-assurance, of acceptance. It is a time when everything in our world truly seems possible, when the search for love is definitely one of our guiding forces and when we are particularly capable of giving and receiving love in many meanings of the word. The time of Shawnodese is a time of learning about relationships.

The paradox of Shawnodese is that while all this open, outward, energetic activity is taking place, while we are learning to trust life and follow our own life path, the old trickster, the coyote, is prepared to do whatever he needs to in order to make us grow inwardly as well.

The coyote means many things to Native people. To some he is trickster in the most powerful sense: a sacred clown who urges life to keep creating itself. To others he is a form of the Creator. Some consider coyote merely a clown, a fool, one who tricks himself more than others.

The animal itself also has many meanings to people. To some, coyote is a nuisance, a thief, and a scoundrel. To others he is a symbol of freedom and mystery. How fitting a totem he is for paradoxical Shawnodese.

The favorite trick of the coyote is one very appropriate to this point on the wheel: making you fall in love, most often with a person very different from you and from how you thought you wanted your mate to be. Attraction is the glue that draws people to these walking, talking, human lessons of life. Love is the cement that binds them together as long as they are willing to learn from each other.

The power of Shawnodese is a mysterious power, a changing power. It is the power that takes that which we yearn for, gives it to us, and then craftily observes what happens. The little sprout of the spring yearns to be the flower of the summer. When it is, the plant must learn the lessons of being fully open and fully vulnerable to the earth, the sky, and all its relations.

When you are under the influence of Shawnodese, it is a good time to explore love, explore relationship, and explore the world around you; to learn who you are and how that compares with who you feel you should be; and to take the first strong steps toward your own maturity.

When you are under the influence of Shawnodese you must be careful not to burn yourself out trying to do everything. You must be careful to use some common sense in your relationships. You must learn how to protect yourself, for this is one of the lessons necessary to grow into a mature human being. You must learn that there is both a time to be open and a time to contain your energy and your feelings within yourself.

Shawnodese is the place of the heart, the place of the emotions. It is here that we come when we need healing of the heart, when we need to learn how to love, when we need to learn to let go of all that is not love: hate, fear, envy, jealousy, rage, and anger.

The Shawnodese stone is the place to come if you are having problems with a relationship or if you are looking for a relationship. The Shawnodese stone, the stone of the trickster, will help you to understand why it is that you are drawn to a person and what you can do to help the relationship grow. This is the position in which you will learn about charm, nurturance, trust, gullibility, humor, and manipulation. The Shawnodese stone will teach you about sexuality and sensuality and how they differ and how they are the same. This is the stone to seek to ask for healing of the emotions and healing of the heart. It is to Shawnodese that we come when it seems like it is too painful to open once again. It is Shawnodese who teaches us it is even more painful not to. The power of Shawnodese is the power of love; the power of the open heart working in conjunction with the discriminating mind. The power of Shawnodese is the power of growth.

MUDJEKEEWIS, SPIRIT KEEPER OF THE WEST

The element associated with Mudjekeewis, the Spirit Keeper of the West, is that of fire. Mudjekeewis, the Father of All the Winds, provides a home for the Thunder beings. The mineral associated with Mudjekeewis is soapstone. The plant is cedar, the animal is the grizzly bear, the colors are blue and black, the season is the autumn, the time of day is the twilight, and the time of life is that when we reach adulthood and maturity. Mudjekeewis directly influences all the moons in the western quadrant: the Ducks Fly Moon (September 23 to October 23; Raven), the Freeze Up Moon (October 24 to November 21; Snake), and the Long Snows Moon (November 22 to December 21; Elk). The major lesson of Mudjekeewis is that of responsibility: responsibility for self, responsibility for the Earth, and responsibility for all of our relations on the Earth.

It is during the time of Mudjekeewis that all of earth's children prepare to give their harvest back to the Earth Mother. It is during this time that the seeds from most plants fall back into the earth in preparation for the seasons that will come. It is during this time of life that people who have been given a vision know themselves well enough to be ready to share the lessons of their vision. Mudjekeewis brings the gifts of maturity, of experience, and of expertise. It is during the time of Mudjekeewis that people find out what their abilities and skills truly are and gain an unshakeable knowledge of what they can and cannot do in life. This is a time when people are not afraid to say that something is unknown to them or beyond their capabilities. It is a time when they have firmly established their habits and patterns, when they finally know themselves well enough to relax in life. The West is a time of strength in human life, a time of balance.

The animal associated with Mudjekeewis is the grizzly bear, one of the strongest of our bear brothers and sisters. Like all bears, the grizzly is very intelligent, cunning, and resourceful. The grizzly bear is a problem solver, one that can use hands and heart to find ways to do things that will benefit both himself and his brothers and sisters in the bear kingdom. The grizzly bear is an animal that sometimes inspires fear in humans in much the same way the truly mature individual can inspire fear in those who are hesitant about reaching their own maturity.

When people reach the time of Mudjekeewis, they have established themselves. They have a career, a profession, a family, and a home. They are stable and responsible. They have reached a point where they are carrying on their backs not only the young ones—to whom they provide teaching, leadership, and healing—but also the older ones, those who are no longer capable of caring for themselves as they once did. While the time of Mudjekeewis appears to be a straightforward time, it does contain a paradox: Although you experience your highest point of strength, you suddenly become aware of the little deaths you see around you; although you feel you could conquer the world, you become aware of your own mortality and what that truly means.

When you are under the influence of Mudjekeewis, it is a good time to find out how you can manifest the powers of Spirit here on earth. It is also an appropriate time to look within yourself and gain the strength that comes from true self-knowledge. The time of Mudjekeewis is the time when you have the freedom and the knowledge to be selfless and idealistic. It is a time when you can understand and move between the different realms of creation, when you can share your strength with others.

When you are experiencing Mudjekeewis, it is important that you use all the abilities given to you for the good of the people. This is a direction in which people do have a lot of power and, as with all power, it can be used for good or for bad.

The Mudjekeewis position is the place to seek if you aspire to maturity. The Mudjekeewis position can teach you about strength, adaptability, responsibility, teaching, leadership, and power. The Mudjekeewis position is one that will help you be truly concerned for the welfare of others. It will aid you in tempering your passion and in assessing the knowledge you have gained from life. You should seek this stone to learn the balance between looking within and acting without. You should also come to this place when you know what your purpose in life truly is, but need help in fulfilling it.

Mudjekeewis brings healing to the spiritual level, healing to all that we consider to be sacred. It is during the time of Mudjekeewis that we can be most effective as spiritual leaders and as ceremonialists. It is when we have enough experience of life to share that we can do the most true teaching. The power of Mudjekeewis is the power of serving: serving with strength, courage, grace, and great ability.

COMMUNICATING WITH YOUR SPIRIT KEEPER

What you need. A shell or bowl; a feather; sage, sweet grass, cedar, or tobacco (to find them try an herb store or crystal shop); matches for smudging; a tape of chanting or drumming; and notebook and pen or tape recorder. Access to a Medicine Wheel is helpful but not mandatory.

Estimated time. Thirty minutes minimum.

1. Begin playing your chanting or drumming tape.
2. In order to center your energy it is good to begin with the ceremony of smudging (see page 12). To smudge you place dried sage or sweet grass or cedar or tobacco or some combination of these herbs in a strong shell or bowl. You light the herbs; when they are starting to burn use the feather to extinguish the flame so that the herbs smolder rather than burn. You draw the smoke from the herbs to you using five motions: one to cleanse your heart; one, your head; one, your arms; one, the front of your body; one, the back of your body.
3. Take some deep breaths and feel yourself connected with the energy of both earth and sky.
4. Think about the four directions, the Spirit Keepers, and their qualities.
5. If you have access to a Medicine Wheel, go to each Spirit Keeper stone as you consider it.
6. If you don't have a Medicine Wheel to use, or if you are using a small wheel, make your walk, your offerings, and the choice of place to sit through visualization.
7. Make an offering to your beginning Spirit Keeper. If you know which Spirit Keeper is most affecting you now, make an offering there also.

8. Sit by the Spirit Keeper stone that draws you most strongly right now.
9. Once seated, whether in body or visualization, take time to breathe and relax again.
10. Imagine yourself in a beautiful meadow. In this meadow you come upon an ancient Medicine Wheel. Note how the wheel looks.
11. Walk around the wheel, paying particular attention to the Spirit Keeper stones. Take the time to notice how each stone makes you feel. Eventually, settle by one of these four stones.
12. Ask the Spirit Keeper of this stone if he or she will communicate with you now.
13. Wait in a receptive state to get an answer.
14. If the Spirit Keeper wishes to communicate with you, allow him or her to come to you. Note how he or she looks, moves, smells, sounds, and feels.
15. Ask the Spirit Keeper whether you are now experiencing some of his or her power.
16. Ask on what levels of your being—physical, mental, emotional, or spiritual—this Spirit Keeper is now affecting you.
17. Ask the Spirit Keeper if he or she has any particular messages for you now.
18. Ask the Spirit Keeper if there are any lessons he or she wishes to impart to you.
19. When the Spirit Keeper has finished, thank him or her for the teachings.
20. Ask whether he or she would like any particular gifts or offerings made by you.
21. Take some time to reflect. When you are finished, walk again through the meadow and return to normal consciousness.
22. Gently stretch and be sure you are totally back in normal awareness.
23. Write or record your experience.
24. Make any offerings the Spirit Keeper asked you to make.

COMMUNICATING WITH YOUR ELEMENTAL CLAN

Follow the exercise for communicating with the Spirit Keepers, substituting the elemental clan stones for the directional ones. Be aware that these keepers can appear in the form of their element; that is as a mountain, a lake, an erupting volcano, a whirlwind, or any other form of the four elements.

COMMUNICATING WITH YOUR ELEMENTAL CLAN THROUGH NATURE

What you need. A notebook and pen or tape recorder. For earth: time to walk on the earth or a handful of soil or a pot full of earth. For water: a body of water such as a creek, river, lake, or the ocean; tap water; or a glass of water. For fire: a candle, a safe campfire, or a fireplace. For air: the wind.

Estimated time. Thirty minutes minimum for each element.

1. It can be very effective to communicate directly with the element now affecting you. You can determine that element by walking around the Medicine Wheel either in reality or through visualization. Be aware of the stone representing the elemental clan that draws you most strongly. Once you determine with which element you are working, proceed to either step 2, 3, 4, or 5.

2. For the element of earth, it is best to actually go out in nature and experience the earth energy. You can do that through putting your hands over the earth and feeling her energy or by lying on the earth and allowing her energy to go throughout your body. If you are not situated to do either of these you can get a handful of earth and sit holding it, or sit near a large pot full of soil.

3. To experience the element of water, you can walk by a river, lake, stream, or ocean and feel how this energy affects you. If weather and water quality permit, you can also go into the water and experience the difference in energy this can create. You can also make contact with the energy of water whenever you wash your hands, take a bath or shower, or take a drink of water.

4. The most common way to experience the element of fire is through a candle. You can sit looking at the flame and see what energy shifts this evokes. You can also experience fire in situations where you can safely build a campfire or by watching a fire burning in a fireplace.

5. To experience the air, become aware of the wind. Feel the difference in energy when it caresses you with a gentle breeze or buffets you with a strong gale.

6. By actually experiencing each of the elements, you will be able to ascertain which one is affecting you most at any given time.

7. Be sure to express your thanks to whichever element is now helping you.

8. Write or record your experience.

**Shawnodese—Spirit Keeper of the South
—by George Monacelli**

4

The Moon and Spirit Path Stones

The essence of the Medicine Wheel is movement and change. To grow, people have to journey as far as they can around the wheel experiencing the lessons, challenges, strengths, and weaknesses of as many of the positions as possible. Each position has some gift to give that will enlarge and enrich their lives.

Although people only experience the Center Circle and Spirit Keeper stones for short periods of time, they spend most of their lives experiencing one or another of the moon positions. People are born into one moon position, which is determined by their date of birth. This birth, or beginning, position determines how a person will be as a child and how they will act during times of transition in their lives. Your beginning position is most comfortable for you. As you travel the wheel you return to it when you need familiarity and a feeling of security. You do not remain in this position but also explore other moon positions as you seek to understand as many lessons of life as you can.

People usually seek knowledge of the Spirit Path stones when they are concentrating on healing the physical, mental, emotional, or spiritual aspect of themselves. The Spirit Path stones gently yet directly teach about the powers of each Spirit Keeper, of the Creator, and of these four distinct levels of human life.

The twelve Moon stones and the twelve Spirit Path stones provide people with reasonable, practical ways of journeying about the Medicine Wheel, ways that strengthen and support them in growing as much as they can, and ways that introduce them to the unseen world slowly and subtly.

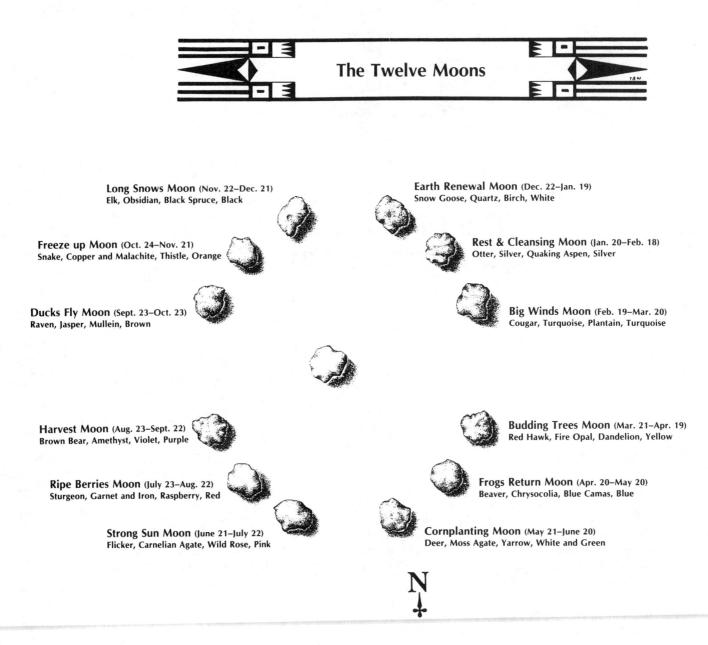

The Twelve Moons

Long Snows Moon (Nov. 22–Dec. 21)
Elk, Obsidian, Black Spruce, Black

Freeze up Moon (Oct. 24–Nov. 21)
Snake, Copper and Malachite, Thistle, Orange

Ducks Fly Moon (Sept. 23–Oct. 23)
Raven, Jasper, Mullein, Brown

Harvest Moon (Aug. 23–Sept. 22)
Brown Bear, Amethyst, Violet, Purple

Ripe Berries Moon (July 23–Aug. 22)
Sturgeon, Garnet and Iron, Raspberry, Red

Strong Sun Moon (June 21–July 22)
Flicker, Carnelian Agate, Wild Rose, Pink

Earth Renewal Moon (Dec. 22–Jan. 19)
Snow Goose, Quartz, Birch, White

Rest & Cleansing Moon (Jan. 20–Feb. 18)
Otter, Silver, Quaking Aspen, Silver

Big Winds Moon (Feb. 19–Mar. 20)
Cougar, Turquoise, Plantain, Turquoise

Budding Trees Moon (Mar. 21–Apr. 19)
Red Hawk, Fire Opal, Dandelion, Yellow

Frogs Return Moon (Apr. 20–May 20)
Beaver, Chrysocolia, Blue Camas, Blue

Cornplanting Moon (May 21–June 20)
Deer, Moss Agate, Yarrow, White and Green

N

THE TWELVE MOONS
·····

Life is a circle, from birth to death to rebirth. Humans, like the seasons, pass through many phases during their lives. The Moon stones of the Medicine Wheel give us a way of understanding and celebrating these changes. The moon during which you were born determines your starting place on the wheel.

Each moon has its own totem in the mineral, plant, and animal kingdoms. These totems help to describe the lessons of that moon and aid humans, either born during or traveling through the position, to understand their own characteristics and lessons. These totems also provide a bridge from humans to all of the rest of earth's children. As you travel the wheel you should attempt to learn as much as you can about the totems of any position in which you stand so you can always grow more knowledgeable about those who share the earth with you. When you experience a new moon position you have the opportunity to take on the characteristics of the totems for that moon and learn from them. The more you learn the farther you can travel on your journey around the wheel.

As you read about the moons remember not everyone standing in a particular moon position will have every characteristic of that position. Each person travels the wheel at his or her own speed, learning the lessons appropriate at any given time. The important thing is for people to keep traveling and not get stuck in one position, using this as an excuse for not being all they can be.

Throughout the book each Moon stone is referred to either by its moon name or by its animal totem. People tend to relate more easily to their animal totems than their mineral or plant ones. The material about the moons and totems—discussed in detail in *The Medicine Wheel*—is highlighted here, with more detail about all of the mineral, plant, animal totems, and colors appearing in part II of the book.

THE EARTH RENEWAL MOON—SNOW GOOSE

The Earth Renewal Moon (December 22 to January 19) is the first moon of the year and the first moon of Waboose, Spirit Keeper of the North. This moon begins at the time of the winter solstice when Father Sun returns from his journey South and begins to bring the warmth that quickens growth in the Earth Mother and all her children. The stone representing this moon is placed one-quarter of the way to the East in the northern quadrant, moving clockwise. The mineral totem for the Earth Renewal Moon is the quartz crystal, the plant is the birch tree, and the animal is the snow goose. The color is white. The elemental clan influencing this position is the Turtle clan.

The Earth Renewal Moon teaches you to be as clear a receiver and transmitter of universal energy as the crystal, as important a communicator of the ancient knowledge as the birch tree, and as respectful of tradition and ritual as the snow goose. This is a position with the potential for great power. The Earth Renewal Moon teaches you to be fluid, yet proper in conduct as well as clear, adaptable, prudent, and wise. People in this position have keen vision, are good ceremonialists, and can take large steps in their personal evolution. Snow goose people need to guard against becoming blocked, against using their enormous power incorrectly, and against being so perfectionist they never have time for fun.

THE REST AND CLEANSING MOON—OTTER

The Rest and Cleansing Moon (January 20 to February 18) is the second moon of Waboose. The stone for this moon is placed midway between the northern and eastern stones. Silver is the mineral totem for the Rest and Cleansing Moon, the quaking aspen is the plant totem, the otter is the animal totem, and silver is the color. This position is influenced by the Butterfly clan.

People experiencing this moon are considered as valuable as silver, as light-hearted as the music of aspen leaves, and as playful as the otter. The otter position can help you truly to like people, yourself included, and to be more humanitarian in your views. This is a time when you can excel in communicating, in developing your intellect, and in romance. The Rest and Cleansing Moon can help you both to develop your psychic abilities and to uncover the clever, bold, humanitarian, and gentle aspects of your own being. Although otter people have the potential to be noble and loving, they need to guard against dreaming so much that none of their noble ideas ever become reality.

THE BIG WINDS MOON—COUGAR

The Big Winds Moon (February 19 to March 20) is the last moon of Waboose, Spirit Keeper of the North. The stone representing this moon is placed three-quarters of the way between North and East. The mineral totem for the Big Winds Moon is turquoise, the plant is the plantain, the animal is the cougar, the colors are blue and green, and the elemental clan influence is that of the Frog clan.

Turquoise can teach people in this position about the real meaning of value and about protection, the plantain can teach them about their healing abilities, and the cougar can teach them about mystery and the need to establish safe territory. The Big Winds Moon can help you discover your own natural medicine power and the depth of your psychic abilities. In this position you will learn about your deep sensitivity, your yearning for spirituality, your hesitation to express your true feelings, and your need for grounding on the earth. People experiencing the Big Winds Moon can be prone to moodiness and to melancholy. They need to learn to temper their sensitivity and to have a greater sense of reality.

THE BUDDING TREES MOON—RED HAWK

The Budding Trees Moon (March 21 to April 19) is the first moon of Wabun, Spirit Keeper of the East and occurs at the time of the spring equinox. The stone for this moon is placed one-quarter of the way between the eastern and southern stones in the outer circle. The mineral totem for the Budding Trees Moon is the fire opal, the plant is the dandelion, and the animal is the red-tailed hawk. The color is yellow. This position is directly influenced by the Thunderbird clan.

The fire opal can teach people in this position about the need for water— the emotions—in tempering their fiery energy. The dandelion can show them the advantages of taking root as well as flying. The red hawk can demonstrate the joy of freedom and of a long, clear view. The Budding Trees Moon will teach you about energy, intensity, catalyzing change, fearlessness, and optimism. Being in this position will show you your leadership ability, the enormity of your own spirit, and the extent of your clear-sightedness. People experiencing the Budding Trees Moon need to learn to channel their energies, contain their emotions, and be more patient with others.

THE FROGS RETURN MOON—BEAVER

The Frogs Return Moon (April 20 to May 20) is the second moon of Wabun of the East. The stone for this moon is placed midway between the eastern and southern stones in the outer circle of the Medicine Wheel. The mineral totem for the moon is the chrysocolla, the plant is the blue camas, and the animal is the beaver. The color is blue and the elemental clan influence is the Turtle clan.

From the chrysocolla, people in this position learn to balance the earth and sky within themselves; from the blue camas, to sustain themselves and others; from the beaver, to make all environments as pleasant as possible. This is the position to explore when you wish to learn about stability, the value of hard work, luck, and your ability to create and maintain an orderly and beautiful environment. The Frogs Return Moon will teach you about perseverance, patience, stability, and practicality. People in this position need to guard against being too stubborn, overindulging, and holding back all their feelings.

THE CORNPLANTING MOON—DEER

The Cornplanting Moon (May 21 to June 20) is the third moon of Wabun, the Spirit Keeper of the East. The stone representing this moon is placed three-quarters of the way between the eastern and southern stones in the outer circle of the Medicine Wheel. The mineral totem for the Cornplanting Moon is the moss agate. The plant totem is the yarrow, and the animal is the deer. The colors are green and white, and the elemental influence is from the Butterfly clan.

The moss agate teaches people in this position to clearly see their link with the mineral and plant kingdoms. The yarrow teaches about both cleansing and strengthening. The deer demonstrates the beauty of grace and quick movement. This position teaches about beauty in yourself, in others, and in your environment and teaches about your own healing abilities. This position will point out any cutting edges in your personality, the necessity of balancing time and energy, and your ability to create. People experiencing the deer position need to learn to be more consistent, less suspicious, and more willing to show some of their own deep feelings.

THE STRONG SUN MOON—FLICKER

The Strong Sun Moon (June 21 to July 22) is the first moon of Shawnodese, Spirit Keeper of the South, and occurs at the time of the summer solstice. The stone honoring this position is placed one-quarter of the way between the southern and western stones of the Medicine Wheel. The mineral totem for the Strong Sun Moon is carnelian agate, the plant is the wild rose, and the animal is the flicker. The color is pink, and the elemental influence is from the Frog clan.

From the carnelian, people experiencing this position can learn about their strong heart connection; from the rose, about their ability both to heal and to inspire; and from the flicker, about their desire for self-expression. The Strong Sun Moon teaches about the importance of the emotions and the need for a strong home base. People experiencing the energy of this position are intuitive and wild in some aspects of being, but conservative and home loving in others. The Strong Sun Moon will educate you about the law of relationship and about family, mothering, and nurturing. While working with the flicker you must guard against wallowing in all your emotions and about fearing to take any stand.

THE RIPE BERRIES MOON—STURGEON

The second moon of Shawnodese, Spirit Keeper of the South is the Ripe Berries Moon (July 23 to August 22). The stone for this position is placed midway between the southern and western stones in the outer circle of the Medicine Wheel. Iron and garnet are the mineral totems for this moon, raspberry is the plant totem, and the sturgeon is the animal totem. The color is red, and the position is influenced by the Thunderbird clan.

Iron teaches people in this position about their strength and garnet shows them their heart is the source of that strength. From the raspberry they learn about their sweetness and the thorns they project to protect this part of themselves from other people. The sturgeon show them their depth and their need to teach. The Ripe Berries Moon teaches them how to work from the heart center, how to demonstrate affection, how to face fears, and how to develop leadership abilities. This moon helps develop courage and power. People experiencing the sturgeon energy need to guard against impulsiveness, arrogance, and a tendency to dominate any scenario.

THE HARVEST MOON—BROWN BEAR

The Harvest Moon (August 23 to September 22) is the last moon of Shawnodese of the South. The stone honoring this position is placed three-quarters of the way between the southern and western stones. The mineral totem for this position is the amethyst, the plant totem is the violet, and the animal totem is the brown bear. The color is purple, and the elemental influence comes from the Turtle clan.

The amethyst can teach people experiencing this moon about good judgment and justice; the violet, about their ability to penetrate to secret regions of the heart and soul; and the brown bear, about their capacity for creative curiosity. The Harvest Moon teaches about discrimination, fair decisions, good sense, perseverance, confidence, and the ability to analyze. The energy of this position is one of balance, rationality, and practicality. This is the place on the wheel that will help you truly understand the concepts of work and duty. In the brown bear place you need to guard against being overly critical of others, or cynical about life.

THE DUCKS FLY MOON—RAVEN

The Ducks Fly Moon (September 23 to October 23) is the first moon of Mudjekeewis, the Spirit Keeper of the West and occurs at the time of the autumn equinox. The stone honoring this moon is placed one-quarter of the way, moving clockwise, between the southern and western stones. The mineral totem for this moon is jasper, usually of the bloodstone variety; the plant is the mullein; and the animal is the raven. The color is brown, and the elemental clan influencing this moon is the Butterfly clan.

From the jasper people experiencing this energy can learn how to draw both the earth and sun energy into their being and how to understand the messages of the heart. From the mullein they can learn about their abilities both to soothe and to irritate. From the raven they will gain understanding of their relationships with groups, and their ability to soar and dive. This is the position in which you can learn what balance truly is, even if you need to experience discomfort in order to do so. People experiencing the Ducks Fly Moon can rapidly go from one idea, concept, or mood to its opposite. This position can teach how to show physical affection and how to be comfortable both in earth and sky. People experiencing the raven energy must be careful not to be totally indecisive, and so changeable they confuse even themselves.

THE FREEZE UP MOON—SNAKE

The Freeze Up Moon (October 24 to November 21) is the middle moon of Mudjekeewis of the West. The stone honoring this time is placed midway between the western and northern stones in the outer circle of the Wheel. The mineral totems are copper and malachite, the plant is the thistle, and the animal is the snake. The color is orange and the Frog clan is the direct elemental influence.

Copper teaches people experiencing the Freeze Up Moon about how to focus their energies and malachite teaches them to be more sensitive to all energies. The thistle demonstrates healing abilities and versatility. The snake teaches adaptability and the capacity to silently travel to places others might fear to go. This is the position to learn how to travel between the different realms of creation and how to become a messenger for the spiritual aspects of life. The snake position will teach you about the extent of your own energy, your ability to create change, your inquisitiveness, your desire for truth, and your keen sight. When working with the Freeze Up Moon you must be careful to keep yourself grounded and not to become too suspicious of people.

THE LONG SNOWS MOON—ELK

The Long Snows Moon (November 22 to December 21) is the last moon of Mudjekeewis and the final moon of the year. Moving clockwise, the stone representing this position is three-quarters of the way between the western and northern stones of the wheel. Obsidian is the mineral totem, the black spruce is the plant totem, and the elk is the animal totem. The color is black and the elemental influence comes from the Thunderbird clan.

From obsidian, people experiencing this position can learn about their ability to perceive and mirror the thoughts and feelings of others. The black spruce teaches how to be soft and strong at the same time, and the elk demonstrates the power of beauty, majesty, and cooperation. This is the position in which to learn about your desire for justice, and your ability to live with the dualities of nature and life. The Long Snows Moon teaches about mental strength, deep fear of emotions, relationships, teaching, and communicating. People in the elk position are insightful, independent, fearless, determined, and open hearted. They need to guard against being overly argumentative and erratic in intimate relationships.

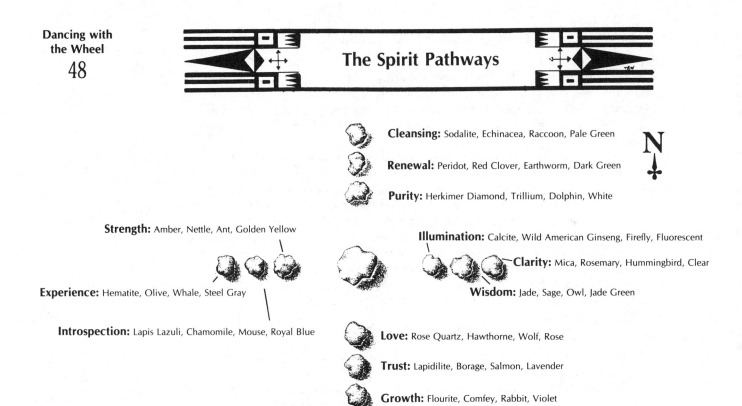

The Spirit Pathways

Cleansing: Sodalite, Echinacea, Raccoon, Pale Green

Renewal: Peridot, Red Clover, Earthworm, Dark Green

Purity: Herkimer Diamond, Trillium, Dolphin, White

Strength: Amber, Nettle, Ant, Golden Yellow

Illumination: Calcite, Wild American Ginseng, Firefly, Fluorescent

Clarity: Mica, Rosemary, Hummingbird, Clear

Experience: Hematite, Olive, Whale, Steel Gray

Wisdom: Jade, Sage, Owl, Jade Green

Introspection: Lapis Lazuli, Chamomile, Mouse, Royal Blue

Love: Rose Quartz, Hawthorne, Wolf, Rose

Trust: Lapidilite, Borage, Salmon, Lavender

Growth: Flourite, Comfey, Rabbit, Violet

THE SPIRIT PATHWAYS
·····

The Spirit Pathways, which lead from each Spirit Keeper stone toward the Center Circle, remind us of the gifts of the Spirit Keepers and teach us about the qualities that we need to go from the outer part of the Medicine Wheel to the center. The Spirit Pathways provide a road map of the physical, mental, emotional, and spiritual qualities that can take us from ordinary reality to the sacred space, to the center of life, to the Creator. People usually come to the Spirit Path stones by choice either to give thanks or to ask for help. These Spirit Pathways are reminders of both our human gifts and our human responsibilities.

The Spirit Path of the North

The gift of Waboose of the North is the gift of healing of our physical being and of our way of relating to the world. This is the healing that allows us to let go of disease and accept health.

CLEANSING

The outer stone in the northern Spirit Path is the one that represents the quality of cleansing. The mineral associated with cleansing is sodalite, the plant is echinacea, the animal is the raccoon, and the color is pale green. Because the North relates to physical healing, the Cleansing stone is the one to seek to detoxify your body; to get rid of any impurities that are keeping you from health.

On the mental level, the Cleansing stone helps to clear out old ideas and to detach from former ways of thinking that no longer fit. Emotionally, the Cleansing stone is one to seek to discharge emotions that are blocked, to have a true catharsis. It is the stone that can rid emotional misconceptions, open people to wider vistas of feeling. It is the stone to go to when it is time to go dig a hole and bury your emotional garbage. Spiritually, the Cleansing stone aids in knowing what exactly is sacred to you. It is the place to go when you are ready to surrender your old spiritual ideas.

RENEWAL

The middle Spirit Path stone of the North is renewal. The mineral associated with renewal is peridot, the plant is the red clover, the animal is the earthworm, and the color is dark green. Physically, renewal is what happens when you dedicate yourself to becoming healthy, well, and fit; when you nourish yourself correctly; and when you make an effort to rebuild and replenish your body. The Renewal stone is a very strong one for healing, rebuilding, and revitalizing your physical being.

The Renewal stone helps to teach a healthier attitude concerning the way you view the world around you or your place in it. It is the stone to go to when you wish to open up to new ideas or to restructure your thinking. The Renewal stone gives new perspective and new ideas. On the emotional level, the Renewal stone is the one to go to if you wish to learn how to love yourself more, how to be good to yourself and to take better care of yourself in terms of your feelings. It is the position that teaches self-love. Spiritually, the Renewal stone is a stone that can help you get in touch with the true foundation of your own beliefs and to formulate ceremonies to bring your spirituality into focus. This is the position to help you renew your belief in the Creator and in the goodness of all life.

PURITY

Purity is the third Spirit Path stone of the North, the one closest to the Center Circle. The mineral associated with purity is the Herkimer diamond, the plant is the trillium, the animal is the dolphin, and the color is white. Purity is a term that often carries a negative connotation in society today. Yet, according to the dictionary, being pure is being free from anything that is different, inferior, or contaminating. This definition of purity has very little to do with what people first think of when they hear the word. To us, purity means being wholesome, fresh, pristine, with the capacity of looking at the world with the eyes of a child.

Physically, you could come to the Purity stone if you wished to look at the world like a child and if you wished to return to a sense of innocence, to enthusiasm. It is also the stone to seek if you feel the need to purify or totally cleanse your body. Mentally, the Purity stone is the one you would come to for help with getting rid of preconceptions or misconceptions, cynicism and sarcasm. Emotionally, purity is the stone to help renew your sense of integrity, to teach about honesty, spontaneity, and receptivity. It is the place of balance and giving, the place to become self-realized.

The Spirit Path of the East

The gift of Wabun of the East is the gift of healing of the mental being. This is the healing that allows us to see truth and to let go of all the lies we have been told and have accepted in our own minds.

CLARITY

The first stone in the eastern Spirit Path is the stone representing the quality of clarity. The mineral associated with clarity is mica, the plant is rosemary, the animal is the hummingbird, and the color is clear. Clarity is a two-edged gift. It can either open the world for you or help you to form a prison in which you place yourself. Sometimes people are so happy to let go of confusion they mistake their first small glimpse of clarity as the whole truth. They hold this little truth so tightly they lose sight of the bigger truth. On the physical level, you would come to the Clarity stone if you wished to simplify your way of dealing with the world, if you wished to live life in a less complicated manner. Mentally, you would come to the Clarity stone if you wished to see things clearly and simply, if you wished to increase your sense of discrimination, if you wished to have more awareness, and if you wished to be able to communicate more directly. You would come to the Clarity stone if you wished to have more lucidity. But beware because it is when the mind believes it knows everything clearly that you lose the true knowledge that comes from the heart.

Emotionally you would come to the Clarity stone if you wished to have more spontaneous, direct, smooth-flowing, unblocked energy. Spiritually you would come to the Clarity stone if you wished to become a more efficient receiver and transmitter of the universal energy or if you wished to feel more connected spiritually.

WISDOM

The second Spirit Path stone of the East is the one representing the quality of wisdom. The mineral associated with wisdom is jade, the plant is sage, the animal is the owl, and the color is jade green. Wisdom on the physical level means knowing what your limits are both in terms of your body and in terms of life around you. It allows you to come to a better understanding of your body and how it works as well as an understanding of life and how it works. Wisdom is knowing what is good for you and acting on that knowledge.

Mentally, wisdom is the ability to discern. Discernment comes when you have had experience and tempered that experience with understanding. It is one thing to have knowledge but it is quite another to know how to apply it. The Wisdom stone can help you learn this very important lesson.

Emotionally you would come to the Wisdom stone if you wanted to increase your maturity and your sense of stability. You would come to the Wisdom stone if you wanted to know what is good for you and if you were willing to act on that knowledge. Spiritually you would come to the Wisdom stone when you truly wanted to become the sage in your own life.

ILLUMINATION

The third Spirit Path stone of the East, the one closest to the center, is that representing the quality of illumination. The mineral associated with illumination is calcite, the plant is wild American ginseng, the animal is the firefly, and the color is fluorescent. Illumination, which is also frequently referred to as enlightenment is, on the physical level, the ability to let the sacred energy—the Creator—flow freely and vitally through you. You would come to the Illumination stone to ask for that gift and to thank the Creator when you have received it even if only for a second. You would also come to the Illumination stone to ask that the creative energy flows through the way you relate to the world around you and thus helps you see the truth and the light of the life that is all around you.

Mentally you would come to illumination when you wanted to know the truth about life, or when you have been given glimpses of that truth. You would come to the Illumination stone when you wanted to thoroughly understand yourself and the universe and when you wanted to come in real contact with your intuitive knowing. On the emotional level you would come to the Illumination stone when you desired to feel the truth of life within your being, when you wanted to allow your emotions to be more free flowing and balanced, and when you were ready to explore the concept and reality of unconditional love and of peace. Spiritually, the Illumination stone can help you live the truth you have gained. You would come to the Illumination stone when you wished to have a divine understanding of life, when you wished to deeply know your connection with the universe, and when you wanted to have the capacity to radiate out to others those truths you have learned.

The Spirit Path of the South

The South is the direction on the Medicine Wheel to go when you want to receive healing on the emotional level and when you want to receive healing of your heart. It is the direction to go to give thanks for relationships or to ask for help with relationships.

GROWTH

The first Spirit Path stone of the South is that representing the quality of growth. The mineral associated with growth is fluorite, the plant is the comfrey, the animal is the rabbit, and the color is violet. On the physical level, growth means change, development, unfolding, flowering, expanding, and maturing. If you wish to mature in your viewpoint of the world, if you wish to develop your physical body, if you wish to open yourself to new knowledge of all that is physical in the universe, you would go to this stone.

Mentally, you would go to the Growth stone if you wished to learn more, if you wanted to expand your knowledge, and if you wanted to broaden and deepen yourself. Emotionally, the Growth stone can help you enrich your emotions, stretch, extend your boundaries, and expand yourself wider than you have before. You would go to the Growth stone if you wanted to experience a broader range of feelings and know how to connect with these feelings and accept them. Spiritually, the Growth stone represents the harvest, evolution, and development. You would go to the Growth stone if you were ready to take responsibility for your own life experience.

TRUST

The second Spirit Path stone of the South is that representing trust. The mineral associated with trust is lepidolite, the plant is borage, the animal is salmon, and the color is lavender. On the physical level trust is having confidence, being sure of yourself, accepting things, and, conversely, being willing to surrender to life. If you need more assurance, if you need to have body acceptance, or if you need to learn about surrender, you would go to this stone. Mentally, the Trust stone is the place to let go of suspicions, to strengthen your belief in something or someone. It is the place of being mentally open and receptive. It is a place of intense learning.

Emotionally, the Trust stone is the place to ask for the capacity to give and receive love and to express yourself fully. The Trust stone can help you increase your vulnerability. Spiritually, you would go to the Trust stone when you wanted to learn to let go and let the Creator help you. You would go to the Trust stone to learn about true faith and the surrender and release that come with it. You would go to the Trust stone to learn about spiritual openness and to learn to expand your conception of what is sacred in the world. This position can give you more confidence in your relationships with other humans or with any beings on the Earth Mother.

LOVE

The third stone of the southern Spirit Path is the stone for love. The mineral for love is the rose quartz, the plant is hawthorne, the animal is the wolf, and the color is rose. On the physical level, love is pleasure. It is expressed in sexual energy, affection, touching, eating, smelling, viewing, hearing, and in orgasm. It is also expressed by feeling the life energy in your body whenever anything moves you: a color, a musical piece, a plant, a tree, a picture, a view. You would go to the Love stone if you wanted to find out about sensuality, union, touching, parenting, and mating. You would also go there if you wanted to find out how to have more pleasure in your relationship with the world and in your own body.

Mentally, you would go to the Love stone to find out about true healing of emotional problems. You would go to the Love stone to find out how to communicate better, how to accept, and how to support yourself and others. You would go to this position if you wanted validation or recognition or if you wanted to learn how to give them. You would go to this stone if you wanted to learn more about honesty, honor, cherishing, and understanding. Emotionally, you would go to the Love stone if you wanted to find out about devotion, tenderness, compassion, or delight. You would also go to the Love stone if you wanted to learn about joy, ecstasy, and passion. This is the place to seek to learn about nurturing, about harmony, and about sharing on the deepest levels.

Spiritually, the Love stone can help you understand the true meaning of devotion, transcendence, unconditional love, and acceptance. You would go to the Love stone to learn about selflessness, service, blending, and having the commitment and dedication to truly serve all your relations. Here you can experience your deep emotional connection with the Creator and the creation.

The Spirit Path of the West

The western Spirit Path is the place to go if you desire healing on the spiritual level of life. The western pathway is the place to show you what is sacred to you and what is truly sacred in the universe. It is the place to gain knowledge about ceremony and about religion.

EXPERIENCE

The first Spirit Path stone of the West represents experience. The mineral associated with experience is hematite, the plant is the olive tree, the animal is the whale, and the color is steel gray. On the physical level, experience means concrete skills, body memory, education, expertise, and learning something by putting your hands on it. Experience is doing and learning through your doing.

On the mental level, experience is learning through trial and error and remembering what you have learned. It is the mental habits and patterns that guide your learning. Emotionally, the Experience stone is the one to go to if you want more stability, more confidence, and more involvement. The Experience stone will let you feel you are a full participant in any sort of relationship. It is also the stone to help you assess your feelings and relax with them. Spiritually, you would go to the Experience stone if you wished to learn about being selective, if you wished to know how to internalize the lessons you have been taught, or if you were searching for more spiritual maturity. You would also go there if you wanted to know yourself better, if you wanted to temper yourself, or if you wanted the ability to integrate and focus the knowledge you have gained through life.

INTROSPECTION

The second Spirit Path stone of the West is that representing introspection. The mineral associated with introspection is lapis lazuli, the plant is chamomile, the animal is the mouse, and the color is royal blue. Introspection is the ability to look within. On the physical level you would go to the Introspection stone if you wanted to retreat, if you desired solitude and quiet, or if you wanted to learn more about your body and how it works internally.

Mentally, the Introspection stone can help you reflect, contemplate, synthesize, take stock of yourself, think before you speak, and let all of your communications be guided by your own wisdom. Emotionally, you would go to the Introspection stone to learn what your true feelings and patterns are. You would go there to integrate your emotions or to see what you have learned from being withdrawn or in retreat.

Spiritually, the Introspection stone is the one that can help you reevaluate your idea of the spiritual. You would seek this stone to learn more about meditation and about containing yourself. It is at the Introspection stone that you would become more aware of the cycles of life, and it is there, too, in the still, quiet place within that you can have direct experience of the Creator, a direct communication with the sacred energy that is within you as it is within all things around you. Here you can find the truth of the universe by looking inside you.

STRENGTH

The third Spirit Path stone of the West is that representing strength. The mineral associated with strength is amber, the plant is nettle, the animal is the ant, and the color is golden yellow. On the physical level, strength has its obvious meaning. It means endurance, stamina, a steady energy flow, and power. To have all these things, you need to know your limits, to be steadfast in your training, and to have an unshakable devotion to developing your own strength. As all this is true of your body, so it is true of the way in which you deal with the world around you. Mentally, you would go to the Strength stone if you needed more mental discipline, if you needed to learn to have the courage of your convictions, if you wished for more security, or if you wanted to become more determined or decisive. You would go to the Strength stone if you wanted to improve your concentration.

Emotionally, you would go to the Strength stone if you wanted to become more centered, more self-aware, more balanced, and more courageous in your way of dealing with relationships and in your way of dealing with love. The Strength stone can help to teach you about your emotional limits and about constancy. It can also help you know what you truly like. It is the Strength stone that will give you security in your relationships and self-control in your actions with the people to whom you relate.

Spiritually, you would go to the Strength stone when you wanted to know what you believed, when you wanted to be centered, when you wanted to gain strong convictions, and when you wanted to explore spiritual self-discipline. It is also the Strength stone you would seek when you wanted to know your true connection with the Creator.

APPROACHING THE SPIRIT PATH STONES

What you need. A Medicine Wheel or the ability to visualize one clearly (for help in visualizing the wheel refer to the Medicine Wheel chart in chapter 1), cornmeal or tobacco to make an offering, and a notebook and pen or tape recorder.

Estimated time. Thirty minutes.

1. It is appropriate to go to a Spirit Path stone when you need to experience the quality it represents. For example, you would go to the Clarity stone if you were feeling confused.
2. It is also appropriate to go to these stones if you wish to give thanks for having experienced their help. For example, you would go to the Experience stone if you had just experienced a new way of dealing with life.
3. To approach a Spirit Path stone you should first make a complete circle of the Medicine Wheel (either in body or in visualization). Then go to the proper directional stone. Enter from this stone, walking to the left of the Spirit Path stones. Stop at the stone you wish to approach, turn and face the outer rim of the Medicine Wheel. Make an offering to the stone.
4. Make your request or give your thanks.
5. Sit by the stone.
6. Be receptive and wait for any message that quality has for you.
7. When you have received what you feel you need, get up and stand to the left of the stone, facing the center of the wheel.
8. Complete your walk toward the center, on the left side of the Spirit Path stones. When you reach the outside of the Center Circle, turn around the last Spirit Path stone, then walk to the right of the stones, exiting the wheel through the same directional stone by which you entered.

WORKING WITH THE MEDICINE WHEEL POWERS

What you need. A Medicine Wheel or the ability to visualize one, a drumming or chanting tape, tobacco or cornmeal, smudging materials, and a notebook and pen or tape recorder.

Estimated time. Thirty minutes.

This exercise can be done either inside around your own personal Medicine Wheel (see p. 60 on how to construct a personal wheel) or sitting outside around a large Medicine Wheel. The purpose of this exercise is to allow the spirits of the Medicine Wheel positions to work with you.

1. In this exercise it is helpful to have a drumming or chanting tape playing softly in the background.
2. Smudge yourself.
3. Take whatever position at the Medicine Wheel feels right to you at this particular time.
4. In your mind's eye begin to circle the Medicine Wheel, first making a complete circle of the outer stones, then going in by whichever pathway seems to draw you and making a circle of the inner stones. After you have circled the inner stones, go to each pathway, walk down it toward the outside and then back up it toward the center. Do this until you have completely circled and honored each stone in the Medicine Wheel.

5. By this time you should be aware of a power that is calling to you.

6. In your mind's eye go to that stone. See what you feel the correct posture is for you at that rock. Should you sit down next to it? Should you kneel? Should you lie down? Should you stand? Visualize yourself making an offering of cornmeal to the Medicine Wheel power calling to you. Tell the Spirit you are grateful it has something it wants to share with you this day. Thank the Spirit for its help in guiding you to the correct position.

7. See yourself put your hands on or over the stone that honors this power. Thank this power for calling to you today.

8. Tell this power that you are now open to whatever message it wishes to give you.

9. Allow the Spirit Keeper of this position to come to you and to tell you whatever it is that it needs to tell you.

10. When your interaction with this Spirit Keeper is completed, visualize yourself going out the same pathway by which you entered. Once again, make a complete circle of the outer stones of the wheel, and come back to the place from which you began. Make an offering of thanksgiving to the entire Medicine Wheel and to the particular power that spoke with you today.

11. Go back fully into your physical being, making sure that you feel yourself totally in your body.

12. When you are totally in your body, gently stretch.

13. At this point, it is good to physically circle whatever Medicine Wheel you have been using and to go to the beginning place that you used in your visualization. Give thanks there. Make an offering.

14. This is an exercise that you can use time and time again. Using this exercise and seeing which stones call to you at any given time is also a way that you can begin observing your progress around the Medicine Wheel.

RECEIVING HELP FROM THE MEDICINE WHEEL

What you need. Smudging materials and a notebook and pen or tape recorder.

Estimated time. Thirty minutes.

This is an exercise to enable you to be more receptive when you ask the powers of the Medicine Wheel to come to your aid. It is also an exercise that can be used to make you more receptive to other powers with which you are working.

1. Smudge.

2. Take some deep breaths and relax.

3. Tell the Medicine Wheel that you wish to work with it at this time.

4. Accept whatever image first comes into your mind, whether it is a position on the wheel, a color, a mineral, a plant, an animal, a season, or a time of day connected with the wheel. If you get an image that obviously has no connection with the wheel, ask for another image to come into your mind.

5. When you have an image, first thank it for coming into your mind and then tell it that you wish to sit with it for a time. Ask this image to help you know how to be more receptive to your own intuitive powers, your own powers of feeling.

6. Hold this image in your mind for as long as you comfortably can. For

some people this will only be a few seconds, for others it will be a few minutes.

7. When the image fades from your mind, allow yourself to sit there in as relaxed and open a state as possible. Don't try to do anything.

8. If any other images come into your mind, note what they are without passing judgment. If you have any feelings either in your body or emotions, note what these are.

9. Sit in this position for at least fifteen minutes. If necessary, set an alarm to let you know when fifteen minutes are up. This, however, is a rude way to be awakened from a time of contemplation.

10. When at least fifteen minutes has passed, get a piece of paper and write down whatever images came to you or record them with a tape recorder.

11. You might notice that as you begin writing them down you remember other images that were a little less in the forefront of your mind.

12. The next time you choose to do this exercise, take out the paper that tells you about your success in doing it the time before and read it over.

13. Keep these papers, as they will tell you about your journey around the Medicine Wheel. They will also show you that the more you allow images and feelings to come to you, the more images and feelings will come.

14. As you do the exercise each time, be sure to end it by thanking the Medicine Wheel and the particular aspect of the wheel that helped you.

**Mudjekeewis—Spirit Keeper of the West
—by George Monacelli**

5

Building Medicine Wheels

In the Medicine Wheel vision we saw that many Medicine Wheels would spread across the land. They certainly have, not only in the United States but also in lands around the globe. People of various nationalities, races, and occupations have learned to use these new wheels in a good manner to help with healing humanity, the Earth Mother, and all of her other children.

The Medicine Wheel in all of its forms has the power and the ability to connect you to life. It will teach you, heal you, and magnify your prayers. If you have not already done so, the time may be approaching when you will wish to construct a Medicine Wheel of your own.

In this chapter is information both on how to construct a basic Medicine Wheel and different forms of the Medicine Wheel. This information provides a guideline for you. However, you should, when it feels right, use your own vision and intuition to guide you in developing ceremonies special to you and your Medicine Wheel, as long as they are not your adaptation of traditional sacred native ceremonies such as the pipe or sweat lodge. As you learned in the chapter on ceremonies and respect, there are some ceremonies that can be self-generated while others should only be done after thorough training with a medicine person.

Constructing any kind of Medicine Wheel is a ceremony. Follow the suggestions from the chapter on ceremonies in addition to what we share here.

BUILDING A MEDICINE WHEEL

What you need. Thirty-six rocks; cornmeal, tobacco, or other offerings; talking stick, wand, or staff; and, if desired, a compass, a rope, a pipe carrier with his or her pipe, a drum, or a rattle. The ceremony can end with a potluck dinner.

Estimated time. One to three hours.

1. Decide on the people who will participate. You can build a wheel alone or you can enlist the help of others. This is a good way to share a special energy with people you know.

2. Gather thirty-five stones and a special rock or other object to represent the Creator. Choose rocks that call to you or feel right to you. If possible, bring the other people who will be involved in constructing the Medicine Wheel with you when you select stones or ask each participant to bring a preselected stone with them. Remember to leave an offering of cornmeal or tobacco for each rock that you take. Set the rocks a short distance from where you anticipate building the wheel.

3. The ceremony will go smoother if the person organizing it tells the people a little about each position, and then allows people to choose the position they will honor, being sure that all positions are represented. It is also helpful to have either the ceremonial leader or someone else with a good sense of spatial relationship point with a staff to the places where the rocks should be laid during the ceremony. In this way you will be sure to have a circular Medicine Wheel. If no one has a good sense of spatial relations you can mark the places for the stones ahead of time, using rope with knots in it to determine where the correct placement of stones should be.

4. Select with care the location for the Medicine Wheel. Pick a spot that feels, good, powerful, safe, and connected with the universe. Choose an area that is private and will be respected by any casual passers-by. It needs to be a relatively flat area, big enough to accommodate the size wheel you intend to build and to give room to walk or stand outside of it.

   If you can't find a spot that is private or isolated then take down the wheel after each time you use it and rebuild it for the next ceremony.

5. Begin construction of the wheel by smudging the people involved, the area, anything that will be used in ceremony, and the rocks piled close by.

6. Have a pipe ceremony if there is a qualified pipe carrier available.

7. Let people express their feelings for the ceremony they are about to partake in by passing a talking stick, or a wand or staff, to each person who wishes a turn to speak.

8. Have some silent time for each person to center themselves.

9. The person organizing the construction should announce that the construction is to begin. He or she should offer a prayer then lead a meditation or a group centering exercise.

10. The ceremonial leader, or the designated person, will carry the stone or object representing the Creator to the center of the wheel. They will offer the stone to the six directions (sky, earth, North, South, East, West) and then place it in its designated spot, and make an offering of cornmeal, then make a short prayer, silently or out loud, to honor the Creator.

Everyone honoring a stone will follow the same procedure of offering the stone to the six directions, making a cornmeal offering, then making a prayer to honor the energy of that position. If you are building the wheel alone, you would place all the stones after offering them to the six directions and making a prayer for each position. You could then make a cornmeal offering to each stone when the wheel is in place. You may also use this method with a group if you prefer. In some tribes a medicine tool like the wheel is said to come alive after cornmeal has been offered to it.

11. After placing the Creator stone people will place the stones honoring the Earth Mother, Father Sun, Grandmother Moon, and the elemental clans. Each person enters the wheel alone, moves in a clockwise direction, and makes a complete circle around the Creator stone in the course of placing his or her stone. For example, if someone standing in the North were placing the stone for Father Sun he would enter from the North, walk clockwise toward the South where the sun stone is placed, place his stone, then walk clockwise to the West, exiting at the North where he entered.

12. People honoring the four Spirit Keepers should next place their stones. They should make a clockwise circle around the outside circumference of the wheel in their walk to make this placement. Begin placement with the North, Waboose; then go clockwise, or sunwise, around the wheel.

13. The people representing the three northern moons—Earth Renewal (Snow Goose), Rest and Cleansing (Otter), and Big Winds (Cougar)—should go to the northern gateway and enter one by one to place their stones.

14. When the northern people are finished, those honoring the eastern moons go to the eastern gateway, enter and place their stones. They are followed by people of the southern moons, then those of the western moons.

15. When all the stones for the twelve moons have been honored, the twelve people honoring the Spirit Path stones should go to the correct gateway for the quality they are honoring. They should line up at the gateway with the person representing the quality closest to the Creator first in line. For example, in the North, people would line up with purity first, then renewal, then cleansing.

16. When all of these people are in place, they enter to the left of the Spirit Keeper stone, walk to the position of the stone they are honoring, and place the stone. Then stand behind it facing the outside of the wheel.

17. The person honoring the quality closest to the outside perimeter speaks first. In the North, that would be the person representing cleansing. Then the person honoring the middle stone speaks, followed by the person honoring the innermost stone.

18. When all Spirit Path stones have been honored, the twelve people circle the stone they have honored then exit the Wheel on the opposite side of the Spirit Keeper stone from which they entered.

19. Everyone should join hands around the outside perimeter of the wheel while the ceremonial leader offers a prayer of dedication.

20. While the people are still standing in a circle, it is good now to give them the opportunity to speak what is in their hearts, whether it be words, a poem, a prayer, or music.

21. If appropriate, have a feast or potluck to celebrate this new Medicine Wheel.

22. If you are making a small Medicine Wheel in your home, follow the same directions, but compensate for the reduced size. If other people help you it might be better to have one person placing all the stones while the other people stand in a circle and make prayers for the different powers they are honoring.

23. If you have six people helping with the ceremony, each of you would honor six positions; if three, each would honor twelve; if eight, four would honor four stones and four would honor five.

GETTING TO KNOW YOUR WHEEL

•••••

Once your wheel is constructed, use it frequently. Many of the exercises in this book are more powerful when they are done around a Medicine Wheel. A Medicine Wheel can help you learn about the powers of the directions, the elements, the totems, the earth, sun, and moon. The more you use the wheel, the quicker your learning will occur. Each position on the wheel can give you new lessons and new understandings.

In addition, the presence of the Medicine Wheel can change the energy of the area in which it is built. It helps to send healing constantly to the Earth Mother and all of her children.

After constructing a wheel we sometimes do an exercise that gives the participants a chance to immediately feel and experience the energy of the Medicine Wheel.

When we utilize this exercise we have witnessed skeptics be positively affected, much to their surprise. It is often with awe that people verbalize how they feel the energy of a Medicine Wheel. Frequently participants are overwhelmed by the sensations. Some of the feelings participants have experienced range from temperature variations such as feeling hotter or colder, to a general sharpening of senses. Some people perceive the energy as thicker, tingly, tangible, pleasurable, tickley, safe, vibrant, blissful, numbing, sharp, refreshing, luxurious, and womblike, to mention a few. The energy of the wheel has elicited goose bumps, hair raising on arms, sweat, and flushed skin. Whatever the response, the overall consensus is that something special happens when stones are placed together in this manner.

EXERCISE TO FEEL THE MEDICINE WHEEL ENERGY

What you need. A Medicine Wheel, smudging or other cleansing materials, and a notebook and pen or tape recorder.

Estimated time. Twenty minutes.

1. Stand outside the outer circle of the Medicine Wheel. If there is more than one person doing the exercise they should stand in a circle, but not join hands.
2. Cleanse and center.
3. Put your hands in front of you, palms facing the earth. Be sure your hands are outside of the wheel. Note how the energy feels.
4. Move your hands within the wheel. Notice any changes in feeling.
5. Step back so you are two to four feet outside the wheel. Put your palms

up, facing the center of the wheel. Again be sure they are outside the wheel's circumference. Push into the wheel, feeling any changes of energy.

6. Put your hands down. Feel how your energy is. Now take a step into the wheel and notice any change in sensations. If space permits, step inside the inner circle of the wheel and notice how that feels.

7. If you are doing this exercise alone, you might wish to write or record your experience. If you are doing this with a group, discuss any differences people observed in themselves.

VARIATIONS IN BUILDING A MEDICINE WHEEL
·····

Wheels can be built any size to fit the needs of a ceremony or situation. While they are most commonly built out of stones or rocks this can vary depending on the nature of the ceremony. There are thousands of Medicine Wheels built all over the earth at this time. Although the majority are built from stones some are made from other materials.

Nature is an abundant source of innovative materials for a Medicine Wheel. Rocks, stones, pebbles, beautiful gemstones, minerals, almost anything that moves you can be used: boulders rolled together in the desert; beautiful, fragrant flowers gently placed on the earth; rocks from the earth found during a walk; expensive stones and minerals; acorns; pinecones; or shells. What you use in a wheel is a personal choice derived in part from the reason you are doing the ceremony or by what Spirit has communicated to you.

TREE MEDICINE WHEELS
·····

Making a Medicine Wheel circle with a tree representing the Creator is a wonderful way to honor the tree people and invite their energies to be part of the wheel. In some instances you might be able to build a wheel in a grove of trees where the trees can represent a number of the positions on the wheel. This makes for even more powerful tree energy. A Tree Medicine Wheel that includes a Medicine Wheel totem tree is particularly powerful in engendering the energy of the position with which the tree is associated.

Working with a Tree Medicine Wheel is good for stimulating your gifts of prophecy and of wisdom. Trees have the gift of carrying knowledge of the past into the present and future, so working with this kind of wheel can encourage your psychic abilities. Some people are able to glean ancient teachings from these planetary elders.

A Tree Medicine Wheel provides an excellent location to hold a moon lodge or men's lodge or for any kind of group activity aimed at unifying people for a common good.

It is good to bring frequent offerings to a Tree Wheel and to leave them at the base of the tree or to bury them in the ground below it. It is sometimes appropriate to place offerings in the tree branches. A good and unique offering is birdseed, which honors both the tree and the birds. We can learn much from the tree beings that firmly plant their roots in the earth while ever reaching for the sun above.

BUILDING A TREE MEDICINE WHEEL

What you need. A living tree or trees, and the materials required to build a Medicine Wheel (see p. 60).

Estimated time. One to three hours.

1. You can build a more permanent Tree Medicine Wheel using stones in addition to the trees(s) or you can use the gifts the tree provides such as pinecones, leaves, nuts, berries, or any fallen branches in place of stones.
2. Follow the instructions for building a Medicine Wheel. When you come to the position the tree represents, the person honoring that power should walk to the tree, make an offering to the six directions, then make a prayer that honors both the power and the tree.
3. If the Tree Medicine Wheel is not in a private place everything except the tree(s) should be dismantled after the ceremony is completed. A special prayer and offering should be made thanking the tree or trees at this time.

TREE MEDICINE WHEEL DREAM CEREMONY

What you need. Smudge materials, an offering, notebook and pen or tape recorder, and, if desired, a blanket.

Estimated time. One hour.

Simply napping inside a Tree Medicine Wheel can provide a lovely odyssey. Trees speak to the deepest levels of your consciousness. This dream ceremony can open you up to these levels in a way that ordinarily is difficult to reach.

1. Smudge yourself, the area, and anything you will use during the ceremony.
2. Make a special offering to the tree.
3. Invite the spirit of the tree to be with you. Make a prayer for whatever it is you are seeking. This can be done silently or out loud.
4. Wrap your arms around the tree, lean your body against it, and really connect with its energy. Allow this energy to come into you while allowing some of your energy to go to the tree. If the tree is very strong and sturdy and you are limber, you might climb up into its branches. Keep hugging or sitting in the tree until you feel a real connection.
5. Find a comfortable place to rest. Be aware of your relationship to the other parts of the wheel. You can curl up at the base of the tree in a blanket or lean against the tree for support. What is crucial is that you are comfortable enough to nap.
6. Make sure you have a notebook close by so you can write down any dreams, images, or symbolism that come to you while you sleep.
7. Lie in the position of your choice. Feel the earth beneath you and the tree close by. Allow this energy to come to you. Be aware of your breathing. Long, slow, regular deep breathing is best.
8. Relax into the surroundings. Let nature nurture you.
9. Smell the aromas of nature, hear the birds, feel the wind caress your body, see the images shift in your mind's eye.
10. Allow yourself to drift off to sleep or into deep daydreaming.
11. Stay in this state as long as comfortable.

12. Upon awakening, stretch your body slowly keeping your mind focused on what you have just experienced.

13. Write down everything you can possibly think of that passed through your mind's eye while dozing or in your awakened dream state even if it makes no sense to you at the time.

14. After writing everything down, take time to interpret what you can right then. Also write any feelings you are having and any other insights or revelations that come to you. Do not think too much about what you are doing. Just let whatever comes to you flow through.

15. When you have exhausted your stream of consciousness through writing do a completion prayer. Give thanks to the Creator, the Medicine Wheel, and the tree for the blessings of the day. It is good to make a final offering.

16. At a later date, go back over everything you wrote down. This information can be very enlightening when properly understood.

17. Go back and visit the Tree Medicine Wheel often, because your understanding will grow along with your relationship with the tree.

GARDEN MEDICINE WHEELS
·····

A Medicine Wheel built among the plants in your garden or a wheel composed of plants encourages the "little people" to come and help you. Gardens planted in circles are said to grow larger, more nutritional vegetables because the "wee spirit keepers" so love to dance and play there. They delight in spreading their good medicine and this helps plants grow and flourish. Some little people are best contacted in a garden setting. In other traditions they are called devas, elves, or garden angels. They sing songs that can make your heartstrings dance.

These spirits encourage joy, laughter, innocence, honesty, and youthful exuberance. They love gardens planted with vegetables, flowers, herbs, fruit trees, or shrubs,

When first planting a Medicine Wheel garden, or any garden, leave offerings for the little people and make prayers every day for a month from one full moon to the next moon. On both full moons dance around your garden. Sing songs and tell stories with friends in the moonlight. The little people love this and will reward you with an abundant array of vegetable or flowers as well as answers to the prayers you have been making.

Thank them profusely with gifts such as tobacco, food offerings, stones, or something that is special to you. Most of all the little people like the offering of a song, dance, or story. They love to be entertained and think humans are their personal entertainment committee. If they find you amusing they return the entertainment. You can hear them sing during a light rain, dance on the wind, and tell dreamtime stories while you snooze during a siesta on a hot summer day.

The best way to thank the little people is to love and care for your garden and the Medicine Wheel there, showing appreciation for them and for the plant kingdom.

Some people have planted a Medicine Wheel garden containing all the plants of the wheel that will grow in a garden in their area, each plant placed in its rightful position. Obviously they do not plant the trees of the wheel unless there is ample room for them to grow.

Other people make a Medicine Wheel garden planting correctly colored plants in each position or in each direction. You can use your imagination and intuition in planning and implementing a Medicine Wheel garden. However you choose to do so, you will find the plants in such a garden grow in a very special way.

A TRAVELING MEDICINE WHEEL

·····

A traveling Medicine Wheel is a small group of stones carried in a pouch or bundle, used to build a small Medicine Wheel. Such a wheel is easy to take with you and can be quickly and unobtrusively assembled. Components of the wheel may vary. Some examples are pebbles, totem minerals, fetishes, corn kernels, gemstones, or seedpods. After assembling your components you should smudge them, offer them to the six directions, and pray over them.

Because of the mobility of traveling Medicine Wheels, ceremonies can take place in a matter of minutes before a mood, energy, or spirit message passes you by.

HEALING WITH A TRAVELING WHEEL

Carrying Medicine Wheel stones in a pouch is reminiscent of the olden days when a doctor carried a black medicine bag. With your traveling wheel you are ready for any situation that demands immediate prayers or this form of medicine.

A Medicine Wheel of this nature can be used in conjunction with other healing methods. Place the wheel close to the location of the person you are working with, preferably near their head or feet. This will magnify and support the other healing techniques being utilized.

If you are giving a massage, placing a traveling wheel under the massage table can enhance the effects of the massage.

In the case of a medical emergency this wheel does not take the place of a doctor or first aid team but can be used in conjunction with other modalities *if circumstances permit.* An emergency is not the time to educate others about your "path." Cooperate to alleviate the emergency making silent prayers until an appropriate time presents itself to do a supportive ceremony.

BUILDING A TRAVELING MEDICINE WHEEL

What you need. Smudging materials and your traveling Medicine Wheel.

Estimated Time. Five minutes.

Follow the basic instructions for building a wheel. Because you have already offered these stones, and prayed over them, you can place them rapidly, adding a short, silent prayer.

Carry smudging utensils with you so that you can smudge, assemble the stones into a wheel, and be ready to do ceremony, make prayers, call for spiritual guidance, or to do a healing at a moment's notice.

You can use a traveling Medicine Wheel to help with meditating, prayer, or focusing; to open yourself up to a power spot; to complement other forms of healing; to connect with wildlife on a wilderness hike; to connect with the spirits of an area that you feel an affinity for; to communicate with Spirit; and to ask

Spirit to heal an area that has met with some form of disaster, such as a blackened forest ravaged by fire or a beach laden with pollution. When traveling in a car or plane you can hold your traveling wheel for safety and protection.

MEDICINE WHEEL FIRE CEREMONIES
▪▪▪▪▪

The element of fire directly allied with the powers of the Medicine Wheel makes strong medicine. Fire has long been a powerful force for releasing negative energies and patterns and setting positive ones. By putting prayers into a fire you immediately release that prayer through the smoke as it curls upward to Spirit. Smoke quickly journeys from the physical to the spirit plane.

BUILDING A FIRE PIT MEDICINE WHEEL

What you need. A Medicine Wheel, a shovel, kindling, wood, flint and steel or matches, sufficient water to extinguish any sparks or fires, and tobacco.

Estimated time. One hour.

1. Dig a fire pit at the center of the Medicine Wheel, in the position of the Creator. This pit will only be used for sacred ceremonial fires.
2. Determine when you will have a fire ceremony at the wheel. Before sunrise to greet the light of day or at dusk when light turns to dark are two powerful times.
3. Choose a fire keeper. This person will stay with the fire at all times.
4. Light the fire in the most natural way possible, using pine needles and pinecones or grass for kindling and using a flint or matches, not a lighter or any kind of starting fluid. Never allow anyone to throw anything into the fire unless it pertains to the ceremony you are doing.
5. Use wood that has been gathered with proper thanksgiving. When you see the smoke circling in all four directions, you know that the fire has been properly prepared.
6. Be very aware of the surrounding earth conditions when you build such a fire so that you do not endanger any of your relations.
7. Do whatever ceremony you have come to the wheel to perform. You should incorporate making offerings of tobacco to the fire as part of this ceremony.
8. When the ceremony is completed, the fire keeper should dismantle any wood remaining in the fire and then put out the coals with water or earth.

FIRE CEREMONY FOR RELEASING THE OLD AND INVITING IN THE NEW

What you need. Pencils and paper, smudging materials, a fire pit and fire, tobacco, and notebook and pen or tape recorder.

Estimated time. One hour.

1. Smudge everyone involved, the area, and anything that will be used in the ceremony.

2. Have each person write on one piece of paper anything they would like to let go of or release in their lives. Some examples are "I would like to let go of my habit of smoking," "I would like to let go of my anger," "I would like to let go of my illness," and "I would like to let go of my attachment to a negative relationship." It is good if each person then goes to the stone that he feels will help him with his resolve and makes an offering.

3. Have each person write down on the same piece of paper something he would like to invite into his life. Some examples are "I invite more joy in my life," "I invite more time to spend with my family," "I invite serenity," and "I invite the means to have a cabin in the woods." It is good for each person to make an offering of thanks to the position that can help bring him this quality.

4. Begin the fire part of the ceremony with a chant to honor the element of fire and the Thunderbird can.

5. Each person should make an offering of tobacco in thanks to the fire and wheel. Each person should give thanks for the purification and renewal the fire brings.

6. Next each person throws his or her prayers in the fire, watching as the paper burns to ashes and the smoke spirals upward to Spirit. As the smoke rises each person should release the negativity he or she asked to release and accept the requested gift.

7. After everyone has done this, gather together for another chant to complete the ceremony.

8. Participants should write, record, and/or discuss their experiences.

9. Never leave a fire unattended. Dismantle any remaining wood. Be sure the fire is completely out and covered with dirt or ashes.

Building and working with Medicine Wheels can be an extraordinary experience that will differ with each wheel you build. If you remain open and willing much healing, transformation, and growth is possible through the tool of a physical Medicine Wheel.

The Big Winds Moon—by Pru See

6

Traveling the Wheel

The essence of the Medicine Wheel is growth. Everything in nature grows and changes. Minerals begin either as visitors from another galaxy, or as tiny grains of matter born on this planet that join together to make ever larger formations. From tiny seeds planted in the earth grow the flowers, herbs, trees, vegetables, and fruits that we receive as gifts of the plant kingdom. From a small one-celled organism grows the mighty grizzly bear or the redwood or a human. All is growth, all is change.

Somewhere in the beginnings of the society that now dominates the earth people became afraid of change. They created philosophies, theories, and religions to convince themselves that there was stability in the universe: that mankind could create things that would be never changing. To really believe such ideas, humans had to close their eyes to the natural world. People who live in a natural way recognize the changes all around them, and know that growth is the law of life. They also recognize that without growth life could not continue. People who are afraid of growth are also afraid of life.

The Medicine Wheel is a tool that can help you to accept, and even embrace, change. It is a tool to enable you to take delight in the many variations that occur in your own life.

The Medicine Wheel gives you a holistic view of the world and of all life.

71

Each of the thirty-six positions of the Medicine Wheel provide you with a some-what different comprehension of all that is around you. It is possible for you to experience life from all these positions and thus gain thirty-five new understandings of life to add to the one that you have today. Imagine how much more versatile your wardrobe would be if you added thirty-five new outfits to it. Now imagine how much more multifaceted your life view will be if you can add thirty-five new viewpoints to that. This is the potential the Medicine Wheel brings to you.

YOUR BEGINNING POSITION
·····

The Medicine Wheel is divided into twelve moons or months. These begin with the Earth Renewal Moon, which starts on the day of the winter solstice, or Earth Renewal, December 22. The cycles of change continue at approximately thirty-day intervals until the year returns to its beginning point. By virtue of birth, each human begins their life journey at one of these moons. Your starting position gives you the gift of the particular strengths, challenges, and life lessons of your birth moon. Your birth, or beginning, moon also determines your initial elemental clan membership and the Spirit Keeper who first gives you protection.

Your birth position on the wheel (see the chart on pp. 4–5, chapter 1) is the one that first teaches you how to view life. For most people, the birth position describes the way they were in their early childhood. At some point people naturally begin to grow and change. So they travel to other positions on the wheel to learn what these positions have to teach.

Your beginning position has the gift of familiarity. It represents the way you first learned to feel, to think, and to pray. No matter how many other ways you learn, you will always feel a certain ease with the view you received from your birth moon. However, this does not mean that you should cling to your beginning position, or fear moving around the wheel. People who have such fears sometimes attribute their weaknesses to how they were born, where they were born, what their beginning position is. These are the people who use their beginning place as an excuse for not changing or growing.

Everyone has moments in which he wishes to stay put. Everyone experiences times when he would prefer to just dig in and remain the way he has always been. It is at these times that people need to encourage themselves to move around the wheel and to experience life from different positions. By going to other positions, you expand yourself. You come to know about your relations on the Earth Mother. It is one of your responsibilities as a human being to learn about the different totems, moons, plants, and elements that describe different places on the wheel. Through this learning, you help to keep your own life in a state of growth; you help to keep the life energy beating within your heart. Such energy will allow you as much change in your life as you can handle. Such learning will help you to progress around the wheel and experience as many manifestations of your own nature, of human nature, and of earth nature as you possible can.

The Medicine Wheel can help you to know you have many possibilities within yourself. However, you have to place yourself in various experiences to realize what is possible. It is by experiencing strength that we can let our own weaknesses fall away from us. Sometimes strength will come from learning about human nature. Other times it will come from learning about the minerals, the elements, the plants, and the animals. If you live in a way that is open to all of the lessons the universe has to teach you, you can be sure that the right lesson will always come to you at the proper time, no matter who the teacher is or what the tool for teaching might be. People who live in this way find that life is beautiful and the earth is a magical place that constantly presents new marvels to them. It is possible for anyone to live like this if he so chooses. The Medicine Wheel is a tool to help you to do so.

One of the reasons it is necessary for you to leave a position on the wheel when you've learned its lessons is that there is always somebody else coming along who needs the lessons of that position. By refusing to move you can block other people from learning what they need to know. If you are willing to move, you not only encourage and aid your own growth but you encourage and help growth in all the people you touch. In this way you learn about the breath of life. You learn both to give and to receive. For you to grow you must reach out and give something of yourself to the universe. By this giving you will be able to experience more of life. Remember—no teacher can teach a person who is selfish. No teacher can teach a person who is not willing to share the knowledge they have already gained from life. If you are the sort of person who has a mind lock that keeps you in one position on the wheel, it is very difficult for you to grow beyond that. This makes it difficult for those around you to come into the position you could have vacated.

To receive knowledge you have to give. It is the giving process that opens you up. When you smoke the sacred pipe in a special ceremony, you first inhale the smoke and then exhale it to the Spirit. In this instance, you are not smoking for yourself, you are smoking for Spirit. It is critical that you give out the smoke. The same is true with all of life. It is critical that you give out what you have received. You can't live just for yourself. When you accept that, you will know one of the truly great laws of the universe. This was one of the laws that traditional native people around the world followed. This was one of the laws that kept them in balance with everything around them.

As you have probably observed from knowing about your birth position on the wheel, you do take on some characteristics of each position but you do not take on all of them. If you were born in the Elk position, for example most characteristics of the Long Snows Moon apply to you, but some do not. You are a unique individual. Some things that we say about each position will fit you. Others will not. This is part of your individuality, and it is important that you respect this.

As you have gone through life you have probably observed there are times your birth position on the Medicine Wheel no longer seems to describe you accurately. For example, you may have been born in the Beaver position. For parts of your life you may have felt this position fit you. But then one day you notice you do not feel as rooted, you do not feel as stable, you do not feel as stubborn, you do not feel as grounded as you have in the past. You notice that your eyes travel skyward and you admire the birds in flight. You notice that a lot of ravens seem to be around whenever you are out in nature. You even have some dreams about ravens. These would be good indications that you have moved from the beaver position to the raven position on the Medicine Wheel. You are now a person of the Ducks Fly Moon. You have taken several steps to a totally new place on the Medicine Wheel and you have a whole new perspective, a new set of lessons, and a new set of helpers.

As you travel to other positions on the wheel, you will find that you are only capable of learning those lessons that are right for you to learn at a given time. This is the reason people circle the wheel, often many different times in life. Each time you return to a position, you learn more about it and open yourself to new lessons that position has to teach you.

METHODS OF TRAVEL
·····

There are many ways of traveling around the Medicine Wheel. No one way is correct. This is a matter of intense individuality. While most people travel the Medicine Wheel in a sunwise or clockwise direction, there are some people who travel moonwise (counter clockwise). Some people travel the wheel by going from one clan position to another. For example a person born in the beaver position might stay with the Turtle, or Earth, clan and move to the other Turtle clan places: Brown Bear and Snow Goose. Another person who was born a Red Hawk might stay with the Thunderbird (fire) clan and next travel to the Sturgeon position then to the Elk. The same movement pattern could apply to the Frog (water) or Butterfly (air) clan birth positions.

Other people might explore all the positions governed by one Spirit Keeper before they move on to another direction.

Yet others move to the complementary position on the Medicine Wheel. Your complement is the position directly across from your birth place on the wheel. In this instance complement means just what it says—that these two positions *complement* each other. It does not mean they get along easily. It means that if you learn to see life from both sides of the wheel you have a whole and complementary view of what life is about. Consequently, moving to complementary positions is not one of the easier ways of traveling the wheel. Other people move around the wheel in what seems to an outside observer to be a random fashion. However, what is random to one person is very specifically directed to another. Any way you move around the wheel is fine, as long as you keep moving.

In working with people as they have traveled the Medicine Wheel, we have observed it is unusual that all aspects of a person will be in the same position at the same time.

What we are describing when we talk about physical, mental, emotional, and spiritual are different rates of vibration. These rates of vibration apply to how we experience, understand, and deal with the world. The physical refers both to our physical bodies and to how we perceive the world around us. When we talk about the physical, we are not only talking about a person's health but also about his occupation, home, view of finances, and view of physical reality. The mental refers to a person's ideas, philosophy, and world view. The mental also refers to a person's method of communication and way of verbalizing life. The mental also refers to the mental health of a person. Emotional refers to a person's capacity to relate to the world and to other people. Your emotional being is the part of you that makes friends, finds mates, relates to children, and relates to any part of the world in a strong and feeling way. Your emotional being also describes your capacity for relationships and gives some indication of how you stand concerning the universal law of relationship. When we talk about the spiritual, we are talking about what a person considers to be sacred. This includes your relationship to the Creator, your relationship to religion, and your relationship to spiritual teachers and spiritual teachings. It also describes your viewpoints about ritual and ceremony. Your spiritual aspect governs your basic ideas about life, about death, and unity.

Because each aspect of your being can move at a different rate of speed you can very conceivably be in at least five positions in relationship to the Medicine Wheel at any one time. You could be one place on the wheel physically and in others mentally, emotionally, and spiritually. To better understand the point that we are making, please look at the chart titled "Jane Doe's Medicine Wheel, January 2, 1990" which you will find on page 75. As you can see

Jane Doe's Medicine Wheel
January 2, 1990

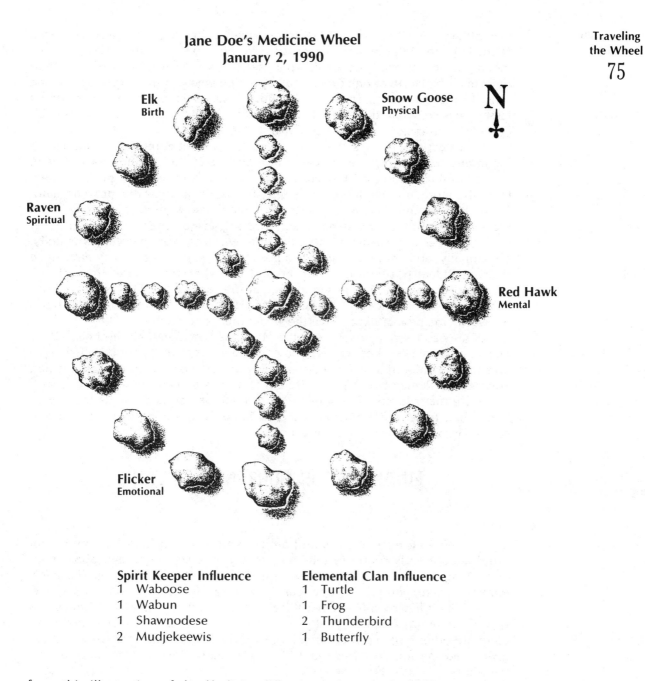

Spirit Keeper Influence
1 Waboose
1 Wabun
1 Shawnodese
2 Mudjekeewis

Elemental Clan Influence
1 Turtle
1 Frog
2 Thunderbird
1 Butterfly

from this illustration of the Medicine Wheel, on January 2, 1990, Jane Doe, who was born an elk, is now a snow goose in terms of her physical being, a red hawk in terms of her mental being, a flicker in terms of her emotional being, and a raven in terms of her spiritual being.

Now being in five totem positions also puts you in relationship with a number of Spirit Keepers and a number of elemental clans. Jane Doe is being influenced by Waboose, Wabun, Shawnodese, and, most emphatically, by Mudjekeewis. She is being influenced by the Turtle, the Frog, and the Butterfly clan positions, although her strongest elemental clan effect at this time is coming from the Thunderbird, or fire, clan. As you can see from the example of Jane Doe, one might be experiencing quite a number of influences of the Medicine Wheel at any one time. That is good, because it gives you more opportunity for growth. It gives you more opportunity for change and expansion.

If you refer again to Jane Doe's Medicine Wheel you will see that with the Spirit Keeper and elemental influences, she is currently being affected by thirteen different positions on the Medicine Wheel. Jane Doe has a fairly balanced chart. It is possible for one person to have all aspects of their being in one moon position at one time, or it is possible for one person to have all of their aspects in the North at one time, or all of their aspects in the Turtle clan at one time. In these instances a person would be experiencing more concentrated lessons in one or another aspect of the wheel. Such intense lessons, although powerful, can make a person feel out of balance.

In evaluating people's Medicine Wheels, it is most common to find people are in different positions in at least three aspects of their being. For example, a person might be in the otter position physically, the red hawk position mentally, the sturgeon position emotionally, but again in the otter position spiritually. It is common for a person to experience two aspects of their being in the same position at the same time. Most people go around the wheel many different times in their life, visiting the different positions physically, mentally, emotionally, and spiritually. It is also possible for people, after they have done their individual positioning, to go around the wheel one more time with all aspects of their being in the same place at the same time. This is a very powerful way to experience the Medicine Wheel. And it is entirely possible this is the way some people experience the wheel their whole lives.

Some people may travel the entire Medicine Wheel in their lifetimes. Other people move slower. Perhaps for you one trip around the wheel is sufficient to do all the learning that you need to do. For others more visits to each position are needed. Remember life is a circle that spirals upward as well as outward. There are many levels of lessons to learn. Each person is a unique individual. Each must travel the Medicine Wheel in his own way and at his own rate of speed. No one way is correct for everyone.

FINDING YOUR CURRENT POSITIONS
.....

If you open your eyes to the world around you, you will find that the natural world is constantly trying to tell you about your own movement, about your own changes, about your own helpers, and about your own totems. The information is there, you just have to learn how to receive it.

Although having a Medicine Wheel consultation or using Earthstones is a very effective way of finding out your current positions on the Medicine Wheel, there are other easy ways to do so. Toward the end of this chapter we will be giving you specific exercises that will enable you to find out where you are on the wheel.

One of the best ways to observe your own travels around the wheel is to use a Medicine Wheel you have built. This can either be a large Medicine Wheel that is out in nature or a small Medicine Wheel you keep on your altar or in some private spot in your own home. In either instance, you can often tell your position just by physically walking around the Medicine Wheel and discerning which positions seem to draw you most strongly. As you move around the wheel you will find you feel much more energy in some positions than in others. These energized positions are most often the ones with which you are working.

If you are not able to have a Medicine Wheel for you to physically move around, move around one in your mind. To do so you would meditate on the Medicine Wheel, visualizing it and visualizing which position is drawing you. For some of you, you will literally see a difference in the relevant positions; perhaps they'll appear a different color, or give off a glow. Others will hear a sound or a note being given off by some positions. Some people feel a difference in the energy of the stones if they visualize themselves putting their hands over them. Yet others might sense a smell emanating from the positions with which they are working. Whatever method you use to determine the positions is fine as long as it works for you.

Some people can tell they are moving around the wheel because they notice omens in nature. For example, some people find stones or feathers or pieces of wood in the shape of their animal totems. Others might look up in the clouds and see there the shape of a plant or an animal that is currently working with them. Others will notice in nature whatever beings are currently part of their wheel. For example, a person who has rarely noticed woodpeckers before might, all of a sudden, see flickers around them all the time. That would be a good indication that the person is in the flicker position in some aspect of their being.

Other people will dream their new positions on the Medicine Wheel. It is quite amazing how many people have dreams about Medicine Wheel totems, even though they have never before come in contact with the Medicine Wheel. Many times people ask us for an interpretation of a dream that is just full of symbols from the Medicine Wheel. These people are dreaming about their own travels around the Medicine Wheel.

Some people can tell about their travels because they will suddenly be attracted to a new color. For example, someone who has always loved pink might suddenly want to have yellow around them. This would be an indication that they are moving from a flicker position to a red hawk position. A similar thing can happen with minerals. Perhaps someone has always wanted to have quartz crystals as part of their medicine. Then one day they find that they are suddenly attracted to copper and malachite. This would be an indication they have moved from the snow goose position on the wheel to the snake position.

This can also happen with plants and with animals. For example, if one day you wake up really craving some raspberry leaf tea or raspberries, this might be a good indication that you have moved to the sturgeon position. Or if you cannot resist the temptation to buy a poster that shows a golden eagle, this is a good indication you are now in one of the eastern positions of the Medicine Wheel.

If you find you are having difficulty clarifying which totems are now affecting you, you might find it easier to figure out the direction or the elemental clan having the most influence on your life. If you can find your current connection with either Spirit Keeper or clan by observation or through one of the exercises we suggest, you at least know you are in one of the three possible totem positions that go with each of these parts of the Medicine Wheel.

You might find that charting your travels around the Medicine Wheel is a very good way both to learn about where you've been and where you might be going. To chart your own progress you can copy the blank stone circle and chart on page 2. As you ascertain your positions, write them and the date on the charts. Some people chart their progress on a daily basis; others find that doing so weekly or even monthly gives them an accurate enough picture of their own travels around the Medicine Wheel. Whichever feels right to you is fine. Most important, following your own progress around the wheel proves to you that you are moving. It also shows you what your major lessons are at any given time, and what challenges you could most easily expect life to be presenting to you.

Some people wish to know whether a particular direction, elemental clan, or totem is affecting them on the physical, mental, emotional, or spiritual level. To find this out, observe what is in your mind or heart when you have a dream, an omen from nature, an attraction to a particular aspect of the wheel, or a meditation concerning the wheel. Usually it will be pretty obvious which aspect of your being is in a particular position on the wheel. For example, if you're walking along the street thinking about a good friend and how you hope your relationship with him will grow, and you happen to see a raven fly over head, that would be a fairly good indication you are in the raven position emotionally at this particular time. If you notice you want to paint your apartment yellow, that would be a good indication you are in the red hawk position on the physical level at this time. If you are participating in a ceremony and you notice you are strongly drawn to a piece of chrysocolla, that would be a good indication you are in the beaver position spiritually at this time. If you are busy having a lively debate about your world view with a friend and all of a sudden you notice there are a lot of wild roses growing outside the window, this would be a good indication you are in the flicker position mentally at this time.

Noticing and keeping track of your own progress as you travel the Medicine Wheel will teach you a lot about yourself as well as about the universe. It will allow you to see the miracle of change as it relates to you own life. As you visit the different positions of the Medicine Wheel, you will notice your way of thinking, feeling, and perceiving everything around you changes. You will find you are capable of growing in ways you might never have dreamed of before.

Most important of all, traveling the Medicine Wheel and observing your own travels can be a lot of fun. It can introduce you both to yourself and to many more of your relations on the earth. Use the exercises that follow as a means to become a conscious voyager in the unbounded sea of your own life.

FINDING YOUR MEDICINE WHEEL POSITION
with a Large Wheel

What you need. Smudging or other cleansing materials, an offering, notebook and pen, or tape recorder, and your personal Medicine Wheel chart.

Estimated time. One hour.

1. Smudge or do whatever cleansing ceremony is most effective for you.
2. Center yourself through some sort of meditation or through standing by the wheel and feeling your connection with the earth while breathing deeply.
3. Approach the wheel at the Wabun stone—the eastern gate—because you are looking for a new way of seeing life, a new beginning.
4. Circle the wheel clockwise, making at least one complete circle.
5. Very slowly start to make another circle around the wheel. As you are circling, ask that whatever position is affecting you at this time reach out to you. Observe carefully everything that happens. See if you feel a pull or a push in the middle of your body, or if chills run up and down your spine. Notice whether you feel heat, cold, wind, or an energy flow in your palms. Notice if you have a different psychic perception in one segment of the Medicine Wheel. If you see auras (energy or color emanations from an object), notice whether the auras of any of the stones seem to change as you walk by them. Be aware of any different sounds or smells emanating from the wheel.
6. Keep circling the wheel until one stone "calls" out to you in one of the aforementioned ways.
7. When it does, go and sit by this stone. Note which stone it is.
8. Ask whether this stone is affecting you on the physical, mental, emotional, or spiritual levels or whether it is affecting you on all levels.

9. Tell the totem spirits associated with this stone you wish to learn whatever lessons they have for you and that you wish to acknowledge their effect on you at this time of your life. Wait for a response.

10. When you seem to have received all of the information you can from this position, make an offering to this stone then complete your circle of the wheel to the eastern gate. Thank the wheel for the help it has given you and for this new beginning.

11. If you feel drawn to receive more information, circle the wheel again. Ask that this time you be guided to whatever position is affecting you on a different level of your being.

12. You can continue this process until you have found your positions physically, mentally, emotionally, and spiritually.

13. Be sure to make offerings to all of the places on the wheel that are working with you at this time and to the wheel in general.

14. Record or write this information. Chart it if you are following your progress.

FINDING YOUR MEDICINE WHEEL POSITION
with a Small Wheel

What you need. Smudge or cleansing materials, an offering, notebook and pen or tape recorder, and your personal Medicine Wheel charts.

Estimated time. One hour.

1. Smudge or cleanse yourself in whatever way is most effective for you.
2. Center yourself.
3. Sit by your small Medicine Wheel.
4. Close your eyes and imagine yourself walking around it.
5. From this point on, follow the exercise in the same way you would if you were physically walking around a large Medicine Wheel circle.
6. Remember to make your prayers and offerings of thanks to each position on the small wheel and to the small Medicine Wheel in general after you have completed your work.
7. Record, write, and/or chart your findings.

MEDITATION TO FIND YOUR POSITION THROUGH REMEMBERING YOUR DREAMS
with Thanks to Shawnodese[1]

This exercise is most effective if you do it just before sleeping. It can help you bring messages about your Medicine Wheel progress back from the dream world.

What you need. Cleansing materials, notebook and pen or tape recorder.

Estimated time. Thirty minutes.

1. Cleanse yourself.
2. Center yourself.

---

1. This exercise is from the forthcoming book *Dreaming with the Wheel*, by Sun Bear, Wabun, and Shawnodese.

3. Using whatever method is most effective for you, relax yourself as much as possible.

4. Now, imagine yourself in a field. Somewhere in this field you know there is a well. Start walking across the field in the direction of the well.

5. When you find the well, you see that it has your own name written on it.

6. Next to the well you find a pad of paper and a pen or pencil.

7. Sit down by the well. Know that this is the well of your subconscious.

8. Pick up the pad and pencil and write the following on it: I (and you fill in your name) now release whatever I need to release and accept whatever I need to accept to remember my dreams now. Sign the paper as you sign a check and date it.

9. Tear off the piece of paper from the pad and fold it up.

10. Throw the folded piece of paper into the well and watch as it goes down.

11. Walk back across the field and see yourself going into your own bedroom and into your own bed.

12. See yourself drifting gently off to sleep.

13. As you sleep imagine that you have a very vivid dream. In this dream, you can see things, you can taste things, you can touch things, you can smell things, and everything is in brilliant color.

14. Imagine yourself waking up from that dream. You are very excited because you've been able to remember your dream.

15. You find a pad of paper and a pencil or a tape recorder next to your bed. Write down or record the dream exactly as it happened. See yourself still very excited at being able to remember and to record your dream.

16. Return to the field, walk back across it and come back into your body. Feel yourself completely in your body.

17. When you are completely in your body, gently stretch.

18. Take a moment to be sure that you are totally present in your body. When you are totally present slowly and gently drift to sleep or sit up if it is not your bedtime.

19. Keep a notebook or recorder by your bed so you can record any dreams you have.

Shawnodese has shared this exercise with quite a large number of people. He has had reports that if it is done faithfully, people who have never before remembered their dreams will begin to do so within five to seven days of beginning to use the exercise.

NATURE'S MESSAGES ABOUT YOUR
MEDICINE WHEEL POSITION

What you need. A safe, natural area, offerings, walking shoes, and, if desired, a blanket, a notebook and pen or tape recorder.

Estimated time. Two hours.

1. Take a walk in as natural an area as possible.

2. While you are walking, consciously open yourself to the powers of nature all around you.

3. This does not mean you go into a meditative state that drives your energy

into your body. Rather it means you allow your energy to reach out and merge with the energy of all of your relations around you.

4. Consciously feel the earth beneath your feet, feel the sun touching the crown of your head. Allow yourself to breathe deeply, letting your breath fill as much of your body as you are comfortable having it fill.

5. Become aware of the mineral kingdom. Are there large rocks in the area? Can you only find small rocks? If it is possible to do so, find a place where you can sit down on the Earth Mother and look at the mineral beings that are there. Observe how you feel while you look at your brothers and sisters in the mineral kingdom. Ask them to deepen your awareness of them. Make an offering to any that have particularly "spoken" to you. Continue walking.

6. Notice whether any mineral beings seem to be in your path. If so, take the time to observe them.

7. Note whether any mineral you see is a specific one mentioned on the Medicine Wheel. If it is, that is a very direct message. If it is not (which is the more likely case), notice whether the stone has any design or pattern that reminds you of something from the Medicine Wheel.

8. If you feel strongly drawn to this particular representative of the mineral kingdom, ask it if it wants to come with you. If it does not, leave it where it is. If it does want to come with you, make sure you leave an offering before you take it. (Do not take every mineral that calls to you as this is tantamount to clear-cutting the mineral kingdom.)

9. When you have finished communicating with the mineral kingdom turn your attention to the plant kingdom. Follow the same process as you did with the mineral beings. However, do not pick plants to take home with you, particularly if you are near an urban area where there are a lot more people than plants.

10. As you continue walking, notice whether any members of the animal kingdom are around you. If so, what are they? Do they seem like they are trying to communicate with you at this time? If so, what are they trying to tell you?

11. If you do not actively see animals, find a place that feels safe, sit down and take a few minutes to go within yourself while you are in this natural setting to see whether there are any animal beings who wish to communicate with you but are not able to be with you in the physical level.

12. As you continue walking, give thanks to all of your relations who have already spoken to you. Ask them if there is anything else you might do to honor and acknowledge them and the many gifts they have given to you.

13. If they make a request of you, please follow it.

14. After you have finished doing whatever your totems have asked you to do take a while just to walk and relax and enjoy the beauty of nature all around you.

15. At a later time, write about or record your experience.

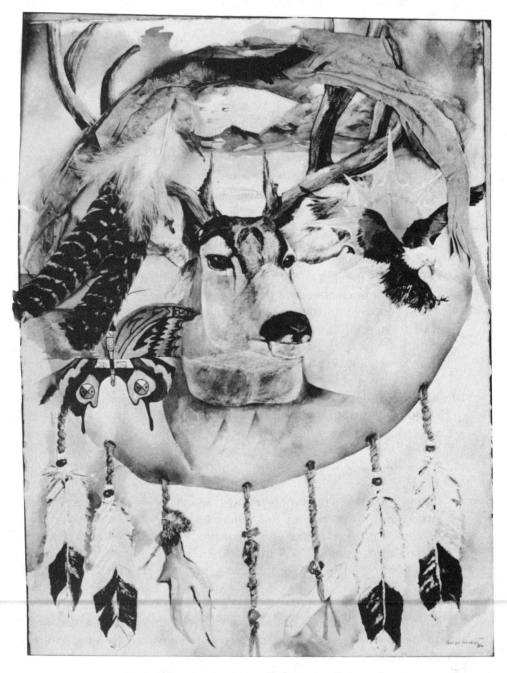

The Cornplanting Moon—by Gwyn George

7

The Thirteenth Moon

In some years there are thirteen moons. Each lunar month consists of the twenty-nine days, twelve hours, forty-four minutes, and two and seven-tenths seconds it takes to go from one new moon to the next. At some point in the history of the society that now predominates on the earth, it was decided that it would be easier and more stable to make up a calendar that would go by the daily cycle mankind decided should divide the year, rather than by the natural cycle into which the moon divides the year. During the Gregorian period, the calendar in use now was adopted. This calendar divides the year into twelve months rather than into the thirteen moons used by most native peoples.

In the original Medicine Wheel book, we realized that for accuracy with the native view, we should divide the year into thirteen moons. We also recognized that because of the uniqueness of so many of the ideas contained within *The Medicine Wheel* a thirteen-moon year might make earth astrology too confusing for some people. However, we knew that the thirteenth moon would eventually present itself in this system of earth astrology.

The thirteenth moon has certainly made its presence felt as we have worked with people on their individual Medicine Wheels. In trying to help people place themselves on the Medicine Wheel, we would often encounter people who would have a difficult time making decisions about one or all levels of their being.

Jane Doe's Medicine Wheel
June 3, 1990

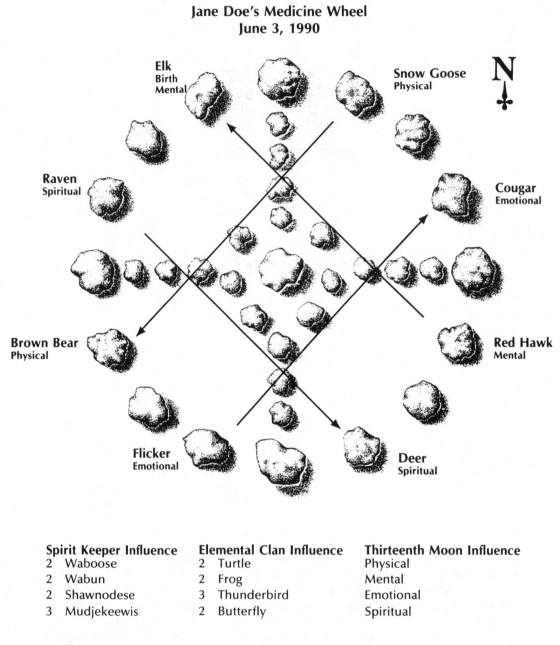

Spirit Keeper Influence	Elemental Clan Influence	Thirteenth Moon Influence
2 Waboose	2 Turtle	Physical
2 Wabun	2 Frog	Mental
2 Shawnodese	3 Thunderbird	Emotional
3 Mudjekeewis	2 Butterfly	Spiritual

When we tried to place them on the Medicine Wheel, we would find they would be in invisible positions. They would be, for example, a Thunderbird person of the North, or a Frog person of the East, or a Butterfly person of the South, or a Turtle person of the West. None of these positions exist. In talking and working with the people who seemed to be in these invisible positions, we found that their lives were currently in a state of great flux. Their old way of doing things was no longer working for them, but they had not yet found their new way.

These are people who are under the influence of the thirteenth moon. The thirteenth moon heralds change. It is the moon that brings times of transition and new opportunity. For people under the influence of the thirteenth moon, the element of change, the element of the thirteenth moon itself is more important in understanding their progress around the wheel than where they have been or where they are going. As the thirteenth moon concept does not easily fit into a society based on a solar calendar, people under its influence find it difficult to fit themselves into such a society.

This Medicine Wheel illustration shows Jane Doe's personal Medicine Wheel for June 3, 1990. When you consult this illustration you will see that although she is in the birth position of Elk, physically she is moving from Snow Goose to Brown Bear; mentally, from Red Hawk to Elk; emotionally, from Flicker to Cougar; spiritually from Raven to Deer. On June 3, 1990, Jane Doe was definitely experiencing a major time of transition in her life.

At that time Jane Doe was under the influence of all Spirit Keepers, but most strongly under the influence of Mudjekeewis. She was also under the influence of all elemental clans, but most strongly under the influence of the Thunderbird. She was under the thirteenth moon influence in the physical, mental, emotional, and spiritual aspects of her being.

This means that on June 3, 1990, Jane Doe was actively working with almost half the positions on the Medicine Wheel. She would have found it difficult to answer a question about what her viewpoint was or to make decisions about what she wanted. The thirteenth moon allows you to see life from so many viewpoints that it is difficult to choose only one.

SEEK NEW WAYS
.....

When you are under the influence of the thirteenth moon, you are in a time of transition, a time of questioning everything you might have previously believed, a time of experiencing deep and lasting change on some or all levels of your being. When you are under this influence it is a good time to seek new vision, to seek new ways of being, feeling, thinking, and doing. It is an excellent time to go on a vision quest if you wish. Because of the thirteenth-moon influence you are more likely to be open to your own innermost thoughts. You are more likely to be able to hear the voice of the Earth Mother as she speaks to you.

It is fairly easy to spot times in your life when you are under the influence of the thirteenth moon. One of the first clues is that you are having unusual difficulty making decisions. For decisive people times of the thirteenth moon are particularly difficult because where they once knew exactly what it was that they wanted, now life no longer seems so clear-cut.

If you are not normally a decisive person, it might be more difficult for you to know you are under this influence. You would have to observe whether you are having more than usual difficulty with decision making over a long period of time or to look for other indications of the thirteenth moon's power. For example, you might have an uneasy restlessness, a feeling that your former beliefs or ways of being just do not fit anymore. You might feel as though whatever foundation you were used to having in life had been taken away from you. If someone were to give you a series of choices you would probably want to choose all of them, or at least most of them rather than just one. You can sometimes see the influence of the thirteenth moon in as simple an activity as ordering from a menu. If you are used to knowing exactly what you want, and you start staring at menus for long periods of time, you might look at some of your other ways of dealing with life and see whether you are in this time of change and transition.

THE MOON INFLUENCE
.....

When you are under the influence of the thirteenth moon the energy of Grand-mother Moon particularly affects you. To understand the thirteenth moon better, you must understand the energy of Grandmother Moon in general. In Native ways, Grandmother Moon was considered to be the leader of feminine life. Part of the reason for this is that Grandmother Moon, like human women, goes through cycles. Sometimes she shines brightly, lighting up the entire night sky. At other times she seems invisible to the human eye. She also experiences all the stages in between, from the crescent of first quarter, to the almost full three-quarter moon. Each phase lights up the earth in a different way. Each phase has a different effect on the waters of the earth. And each phase has a different effect on the waters—the emotions—of human beings.

People who work in the medical and security professions have told us that during a full moon their business is usually brisker. More people are admitted to hospitals when the moon is full and more people commit crimes. It is no accident that the loon is the animal associated with Grandmother Moon and that one of the words that this society uses to describe someone who does not fit with the society is *loony*. Grandmother Moon lights up the shadow side of life. She illuminates those parts of our being that are frequently hidden. Sometimes people hide these things because they are afraid of them. That fear can stem from real reasons, or because these parts are unfamiliar. In some people, the parts of themselves they most fear are the softest and most vulnerable ones. In other people the hidden parts carry repressed violence, unexpressed rage.

The soft light of Grandmother Moon allows people, if they wish, to examine these hidden parts of themselves. While it might be too frightening to look at what is suppressed in the full light of day it is not as frightening to begin quietly to look at it in the soft light of night. It is the unexamined parts of being that often control people. If people have the courage to find out what lies hidden within, they also come to a much greater knowledge both of the hidden parts of nature and the hidden parts of society.

Examining the shadow side of life does not mean that people have to allow it to come out into the light of day. There are some parts of everyone's being that are better left examined, but hidden from the view of others. But there are other parts of being—wonderful, soft, gentle parts—that should be examined and then brought out into the light. It is these parts that can help people to know their true relationship with the earth and with all of their relations on her.

A critical lesson during times when people are under the influence of the thirteenth moon is not to fight change, not to fight the innate desire for self-examination. The more you strive to keep things hidden from yourself, the stronger they become. It is people who refuse to look at the shadow part of their being who often do terrible things. People who know what lies within them are much less likely to unthinkingly allow these thoughts or feelings to come out at some point in the future.

Although everyone fears change and what it can bring, it is very much a fact of life. If you can use the influence of the thirteenth moon to explore change and how you respond to it then you learn how to flow with these times and how to grow from these times. When you learn to accept the fact that your life will go through many times of metamorphosis, you can use transition in a much more positive way: to experiment with new ways of doing things and with new ways of thinking and feeling, both about the earth and about what you consider to be sacred.

This is a society that worships control, that tries to tell people life can be unchanging. This is a society that strives to make a sixty-year old look like a twenty-year old. It is always difficult to hold a different set of beliefs from those held by the majority of people around you. But most people know, deep within, that change is part of life, that at sixty you have a different set of values and a different set of beliefs than those you had at twenty. What people need to admit is that there is as much beauty in the later stages of our lives as there is in the earlier ones. What stops people from doing so is the fear of going to the North, the fear of going to the time of transformation, the fear of death.

In a natural world people saw death as part of life. In a famous speech, Chief Sealth, after whom the city of Seattle is named (Sealth is the Suquamish spelling; Seattle, the English), says, "The dead are not powerless. Death—did I say? There is no death. Only a change of worlds."

By embracing the influence of the thirteenth moon when it comes to you, you will gain more ability not only to deal with change in your life but to embrace it. By embracing change you will also come to have less fear of death, that which appears to be the ultimate change. By using this tool of the Medicine Wheel you will be able ever more strongly to embrace and love life.

The more you understand Grandmother Moon, the easier it will be for you to work with the times when the thirteenth moon is influencing your life. If you spend time with the moon in her different phases you will grow to know her better. This will help you to understand all of her reflections within you.

The new and full moons are especially beneficial times for acknowledging and improving your relationship with Grandmother Moon. Native people honored the moon and often did ceremonies to acknowledge her. The possibility of doing moon ceremonies is one that is still open to people today. Moon ceremonies are a very good place for people to begin becoming more comfortable with incorporating ceremony into their own lives. What follows are two ceremonies to help you honor Grandmother Moon and your relationship with her. These ceremonies have also appeared in *Lightseeds: A Compendium of Ancient and Contemporary Crystal Knowledge*, written by Wabun and by Anderson Reed.

FULL MOON MEDITATION CEREMONY

This ceremony came to Moon Deer of the Bear Tribe. When she used to live in Cincinnati, Ohio, she performed this ceremony monthly for quite a number of years with a good-size group of people there. This ceremony can either be done inside or outside. Moon Deer often prefers to begin indoors and then move to the great outdoors.

> **What you need.** A crystal, one that wants to work with the moon energies, or a feather; smudge, or other cleansing materials. In preparation for this ceremony you should consult an astrological or moon calendar to determine what element is affecting the moon during this particular cycle. Depending on what element is affecting the moon you will need a bowl of water (water sign), a candle (fire sign), or another crystal (earth sign).

> **Estimated time.** One hour.

1. Cleanse yourself and all others who will be participating.
2. Begin indoors with a silent meditation in which you allow your mind to become a basket, capable of receiving whatever thoughts or images come to it.
3. Ask everyone to receive images about this particular moon. Then pass the moon crystal or feather from one person to the next. Ask each person

to share whatever images he or she wishes to express. The ceremony leader takes these collective images and weaves a name for the coming moon. This name represents the collective energies of the people participating in the moon meditation. If you are doing this ceremony by yourself, you alone select a name for the moon cycle to come. Examples would be "Gift-giving month" for December and "Spring-cleaning month" for March. It is our belief this is how many of the names for the moons that were used in the Medicine Wheel originally came into being. They were the collective visions of the people that, over time, became woven into a permanent tapestry of names for the moons.

4. If the group goes outdoors at this point, put the crystal or the feather in the center of the circle. If you remain indoors do the same. If the moon is currently in a water sign, a bowl of water should be placed near the crystal or feather; if a fire sign, a candle; if an earth sign, a crystal; if an air sign, participants draw their breath over themselves as if they were smudging with it.

5. The leader of the ceremony begins a chant or song.

6. Each person present then makes a prayer to the moon and sends out positive images to the other beings on earth (this means all the beings, not just the human ones) and to the earth herself.

7. Participants may also give thanksgiving to the moon for the energy she gives to them and to all of the other beings on the planet.

8. The group leader acknowledges the sign the moon is in by either lighting the candle, shaking the energy of the crystal into the water, touching the crystal or feather to the earth, or asking people to smudge themselves with their breath.

9. Someone may end the ceremony with a chant, song, drumming, or rattling.

10. When finished, the facilitator should remember to cleanse and renew the crystal or feather.

BEAR TRIBE FULL MOON CEREMONY

This is the ceremony the Bear Tribe uses and teaches to honor the full moon. It can also be used to honor the new moon. Ideally the ceremony is conducted in a safe, beautiful, outdoor setting where the moon will be visible. However, if such a place is not available to you, you can hold the ceremony indoors.

What you need. Cleansing materials, a glass or stoneware bowl that will hold water, water, cornmeal, a moon ceremony crystal, and, if desired, drums or rattles.

Estimated time. One hour.

1. The person facilitating or leading the ceremony chooses a gateway through which participants will enter. The facilitator enters first and walks once moonwise (that is counterclockwise, or to your right) around the circle.

2. When she returns to her beginning position, the facilitator waits until the circle has formed. She then goes to the center, offers the water to the moon then pours it into the bowl. She also offers this bowl to the

moon then sets it down in the center of the circle. She offers the crystal to the moon, then sets it down next to the water. She does the same with the cornmeal.

3. She prepares the smudge and proceeds to smudge everyone in the circle.

4. Participants may chant or sing while the smudging is happening, or they can do so afterward.

5. The facilitator goes to the center, gets the cornmeal and comes back into the circle. She takes a pinch of the cornmeal and offers it, along with any words, chants, poems, or prayers she wishes to share, to the moon. She then passes the cornmeal to the person on her right who takes a pinch and makes her offering of cornmeal and words to the moon. The cornmeal continues around the circle.

6. The facilitator goes to the center of the circle and picks up the crystal. She raises it above her head, point facing the moon, and either silently or aloud asks the energy of the moon to come into it. She then brings the point of the crystal over the bowl of water firmly shaking the crystal toward the water four times. She raises the crystal to the moon again and repeats the offering process for four complete rounds. This draws the moon's energy down into the water.

7. She offers the bowl of water to the moon. She asks the moon to bless the water so that it brings clear, vivid dreams to everyone. She then takes or passes the bowl of water around the circle moonwise. Each person takes a sip of the water, asking silently that the water help her or him to receive, understand, and speak the truth of the moon.

8. The facilitator offers the water to the moon again. She asks that the earth and all her children have enough water to drink in the cycle that is now beginning. She pours the remainder of the water on the earth.

9. If people wish, they can now sing or chant again to Grandmother Moon.

10. The facilitator gathers the tools used in the ceremony. The participants leave the circle in the same way they entered, moonwise, with the facilitator being the first out. This allows everyone to complete their walk around the circle.

11. The facilitator cleans all the ceremonial tools so that they will be ready for the next use. If you have a moon crystal it is good to keep it in a place where it will see the light of the moon during all of the moon's phases.

IMAGINING CHANGE EXERCISE

This is an exercise that can be used by anyone, but will be particularly helpful for people who feel stuck in their lives. In this exercise you will randomly choose a position on the Medicine Wheel that you know you are not in now. After you have chosen the position you read the information about this position; about its totems in the mineral, plant, and animal kingdoms; its Spirit Keeper; and its elemental clan to prepare for the exercise.

What you need. Smudge or other cleansing material, notebook and pen or tape recorder.

Estimated time. Thirty minutes.

1. Set aside a quiet half hour.
2. Cleanse yourself using whatever method is best for you.
3. Center yourself.
4. Now imagine yourself going to a lovely field and finding a large Medicine Wheel there. You make your circle around the Medicine Wheel and then you sit down by the stone honoring the position you have chosen. As you sit by the stone you ask all of its helpers to come to you.
5. First you imagine or visualize the Spirit Keeper of that position coming to you. Know that the Spirit Keeper has a lesson and a message for you. Allow the Spirit Keeper to give you that message and to teach you that lesson. Make your thanks to the Spirit Keeper.
6. Now visualize or imagine the elemental clan totem that is affecting you. Know that the elemental clan totem has a lesson for you. Make yourself receptive to this lesson. When you have received it, thank the totem and allow it to go.
7. Now do the same with your mineral totem.
8. Now do the same with your plant totem.
9. Now do the same with your animal totem.
10. Now do the same with your color.
11. When you have received the lessons and messages from all of these helpers for this particular position on the Medicine Wheel, allow yourself time to imagine or visualize how you feel after having received all these lessons. Ask yourself how you would see the world differently. Ask yourself whether you would have a change in occupation if you were in this position on the wheel. Would you have a change in home? Would you have different philosophical ideas? How would this position affect your relationships with those around you? How would this position affect what you feel is sacred in the world? How would this position affect your ceremonial life? Your religious life?
12. When you know that you have a strong picture of how you would be in this position, thank the stone and all of its helpers for the many gifts that they have given you. Visualize yourself making an offering to this stone and then complete your way around the circle coming back to the gate through which you entered.
13. Take time to thank the entire Medicine Wheel for the help it has given you and for the tool that it is in your life. Now imagine yourself going back through the beautiful field and returning to your body.
14. Gently stretch, and when you feel yourself totally in your body get up from wherever you have been doing this exercise and return to your daily life, taking with you the new insights that you have gained.
15. This exercise can also be done around a large Medicine Wheel, if one is available to you.
16. You may write or record the impressions you received.

The Ripe Berries Moon—by Pru See

Creating Medicine Wheel Tools

Medicine tools are a gift from the Great Spirit. They are tangible objects that help you to discover and understand your spiritual reality. Medicine tools can help you learn spiritual secrets about yourself and the universe while allowing Spirit to communicate to you and through you. The Creator has given us medicine tools to aid us in communicating with the universal spiritual current that flows though life and is life.

When setting out to accomplish any quest or to assist others on their paths it is helpful to have tools that can support and guide you. Medicine Wheel tools can help you both in understanding the wheel and in using the wheel as a way to help you change and grow. Such tools function as a key that will assist you in the transitional period between idea and reality. They act as a catalyst in the creative process of building your knowledge of the Medicine Wheel and the universe.

Like all medicine objects they are powerful tools that help you connect with Spirit and thus do the work Spirit intends you to do. The more you understand you are Spirit's tool, the more powerful your Medicine Wheel tools will be.

Tools such as a screwdriver are fueled by muscle power. A car is fueled by gasoline. Bodies are fueled by food. Medicine objects are fueled by Spirit. It is when people forget the source of power that they can get into trouble with their tools. It is here that the powers of light and dark can struggle. It is good to embrace what power and tools are available to you, but always honor their source. Being humble about this loving force is the key to having it flow through you and your medicine tools.

Keep in mind that it is not appropriate to touch another person's medicine objects without their permission. If someone touches our medicine objects we don't usually make a big fuss. We just politely explain the proper procedure to him, and then reempower the tool.

If a woman is on her moon, it is her responsibility to find out if she should touch a medicine tool. Some Natives feel that a woman's power is so strong at this time that it can influence the outcome of certain ceremonies, or change the energy of a medicine tool.

While constructing your medicine tools remember this construction is a ceremony. Follow the basic ceremonial guidelines outlined in the chapter on respect. Center and cleanse yourself, your area, and any materials you will be using. When you finish creating any tool you should cleanse it again and do one of the bonding ceremonies that follow. How you make your medicine tools is as important as how the finished product looks. While the Creator loves beauty, she is even more impressed with pure intentions and well-meaning heartfelt prayers.

BONDING CEREMONY 1
(Also Called Give Away to the Universe Ceremony)

When you receive or create a new medicine tool it is important for you to merge your energy with it, thus creating a bond. In doing a bonding ceremony you should repeatedly pray that you and this tool may work together to bring only the highest good to any ceremony, person, or situation with which it is used. It is good to give thanks for the opportunity to work with this medicine. You should realize that while this object has been placed in your care, you do not own it. Like you, it is a tool of the Creation.

> **What you need.** Smudge or other cleansing materials, the medicine tool, and notebook and pen or tape recorder.

> **Estimated time.** Fifteen minutes.

1. Cleanse and center.
2. If you are doing this ceremony around a Medicine Wheel, enter it by the directional gateway that most clearly coincides with the tool's purpose. Go to the Center Circle.
3. Offer this tool to the Creator, making a prayer that Creator will use the tool and you for the highest good.
4. Bend down and touch the object to the Earth Mother, making a prayer that the earth will use this tool and you for the highest good.
5. Turn to the North, and extend your arms holding the tool. Pray that Waboose will help you and this tool to work for the highest good.
6. Turn to the East and repeat the process, then turn South, then West, repeating your prayer to each Spirit Keeper.
7. When you have completed your circle hold the tool and be still. Listen for any messages from your relations about how this tool can be used.
8. If you wish, write or record your experience.

By giving your medicine tool away to the universe, with the proper sincerity and intent, it can become truly yours to use, respect, and honor.

BONDING CEREMONY 2

Before the first use of a Medicine Wheel tool it is good to do a bonding ceremony to state the intended purpose of the medicine tool as well as give thanks for the opportunity to work with this medicine. Here is one form of a bonding ceremony.

What you need. Same materials as in bonding ceremony 1, plus an offering.

Estimated time. Fifteen minutes.

1. Smudge yourself, the area, and everything you'll be touching during the ceremony.
2. Place the medicine tool in front of you.
3. Say a prayer inviting in the spirit and medicine of the tool. For instance, "Great Spirit, this little one would like to invite in the medicine and powers of this medicine wand. The intended purpose of this wand is for healing and dreaming work. I pray that the medicine and spirit of these energies enter the wand."
4. Pray to be bonded with this medicine tool for the purposes of the highest good. For instance, "I pray to be bonded to the spirit and medicine of this wand for the purposes of healing and dreaming for the highest good of all those ever involved or in contact with this wand."
5. Then make a prayer of gratitude as well as an offering to give thanks for this gift of Spirit. For instance, "I give thanks to the Spirit that moves in all things and the Spirit that now lives within this medicine wand." After you give thanks, make an offering. We often end our prayers by saying, "It is good. It is done. Ho!"
6. Write or record your experience.

MEDICINE WHEEL POUCH

A Medicine Wheel pouch should be one of the first medicine tools you make. It provides protection as well as gives you a way to carry items that enhance your personal medicine. You may make your pouch out of either leather or cloth.

What you need. Scissors; needle; thread; material for pouch; pencil; ruler, compass, or glass; and a piece of thick paper or cardboard. If you are using leather you will also need sinew or strong thread, an awl, a hole puncher, a leather needle, a knife or very sharp scissors, and a board to place under the leather while punching holes or cutting. Also assemble any decorative items you will want, such as beads, paints, and buttons.

Estimated time. Two hours.

1. Make a pattern. To do this lay a piece of paper on a flat surface. With a ruler, compass, or glass draw a rectangle or circle the size you would like your pouch to be. Add an additional quarter of an inch all around so you have material for the hem.

Three and a half inches by one and a half inches plus an additional quarter of an inch for the hem is a good size for a rectangular pouch, although it can be bigger or smaller according to your preference. A three-inch circle plus the hem is a good size for a circular one.

2. Cut the cloth or leather using your pattern as a guide. To do so turn your material inside out. Fold the cloth in half or lay one piece of cloth on top of the other so you have a double layer. Smooth out any wrinkles. Lay the pattern on top. Cut around the pattern through both layers of cloth. If the material is too thick, cut each piece separately being careful to follow the pattern exactly so the two pieces match.

3. Pin your pouch. You can pin the two pieces of leather or cloth together to keep them in place if they separate easily.

4. Determine which is the top of the pouch. If you are using cloth, fold over enough material so that when your pouch is complete your thong will easily slide through the opening. If you are using leather, you'll need enough room at the top to punch holes.

5. If the pouch is cloth, sew the fold into place. The fold and stitching should be facing outward.

6. Sew the pouch together. Start below the opening for the thong and work your way around to the other side. With cloth, always make sure you go over the stitches at least twice so that the pouch will be strong and hold up well for many moons to come.

   If the leather is very thick you may want to punch holes with the leather punch or use an awl to thread the sinew or leather strips through. When punching holes place the board underneath so you will not damage the tabletop or yourself.

7. Turn the pouch inside out. After reversing the pouch, poke down the corners really well so that the pouch has a nice clean, finished look.

8. Hang the pouch from a thong. The thong can be made from thick yarn, ribbon, a long strip of material, or leather. Make sure you cut this long enough so you can easily get it over your head. To help thread the thong through the cloth pouch, take a very small safety pin and attach it to the end. Use the pin to grip as you thread the thong through the opening at the top of the pouch. Pull the thong completely through the opening, remove the pin, then tie the ends of the thong securely together.

   For the leather pouch, make holes to string the thong from. Punch holes across the top of the pouch. If the leather is not too thick you will be able to go through both layers of leather. If it is too thick, punch three to four holes at the top of both pieces of leather.

9. Add any bead work, painting, or appliqué you desire, using a Medicine Wheel design.

10. For more decoration you can string sinew through a totem stone that has a predrilled hole. Attach it to your pouch by threading the sinew through a leather needle and sewing it directly onto the pouch. Or you can add bead work using the totem colors with which you are currently working. Sew the beads around the seam of the pouch to make a colorful border. Paint a design of a totem animal or plant on the front of your pouch.

11. Smudge yourself, your new pouch, and anything you might be putting into it. Give the pouch away to the universe. Call to the medicine you want for yourself and your pouch. Pray again for Creator to use this tool

to help you, protect you, and heal you. Give thanks to the powers that have and will help you.

12. Perform a bonding ceremony.

What goes in your bag depends on you and what Medicine Wheel positions you are working with at the time. Common items would include the stones, herbs, or fetishes relating to the places you are exploring on the wheel, or ones you need for help and healing. Some examples would be turquoise for protection, carnelian for energy, pipestone for peace, obsidian for mirroring the thoughts of others, wild rose to uplift your spirit, plantain for overall health, and yarrow for strength.

If you are working with the bear for protection, justice, or courage you could place a small bear fetish carved from stone, wood, or other natural material in your pouch. Using fetishes is an excellent way to connect with your animal totems without sacrificing the life of an animal for claws, feathers, teeth, and so forth. So is locating a stone or a stick with the shape of a bear, snake, beaver, or other Medicine Wheel animal on it.

Frequently a small amount of sage, cedar, and sweet grass are added to a Medicine Wheel pouch for cleansing, clearing any negativity, purification, and drawing the good spirits to you. Other common items in pouches are the three sisters—corn, beans, and squash—to connect you with the earth and bring abundance.

MEDICINE WHEEL BUNDLES OR BAGS

A medicine bundle is usually a large piece of cloth or hide wrapped around medicine objects and then securely tied with a thong, yarn, or string. The material used for the wrap is considered sacred and should not be used for anything else. Be sure to smudge the material and whatever you use to tie it up before you wrap it around your medicine objects.

A medicine bag is just what it sounds like. It is a special bag for storing medicine objects. When you determine that something is a medicine bag it should become sacred. It is not appropriate to then use it for storing other belongings. It is not a purse or knapsack and should not be used as such. Only objects directly relating to your Spirit Path should go in it.

You can make it from hide or cloth or it can be ready made as long as it is used for this purpose only.

What you need. Same materials needed for making a medicine pouch.

Estimated time. Two hours.

If you want to make your own medicine bag follow the directions for creating a medicine pouch with the following differences:

1. Determine how large you would like the bag to be then make an appropriate pattern.
2. Always pin the two pieces of material you are using to make the bag because the size will make the material separate. That separation makes it difficult to sew the bag together neatly.
3. Punch the thong holes first. To accomplish this after the bag is completed will be awkward because you are working with more material.
4. Perform a bonding ceremony.

MEDICINE WHEEL NECKLACE

A medicine necklace is a physical manifestation of prayers you are making or energies you are calling to be with you. A simple form of a medicine necklace can be made by taking beads representing the Medicine Wheel stones you are working with and stringing them together. Wearing such a necklace is a way of honoring the different totems currently playing a part in your life. For instance, if you want to purify your spirit you would bead the necklace with malachite, making a prayer for purification with each bead that you string; for transmitting and receiving energy you would use crystal; for inspiring hope or connecting with the sun, moon, or fire you would string opals. Use the mineral wheel chapter as a guide for other medicine you might want to work with.

What you need. Beads that have holes going through them, strong string, thread, or thin fishing line, and, if desired, shells, stones, wood, fetishes, and hook and clasp.

Estimated time. One hour.

1. Quiet yourself, then invite Great Spirit to be with you. State clearly what you are seeking.
2. Make your necklace with ceremony. Begin stringing the necklace. With each bead that you string make a prayer stating what it is you want or feel thankful for.
3. When the necklace is the appropriate length, tie the string with strong knots so that it won't come apart.
4. Perform a bonding ceremony.

For a more complex necklace add shells, stones, wood, or fetishes with a proper hole in them to the stone necklace. If you want a shorter necklace, tie each end of your thread to a hook and clasp, which can be obtained at a jewelry supply store.

MEDICINE WHEEL WAND

Wands are very personal and powerful tools. Take time constructing yours. Contemplate and dream about it before beginning. While doing this keep in mind what you intend to use the wand for. Is it for healing, journeying, or energizing? Clarify the wand's ceremonial focus. As you are told what the different elements of your wand are to be, gather them. Keep them close to you at night. When you have the elements of your wand, set aside a good block of time to blend them together into a significant medicine tool.

What you need. Although wands are a very individual endeavor, there are some common basic components. The wand itself will most likely be made from wood although it certainly does not have to be.

Wood for the wand itself is usually between seven and twelve inches long, relatively straight, and about an inch to an inch and a half wide. If the wand is to be used for dowsing it should be forked at one end. Sometime wands are branched at one end if they are to be used for creativity, movement, change, or "stirring up" energy.

Use fallen branches or wood from a dead tree for your wand. Do not cut into a living tree. The wood used should enhance the wand's purpose.

For example, wood from the birch tree would be used in conjunction with elder or ancient wisdom. Birch also brings guidance, cleansing, healing, and release. Wood from the quaking aspen is good for soothing, calming, and relaxing; it also has healing qualities. Wood from the wild rose is excellent for stimulating unconditional love. It soothes you on the spiritual plane and gives you a feeling of positive spiritual well-being. Black spruce wood is good for releasing congestion on all levels. Black spruce also encourages movement. Wood from sagebrush will bring the trickster into your life and open you to your heart energy. Olive wood will strengthen your purpose, ground you, and help you to remember your experiences.

After you determine the wood for your wand you will want to decide what to put on it. Some people use stones representing specific properties. Others paint symbols or pictures of different animals to call in the powers of a four-legged totem. For instance, a paw print of a cougar would give protection, whereas a picture of an otter would stimulate intuitive powers. A long snake painted down the length of your wand would encourage balance and purify your spirit. A turtle could represent the element of earth; a frog, water. Wands can also be cut from gemstone. The type of gemstone used contributes to the properties of the wand. For example, a wand cut from lepidolite could be used for grounding; balancing; and creating a calm, stable environment. A wand from adventurine could be used for healing or bringing prosperity. A long natural quartz crystal with its six-sided point could be used for healing; for transmitting, receiving, or generating energy; or for manifestation.

The possibilities are endless. Besides the wood and other decorative and healing agents you will need: glue, yarn, thin wire, wire the thickness of a coat hanger, leather or other material to help keep the elements of your wand together, a knife, needle-nosed pliers, and, if desired, paint and brushes.

Estimated time. One week to one year to gather materials; four to eight hours to make wand.

1. Quiet yourself and give thanks for the elements you have gathered and the ceremony you are undertaking.
2. Invite in the totems and Spirit Keepers you would like to empower your wand. To do so, clearly state something like, "Snake, bringer of balance and spiritual purifier, I ask you to be here with me to empower this wand. Malachite, discourager of weakness, please be with me today to weave your medicine into this wand." Each prayer should be directed to whatever energies you are asking to be present.
3. Use glue, leather strips, yarn, sinew, or wire to blend together all the elements of wood, stones, painted symbols, and pictures, while making continual prayers for empowerment of the wand. Every action should be accompanied by a heartfelt prayer for the intended medicine of the wand. Only use the elements you desire to. A wand can be very simple and very effective.
4. Although your wand will be very individual, a good place to start its construction is by decorating the end of the wand that will be the handle. Glue a leather or cloth strip at the handle end.
5. Then wind colored yarn, string, or sinew at the top and bottom of the leather to secure the material further as well as to honor the colors you are using.

6. Tie a thong or yarn at the very end of the wand. You can hang bells, beads, stones, or other items from this.

7. Secure a two-inch or longer crystal or oblong stone to the opposite end. Brace the stone with wire. Upon completion at least one inch of the stone should remain exposed and at least one inch should be secured in the girdle of wire and glue. With the thin wire, vertically attach four pieces of two-inch wire (coat hanger thickness). One inch will nestle against the wand, the other inch will brace the stone in place. If the wand is wood, carve thin diagonal grooves with a pocket knife in which the four thicker wires will fit. Take the thin wire and wrap it horizontally around the thicker wire brace a number of times until it makes a long girdle for the stone. The thin wire should wind in neat circles around the wand, beginning at the wood end and coming up to cover the one inch of wire securing the stone in place.

8. To secure the stone or crystal further you can then use epoxy or glue over the wire and around the places where the stone and wire make contact.

9. Cover the wire by winding colored yarn, leather, or sinew over it.

10. Decide if you would like to place other stones on your wand. If so carve grooves for these with a pocket knife. Glue these stones into place with epoxy or glue.

11. In the space that is left on the wood, you can paint any symbols you would like to include on your wand.

12. Be sure to thank the Spirit Keepers and totems once again for their blessings and good medicine.

13. Perform a bonding ceremony.

MEDICINE WHEEL STAFF

What you need. Same materials as for the wand, except the wood must be longer.

Estimated time. Same as for the wand.

A Medicine Wheel staff can be made in much the same way as a wand. The obvious difference is that a staff is longer. This means you would use a branch or other pole that comes up to your waist or shoulder, depending on your preference. Never use wood from a live tree for this purpose. A plain unadorned branch that has fallen from a tree can be used as a staff. Driftwood also makes a beautiful staff. However a wooden dowel from the hardware store is a good substitute if a long, sturdy branch or piece of driftwood is not available. How you decorate your staff is a personal choice determined by its purpose, medicine, and use. You can put a stone at the end of your staff if you wish, using the same instructions for the Medicine Wheel wand. You can also insert stones or paint symbols on this staff.

HOW TO USE A
MEDICINE WHEEL WAND OR STAFF
•••••

After you create your Medicine Wheel wand or staff, allow it to guide you as to its best use. Sleep with your wand or lean your staff close to your bed so you can become familiar with it. You can also lay either the wand or staff under your bed while you sleep. Keep a notebook close to your bed so that you can record any dreams these tools might inspire.

Wands and staffs can be used for energy balancing, dream work, healing, ceremonial dancing, weaving or cleansing energy, massage work, praying to connect with Spirit, full moon or other ceremonies, and work with the elementals. A wand can also be used as a talking stick.

If you have streamers of bells attached to either a staff or wand you can also use it as a musical instrument and a sound healing tool.

Hiking with a Medicine Wheel staff is a wonderful way to honor nature and make medicine while taking walks or gathering herbs.

MEDICINE WHEEL RATTLES

Rattles are powerful tool for communicating with Spirit and enhancing your prayers and almost any ceremony: particularly ones with song or dance. Different rattles invite in a variety of energies depending on their sound, what they are made from, how they are made, and how they are decorated. If a rattle is for spiritual purposes rather than simply a musical instrument, it should be made in a ceremonial way and treated with respect. Begin all rattle making by following the basic ceremonial guidelines. Some people choose to make special pouches or bundles to wrap their rattles in when they are not using them.

Bell and/or Seashell Rattle

What you need. A sturdy stick; bells or seashells; sinew, string or colored yarn; and a power drill with a small bit.

Estimated time. Two hours.

1. Use a sturdy stick. Choose a wood compatible with the medicine of this rattle.
2. String bells and/or seashells to the stick tying them with sinew, string, or colored yarns to make an interesting pattern. Use a power drill with a tiny drill bit to make the holes in the seashells and wood. Hang as many bells and seashells as you want. Keep adding them until you have the sound you desire.

Make the rattle out of just bells or seashells, or combine them to get a third sound. Bells represent the element air, and seashells represent the element water. The wood represents the earth.

Gourd Rattles

You can make a variety of types and sizes of rattles out of gourds with a wooden stick for the handle.

What you need. A stick, a gourd, a knife, small stones, glue, paint, brushes, and, if desired beadwork, leather, and stones.

Estimated Time. Two to four hours.

1. Choose a stick to use for a handle.
2. Carefully carve a hole the size of the handle into the base of a dried gourd.
3. Insert small stones or other objects to act as noisemakers. Slide the handle into the hole.
4. Secure the handle with epoxy or glue. Then decorate your rattle by painting symbols on it or adhering stones to it. You can apply colorful beadwork to the handle or wrap it in leather strips.
5. Perform a bonding ceremony.

Gourd rattles can be used for many purposes in part determined by how they are decorated. For instance, a gourd rattle could be used for giving thanks for a good harvest or praying for a "good hunt."

Ready-Made Central or South American Rattle

If you are not craft oriented or do not have gourds available, try buying a ready-made, inexpensive Central or South American rattle. You can paint over the usually touristy decorations. This is a way to support a Third World economy as well as to personalize a well-made, pleasant sounding rattle.

Four Directions Rattle

What you need. A gourd rattle, paint, and brushes.

Estimated time. One hour on each of two consecutive days.

1. A simple four directions rattle can be made by painting a gourd or ready-made rattle a color with which you are working.
2. Let it dry then paint stripes or other designs in the colors of the four directions around it. Use white for the North, red or gold for the East, yellow or green for the South, blue or black for the West.
3. Perform a bonding ceremony.

MEDICINE WHEEL MASKS
......

Human beings have used masks since the earliest times for ceremonial dancing, healing, inducing trances, shamanic journeying, driving illness from a home, channeling, portraying spiritual beings or elementals, and communicating and connecting with the spirit plane.

Masks have been used for different occasions such as maternity, birthing, death, coming into manhood, a woman's first moon, dawn or dusk, changing of the seasons, harvest, or initiation rites. In many ceremonies one is presented with what is traditionally spoken of as "a different view" from behind the mask.

Working with masks helps one understand symbolism. While wearing a mask you can lose yourself and become what is being portrayed by the mask. You do not hide behind a mask. You become something more. Masks cannot be completely explained, they can only be experienced. Some who work with masks feel they are a physical manifestation of the more elusive levels of reality. Each mask will have a name and personality of its own. What masks are made from and what is applied to them after they are made varies greatly. Many tribes, such as the Iroquois, made corn husk or bushy face masks along with wood and stone ones. Pacific Northwest Coast tribes made and wore elaborate wooden carved masks, which they painted and decorated exquisitely. In more recent times masks are made from papier-mâché.

As with the other Medicine Wheel tools, embellishments are all applied for a specific reason. Mask making is an art that can be very complex. For most people, buying an already constructed mask to represent the medicine with which you are working may be the best alternative. If you do so, be sure to do a welcoming and bonding ceremony after you obtain a mask.

Most areas of the country have some form of instruction in mask making available. Taking a course is a good idea if you want to make your own Medicine Wheel masks. However, if you cannot do so here are instructions for a simple mask.

MAKING A MEDICINE WHEEL MASK

What you need. Clay you can bake in your oven (get enough to cover your face with about a half-inch thickness, plus additional clay for any exterior expressions or features you may want to add to the mask), newspaper, old clothes, smudging materials, bowl of water, a rolling pin, a small sponge, petroleum jelly, any clay sculpture tools you can obtain, a pencil or awl, and leather or yarn ties. Collect any embellishments you wish to hang from the mask such as beads; stones; feathers; dried corn, beans or squash; or herbs. The herbs can be placed in small squares of cloth, tied with yarn and then hung from prepunched holes after you bake and paint the mask. Also get paint and brushes in advance if you want to color the mask.

Estimated time. Two to eight hours.

1. Cleanse and center.
2. Roll a large piece of clay into a ball. Then, with the rolling pin, roll the clay out into a piece big enough to fit over your face. You may need to use the sponge to slightly dampen the clay or gently smooth it in places. When you are finished the clay should be about half an inch thick and firm enough so that it does not crack or split.
3. Prepare your face by applying a generous coat of petroleum jelly, being especially generous over the eyebrows, and other areas of facial hair. Take a deep breath and hold it, then place the clay over your face. With your hands quickly but gently press the clay so that it conforms to your features.
4. Carefully remove the mask and let it stand for a bit to harden.
5. Cut or punch holes for your eyes, nose, and mouth.
6. Add any additional features you've been guided to include. Punch any holes that you may want in order to hang feathers, beads, or herbs from the mask. To punch these holes use a thin tool or a pencil. It is usual to have the holes around the forehead or across the jaw line although you should put them where you have been guided to.
7. Make a hole by each ear so that you can attach ties with which you'll tie the mask around your head when you wear it. Make the holes far enough in from the edges so that they do not rip easily.
8. Bake the mask according to the instructions that come with the clay.

9. When the mask has cooled, paint it, then add any other embellishments.
10. Perform a bonding ceremony.

MEDICINE WHEEL SHIELDS
·····

Like masks, shields have been very important to humans since the dawn of time. For any battle it is wise to seek protection. Shields have been a protective force in battle, be it physical, spiritual, mental, or emotional.

The types of shield are as varied as are their uses. Besides protecting self, home, or family, shields can be used to heal, to dream, and to connote family clan, lodge, or society affiliation. Shields can be used to form an alliance with one's personal or tribal animal totem and to tell stories or record important events.

Because shield making is complicated you might prefer to purchase a shield from a good shield maker, then add new elements to it as you travel the wheel. However, if you wish to construct your own shield, following are simple instructions.

MAKING A MEDICINE WHEEL SHIELD

What you will need. A hoop, hide or cloth, string or leather strips, needle, thread, paints, stones, herbs, feathers, wood, and other objects you desire.

Estimated time. One to four hours.

1. Smudge and center.
2. If willow is readily available make a hoop from it. Tie it in a circle the size you want. Use sinew, string, or leather strips to fasten it. If willow or another supple wood is not available, embroidery hoops purchased at craft shops work just fine.
3. Stretch elk skin, deerskin, cloth, or canvas across the hoop. Tack the hide or cloth in place using a needle and thread or a leather needle and sinew.
4. Before painting symbols on the shield, quiet yourself. It is good to smudge again at this point. Paint the story, emblems, or symbols currently affecting you onto the shield.
5. Hang or sew on any embellishments you are drawn to use.
6. Perform a bonding ceremony.

STORING AND PROTECTING YOUR MEDICINE WHEEL TOOLS
·····

It is important to store and protect your medicine tools carefully when you are not using them. These are not art objects hung on display to be touched or fondled by all who see them. If you are guided by Spirit to hang objects such as your shield or mask, place them in an area that is secluded or put up a sign that says Don't Touch! Stand firm in making people respect your objects. If you are told to hang something but not talk about it, do as Grandmother Evelyn Eaton suggests in her book *I Send a Voice:* put up another sign that says Don't Ask!

Most medicine objects can be kept in medicine bundles or bags during the time you are not using them.

Cleansing Medicine Tools

It is important to cleanse your tools after every use so as not to drag energy from one ceremony to the next. There have been cases where pain was released into a medicine tool in one ceremony. It was then accidentally transferred to another person in a following ceremony due to the medicine tool's not having been properly cleansed after the previous ceremony. Tools can be cleansed by smudging with mixtures of sage, cedar, and sweet grass, by water (if appropriate) by sound, by breath, and by prayer.

MAKING OFFERINGS TO MEDICINE TOOLS
.....

Periodically smudge and offer your medicine tools to the universe, reaffirming their intention and purpose. Acknowledge the medicine they give you by making offerings to them. Most medicine tools will tell you what they like for offerings. For instance, many masks like both tobacco offerings and being sung to. Wands respond well to basking in the morning dawn or the light of a full moon. Shields like being covered or wrapped in soft materials. Always use a natural material rather than synthetic.

Offerings

Some common offerings are tobacco, cornmeal, birdseed, kinnikinnick, salt baths, songs or chants, drumming, flowers, a piece of your hair, cleansing in streams or water (if appropriate to the materials the tool is made from), smoke or incense, and food left out in an area for the spirit of the medicine tool.

MAKING AN OFFERING ALTAR

What you need. A quiet place in nature, smudging materials, your medicine tool, offerings, and, if desired, drum, rattle, and soft flowers.

Estimated time. One hour.

1. Find a place in nature where you will not be disturbed.
2. Smudge yourself, everything that will be touched during the offering, and the area.
3. First place the medicine tool on the area designated to be the altar. Lay the offering around it, such as flowers, food, cornmeal, salt, and so forth.
4. Make a prayer stating what your purpose is such as, "I make this offering to honor the medicine of this mask. I give thanks for this medicine and the spirit of the mask. Ho!"

5. Try some of these methods for connecting and thanking the spirit of the medicine tool.

- Take time to be with the energy. Sit quietly. Make prayers of gratitude.
- Gift the spirit of the medicine tool by means of drumming, dancing, or singing for it.
- Close your eyes and clear your thoughts so any messages may come to you. Be aware of any images or signs.
- Rub the medicine tool gently with soft flowers such as rose petals or dandelion fluff.
- Hold the medicine tool gently to your heart while you hum or sing for it.

6. Make a completion prayer.
7. Remove and appropriately bundle the medicine tool and any other personal items such as smudge bowl, fan, or herb pouch.
8. Leave in place on the altar any offerings such as food, flowers, stones, or cornmeal.
9. Leave quietly and respectfully.

Keep in mind when you are honoring the spirit of your medicine tool you are giving love and thanks to the spirit or energy of the tool. It is important to be respectful of the medicine tool, but to remember you are not idolizing the physical shell of the tool. What is being acknowledged through this form of prayer and offering is the energy and life force that sends breath, healing, and life via means of the medicine tool. The medicine tool is the physical face representing a need that humans have. The medicine of these tools is all around us. It is the life force focused for an intended purpose. Medicine tools are a gift from Spirit to harness spirit energy in a form that is tangible to humans. These tools and the Spirit Keepers connected with them are like agents of the Great Spirit to guide us to "see" with our hearts and channel the light so that we may, as Evelyn Eaton has said, "Go shining!" Our prayer for you as you work with Medicine Wheel tools is to "go shining" toward your enlightened path, toward the healing that needs to be brought forth, and toward the light of the Creator and the Earth Mother.

Ducks Fly Moon—by Gwyn George

9

Healing with the Wheel

There are many ways of using the Medicine Wheel to promote healing. Studying the Medicine Wheel has brought healing to some people; building a wheel has brought healing to others. Using the wheel for ceremony, meditation, prayer, and contemplation has helped many other people become more whole and healthy on all levels of their being.

The Medicine Wheel gatherings have brought miraculous healings to a large number of people, some with serious problems. It is always amazing to see how strongly the Creator can work through this Medicine Wheel tool to help those who really are seeking help.

At the first twenty-five Medicine Wheel Gatherings Wabun's Rainbow Crystal Healing Ceremony was used on Sunday mornings as a healing tool for participants. It was always very powerful. It is presented later in this chapter for those of you who would like to use it at your own wheels. Then, because Wabun's travels around the wheel took her away from the gatherings for a time, Sun Bear's Healing Ceremony, which consists of blessings with fan and feathers and prayer by Sun Bear and some of the other teacher/healers present has been used. That ceremony has also had dramatic results. It seems that the energy of the Medicine Wheel itself can promote healing in those who are open to feeling such energy.

For those who might find it difficult to feel that energy, what follows is a healing ceremony Crysalis has developed to help people experience the Medicine Wheel as a sensory tool for healing.

THE MEDICINE WHEEL SENSORY
HEALING CEREMONY

·····

The Medicine Wheel Sensory Healing Ceremony is one method used to promote individual healing and energy balancing. It can also help you to connect and learn about your spirit guides and protectors. In addition, this ceremony will help you expand your five senses: sound, taste, smell, vision, and touch.

During this ceremony participants have said that their spirit guides or plant, mineral, and animal helpers have made themselves present. This ceremony has also been used for developing the five senses. It can help you to connect with and explore different aspects of the wheel. It can be used for locating your place on the wheel as well as getting to know the totems of the wheel.

For some it has been subtle, relaxing, and calming; a pleasant experience of communing with nature and opening and deepening the senses. Other people have experienced deep levels of healing and intense connections with the spirit forces. At more than one ceremony there have been weather changes. At one in particular, after inviting in the elemental forces, a breeze picked up and the area became filled with blustering wind and light rain.

There are people who have said, for them, nothing at all happened that they were aware of, although they were able to feel the difference between the energy inside and outside of the wheel.

This is not a ceremony to be shared cavalierly with large groups, or with those ignorant of the power of ceremony. The more you practice this ceremony the more it will benefit you in your life. Make sure that participants are well grounded before completing the ceremony.

When first sharing this ceremony, Crysalis saw that afterward some participants experienced migraine headaches, stomach aches, and a feeling of being disconnected. She noticed this would happen if the participants did not properly ground or discharge the feelings that came to them during this ceremony. Consequently, she now allows proper time and attention to make sure all participants have the opportunity to ground themselves and release any emotion built up during the ceremony. It is the responsibility of the facilitator to observe carefully the needs of the participants so that discomfort can be avoided.

Some participants have experienced healing on many levels from this ceremony. There is documentation of healing that has taken place on the mental, physical, emotional, and spiritual planes. The ceremony does not, however, take the place of a physician. If you have health problems, see your doctor.

It is a good idea to reread chapter 2 before doing this ceremony. We encourage you to keep your healing wheel simple initially. Use local rocks from the forest and from the streambeds. As you continue working with the wheel you might want to make the wheel out of the actual totem stones as you acquire them.

Later still as you become comfortable with the ceremony, you might try constructing some of the other types of wheels described in chapter 5.

Preparations

You will need at least two to four hours for this ceremony. This includes time to prepare, time to do the ceremony, and then time to clean up. It is best not to have any time constraints. This is an extremely potent healing. Do not underestimate its power. Go slowly. Never end a ceremony prematurely and without grounding. All participants should have some knowledge of the nature of ceremony and they should respect it. If you have any uncertainty about doing this ceremony, do not do it. Work with the many other ceremonies in this book. When you feel ready and confident then consider working with this medicine. This ceremony is not for everyone, nor does it need to be. If you are supposed to work with this ceremony you will clearly know it. If you are not sure ask Spirit, and Spirit will guide you.

Decide who is orchestrating the ceremony. Until you have done this ceremony enough that you are comfortable with it, do it by yourself or with four key people: a facilitator, a support person, a drummer, and the participant (the person going into the wheel for healing and help).

If you need this form of ceremony for healing, opening up to Spirit, and experiencing your five senses then you should be the participant and let someone else facilitate or be a support person.

Being a facilitator or support person is a lovely way to do service and extend your healing abilities. Either of these roles is a gift to the participants and by its nature rewarding. It has been stated by people who have been in these positions that although they did not expect it, they too felt healing and a deepening connection with Spirit.

As a facilitator or support person do not project what you think the participant needs or what you want the outcome of this ceremony to be. You are merely the tool guided by Spirit that sets the healing in motion. It is imperative that in your prayers you consciously turn this healing over to Spirit and not limit or get in the way of the ceremony.

If you are not clear that this is between the participant and Spirit then you may not be ready to facilitate or support. Try being a participant first so you have a better understanding of the experience and the needs of the participant.

THE FACILITATOR

This person leads, facilitates, and orchestrates the process of the ceremony. This person is responsible for what shape it takes, what medicine objects, instruments, herbs, and aromatherapy is used. Be clear these are the responsibilities of the facilitator when working with a support helper, because any confusion can be unsettling for those involved in the healing process. The main facilitator may delegate parts of the process to the support person(s) who will be helping with the ceremony.

Keep the ceremony simple and organized. Do not stretch yourself or the support persons too thin. Doing so is a great disservice to those participating, and thus irresponsible. Do less rather than more until you have repeated the ceremony enough that you flow naturally with the energy of the wheel.

This can be a very moving and emotional ceremony for those involved if they have good support. It is the facilitator's role to insure this support.

SUPPORT PERSONS

If you are working with more than one participant, there should be a support person for each participant going into the wheel. It is imperative there are enough helpers to make sure each person has appropriate support and attention. It is the support person's role to give the participants their undivided attention.

Do not ask the participants to speak or respond to the support people at any time during the ceremony. The supporters should do what the facilitator instructs as gently, calmly, and unobtrusively as possible.

Support people should only touch the exterior limbs of the participant's body. They should move slowly and not touch the participant in any way that could even remotely be perceived as intrusive. When touching the participant keep in mind that he will feel your touch about six to twelve inches from his body so move slowly, calmly, and gently. Release and move away from the body in the same manner.

Keep in mind this is a ceremony for them, not you. This is not the time to put your own needs ahead of others.

THE DRUMMER

Drumming a heartbeat song throughout the ceremony is very powerful and can deeply enhance the experience. The rhythm should be of the collective heartbeat of the participants. The ceremony can take place without a drummer, with the rhythm provided by a rattle; however, a drummer is preferable whenever possible.

PARTICIPANTS

If you are looking for an opening of your senses, healing, or a deeper connection with Spirit, then this experience could have value for you as a participant.

TOOLS

You will need to gather available tools for this ceremony. It is not expected nor encouraged that you attempt to use all the tools suggested. It is better to use less initially so you can experience the individual power of each tool. Keep in mind that this ceremony is about connecting with Spirit. It is not an opportunity to play "show and tell." Here are some suggestions for tools:

Sound. Use your favorite natural instrument: rattle, drum, flute, whistle, chimes, diggerydoo (an Australian native instrument), rainstick (an instrument used in South American rain forests), or bells of various kinds. Playing an audio tape is all right if the music is of a natural sound such as drumming, flute playing, the wind, the rain, or the ocean.

Taste. Prepare a cup or thermos of hot tea made from available Medicine Wheel herbs. Choose a tea or tea blend with properties pertinent to the purpose of the ceremony.

Smell. Use whatever form of Medicine Wheel plant aromas you prefer: smudge, the natural plant, oils, essences, sachets, or resins. Choose the herbal aromas that will best serve the participants with whatever problems they are having. Medicine Wheel candles can also be used to heighten the sense of smell.

Sight. Visual stimulation is provided by the stones of the wheel, by the presence of all the medicine tools, and, most important, by nature herself.

Touch. Wands, stone massage tools, special gemstones relating to the wheel, masks, pouches (especially those made in soft or textured materials), and ceremonial jewelry can all be used to stimulate the sense of touch in this part of the ceremony.

Gifts from nature that represent aspects of the wheel can also be used, such as a soft wild rose or fluffy dandelion, an acorn, a pinecone or pine needles, or a fallen branch from one of the plant totems trees.

You will also need blankets (one blanket should be used for the altar, and participants should bring a blanket to lie on), smudge utensils (bowl, fan, and so on), pipe (if you are a pipecarrier), and rocks for the wheel (more on the rocks will be discussed shortly).

Decide on a location to build the Medicine Wheel if you do not already have one. Although it can be inside or outside, it is preferable to be out in nature. However, it should be a place where you will not be interrupted. You will need an area that will be large and flat enough to build a Medicine Wheel that the participants can comfortably lie in. If you already have a Medicine Wheel you can do the ceremony there.

If you are building the wheel for the ceremony, determine the size of the wheel and stones. This can vary according to how many persons are to go into the wheel for healing. As already noted, the wheel should be large enough for the participants to lie down comfortably. Pick stones big enough so that the wheel itself is visually apparent and doesn't get lost when filled with the participants.

You can use any kind of rocks or stones. It is particularly powerful if all persons involved as either facilitator, support person, drummer, or participant bring at least one stone each. It helps build the power and connecting forces of the wheel. People may find these stones during walks in the woods or while interacting with nature or they may use a stone that already has special meaning to them. After the ceremony they can take these stones home with them. The stones will continue to carry the energy and the healing qualities of the ceremony with them. Frequently, these stones are then used by the participants and facilitators in Medicine Wheels that they build at their homes.

Build the ceremonial wheel following directions for "Building a Medicine Wheel" in chapter 5.

THE CEREMONY

Reread the chapter on ceremony and respect before beginning this ceremony.

1. Place everything you will be using on a blanket. This will be your altar.
2. Smudge yourself, all participants, the completed wheel, the surrounding area, and everything that will be touched during the ceremony. If available use Medicine Wheel herbs in your smudge mixture. Draw in this herbal medicine by doing a thorough smudge of everyone.
3. Next have all participants smudge themselves with sound. Smudging with sound clears and purifies the vibratory level, setting up a pure clear energy, conducive to healing and Spirit work. Use musical instruments such as rattles, drums, whistles, flutes, chimes, and so forth. To do this sound smudge, work with the instrument, such as a rattle, to send the sound out over your body drawing out any unnecessary energy. Bend your knees slightly and breathe long, slow, deep breaths. Start at the top of your head and work your way down to your toes. Shake this energy into the ground being careful not to throw it out into the circle or on someone else. Then reach above and then behind you to do the same thing down

your back, again shaking the energy into the earth when you reach your feet. If you have drums or flutes, use them to do this for each other. Bring the sound as close to your body as possible to feel the vibration fully.

4. Sound smudge the area with the instruments. After each person is thoroughly smudged with sound, smudge the Medicine Wheel and surrounding area with the musical instruments. Smudge everywhere, as high up as you can reach and as close to the ground. Smudge the perimeter of the wheel so that anywhere that someone involved in the ceremony might walk has been cleansed with sound vibrations.

5. Place candles in sturdy candle holders at each of the directional stones and/or in the center around the Creator stone. Acknowledge the element of fire as you light the candles. The colors and herbs used in the candles are determined by the needs of the participants. Using candles is optional. If you do not use them, then acknowledge the element of fire when you light the smudge.

6. Now the participants can enter the wheel. Ask them to sit on their blankets. They should already know this is a sensory ceremony and that different parts of the ceremony will be for possible healing on the spiritual, mental, emotional, or physical plane; for connecting with Spirit; and for getting in touch with different aspects of their five senses. Briefly remind them of all this. Then make a prayer to Creator and invite the powers of the Medicine Wheel to be there and answer the prayers of the participants. Acknowledge the elemental energies—earth, water, fire, and air—and the animal, mineral, color, and plant totems. Give thanks for the gifts of sight, taste, sound, smell, and touch. Make a prayer turning the ceremony over to Spirit. It can be as simple as, "Creator, please guide this ceremony for the highest good of all involved." End your prayer with "Ho!" You will continue to follow the structure of the ceremony but recognize it is Creator that is the source of all that happens during the ceremony.

7. If you have a thermos of tea made from Medicine Wheel herbs now is the time to give participants a cup of it. You can explain out loud to the participants that this is to open up their sense of taste, to connect them with the plant kingdom and bond them with the element of water. This step is optional. If you are using ceremonial jewelry this is when the participants should put it on.

8. While they are drinking their tea, have them connect with their gift of sight. Encourage them to soak into their consciousness the visual impact of the Medicine Wheel, the candles, and, if outside, all of nature.

9. If you choose to do the Floating Flower Petal Ceremony (described in chapter 13), bring them the bowl of flowers. Let them know that this exercise is for opening up to sight, color, and smell. Have them follow the directions given in that exercise.

10. Next ask them to lie down and close their eyes. Encourage them to *feel* the support of the Mother Earth beneath them. Ask them to be aware of their breathing and to take long, slow, deep breaths. Find out if everyone is warm enough. If not, bring them blankets. Encourage them to connect with their sense of touch by really *feeling* the earth cradle and nurture them. Invite them to use their hands to touch the ground close by them. They should not open their eyes to do this.

11. Begin the ceremonial drumming. Whenever possible have at least one person who drums throughout the whole ceremony. This person walks slowly around the circle drumming to the sound of the collective heartbeat. Begin the rhythm by having the participants use their left hand to find their heartbeat and with the other hand gently but firmly pat their chest to their life pulse. If there is more than one participant the patting will eventually come in unison. When this pulse becomes a rhythm of its own, the drummer then joins in the heartsong. The drummer continues this throughout the entire ceremony. The participants may stop patting as soon as the drummer has a strong heartsong going.

    If you have many extra helpers you can use more than one drum and rattles, too. It is important the rhythm is done very softly but in a consistent manner so as not to interfere with the other instruments that will be used during the ceremony, or to jar the participants. Any loud noises or fast movements are extremely amplified when in this quiet state of consciousness.

    If you do not have a drummer begin the ceremony yourself in this manner with drumming and/or rattling. If you have no instruments begin the ceremony with the heartsong using just your palm as your instrument, gently patting your chest.

12. Allow the participants a few moments to acclimate to the energy of the circle and the sound of the drumming. Then begin with aromatherapy. Have the support persons enter the circle by the closest pathway. Sit or stoop close to the participant's head. Set the aromas you have chosen to enhance the purpose of the ceremony close by so there is as little disturbance as possible to the participant. Amber, associated with the Strength stone, usually comes in chunks or little boxes; however, most aromas are in oil form. The support person should hold the aroma under the participant's nose as close as possible being *extremely* careful not to spill any oil on the participant. Gently ask the participant to breathe long, slow, deep breaths. Let them breathe in an aroma for two to four breaths. When the support person is done they should pick up the aromas, and leave the wheel quietly, returning to the altar to await the next instruction from the facilitator.

13. If available, place on the ground at the participant's head any enhancing medicine object you might have such as a dream pillow, dream catcher, or double-terminated crystal. If you have more participants than dream medicine tools then place what dream tools you have in the Center Circle of the Medicine Wheel. Quietly say a prayer out loud asking that the participants' dreams will be enhanced, remembered, and understandable, and that each person will connect more deeply with the secrets of their subconscious.

14. Now place a medicine tool or objects from among those previously listed in the tools section of this chapter (page 112) into the participant's hand. Be gentle and remember that in the participant's quiet state of consciousness any fast or rough touch can seem like a serious invasion or intrusion.

15. At this time the support person should be instructed to smudge the participant's energy field with one of the sound instruments. They should start at the participant's head and work down to their feet. This should be repeated two to four times depending on the time frame and how large the group is.

The order for using sound instruments should be a rattle first then light, lovely sounds such as flutes, soft whistles, or fairy bells then building to louder more confrontive instruments such as a diggerydoo, conch, gong, chime, or drum. Toward the end of the ceremony repeat a light, gentle sound with a rainstick, fairy bells, or flute, ending once again with the rattle.

16. Repeat the aromatherapy described in Step 12; use a different aroma if one is available.

17. Repeat the medicine tool placement described in Step 14; using a different medicine tool. If you have only one tool then leave it in place.

18. Repeat the sound smudging described in Step 15, following the sound sequence outlined in that step. If you have only one instrument then repeat with that sound.

19. Remove the medicine tool the participant is holding. If you have a medicine mask now is the time to gently place this on the participant's face. Guide their hands to hold the mask so that you do not cause them undue discomfort. Be aware and respectful at all times of the participant's comfort and highly charged state of being.

20. Repeat the aromatherapy described in Step 12, then the medicine tools and touch sensory step described in Step 14, and finally the instruments creating sounds described in Step 15, until you have used all of your available tools except the final rattle smudge. Remove all medicine objects or masks at that time. Before continuing, look around to make sure that no participant is still holding a medicine object or wearing a mask. If there are any remaining, remove them.

21. If you are a qualified pipecarrier, now is the time to do a pipe. So participants are aware of this transition announce quietly that you are beginning the pipe but there is no need for them to move. Smudge participants from head to toe at this point. If you are not doing a pipe, smudge them anyway with available Medicine Wheel herbs including sage, sweet grass, and cedar.

22. After completing the pipe and/or the smudge, it is then time to do a final rattle smudge.

23. At this point begin grounding exercises to gently but firmly bring participants back to the physical plane. Always end by placing your hands first softly then firmly around the participant's ankles. Begin by applying gentle pressure, then firmer, increasing until you feel a solid grounding energy connecting the participant strongly with the earth plane. Do this for at least a minute then gently release. You do not want to awaken the participant or have any kind of verbal exchange. This is to reconnect them with the physical plane, not with you personally.

    Other exercises for grounding that can be used are laying-on-of-hands, polarity, a shoulder rub, a soft forehead touch, or a gentle head massage. Remember, keep your touch to the head, neck, and exterior limbs of the participant's body. Move slowly, calmly, and gently. Do not do any exercises that suggest the participants should move or talk.

24. After all participants have been grounded then the facilitator and support persons should all gather and join hands in a half circle at the exterior of the wheel by the altar.

25. The facilitator should then share out loud a completion prayer such as, "The ceremony is completed. We give thanks to Spirit for what has taken

place here today and to all the elements and energies that have been present. We give thanks for this ceremony and this healing circle. It is good! It is done! Ho!" Then say to the participants that it is time for them to return to the physical plane, that they should feel the Earth Mother beneath them and connect with that physical plane energy. Continue by stating they have been on a powerful journey but the journey has come to an end and it is time to bring their energy and bodies into strong relationship with the physical earth plane. Instruct them to open their eyes and sit up but not to leave the wheel. Give them time to do this.

Carefully observe the participants to see if anyone may need special attention or further grounding after the ceremony. Some signs of this may be a slightly dazed look, a lot of white light or energy around the head, or agitation of any kind. For the most part you can anticipate that the participants will have sleepy grins and dreamy or awestruck expressions on their faces. Most likely they will be slow moving.

26. Now it is time to ground yourself and the other support persons. Invite the other support persons to bend their knees slightly, let their arms swing loosely and take four long, slow, deep breaths. With each exhale, ask them to send any last prayers or energy to the participants. Then invite them and the participants to take four long, slow breaths together. This time ask that everyone send a prayer of thanks, healing, and energy to the facilitator and support persons.

27. By now everyone should be grounded and present. State that you will pass a talking stick around the circle. When they have the stick each person should express what it was like for them. When others have the stick they should listen. First start with the participants, then the support persons, and end with the facilitator. State that each person has three to five minutes to speak. This is crucial to the process so be sure you allow for time to do this.

28. After everyone shares, take a moment to remind the participants this is a powerful experience and emotions can surface for some time afterward. Encourage them to be ready with the appropriate support in the coming weeks. Say that if they are in therapy, be sure to check in with their therapist in the following week, if they are in a twelve-step program be sure to go to their meetings, if they do cocounseling, women's or men's circles, or whatever form of support to be especially on top of it in the next two weeks. If they are not doing any kind of self-examination, encourage them to consider it at this time. Remind them that because of the ceremony their dreams can be very powerful and enlightening so they should keep a notebook by their beds so they will not forget them. Tell them it is a particularly good time to work with dream tools and, if they do not know how to interpret their dreams, to find someone knowledgeable to do this for them. Tell them to be kind and gentle to themselves as they have just gone through a powerful experience.

End by singing a chant together. Ask them to leave the circle by the pathways and then, if it is not a permanent wheel, take it down. If anyone seems to still be ungrounded or agitated, ask them to stay and work with them further.

For some people, this ceremony can be very emotionally charged so let the support persons know they should be ready to do additional grounding exercises or go sit by a person and really listen to what is going on for them. This is not a time to give advice, or caretake and not allow someone the space to feel his or her experience. However, if someone is emotionally stretched, be ready to help him or her and do not leave that person imbalanced or dangling. The ceremony is not completely over until all participants are grounded and present on the physical plane.

It is up to the good judgment of the facilitator to know when someone needs to discharge emotionally in a productive manner or when someone is not grounded and further discharging will only create more imbalance. This is not a therapy session, nor should it imitate one.

If you do not feel you are aptly equipped to make these kind of judgments and deal properly with the situations that may arise from this powerful ceremony, do not take on the responsibility of the facilitator. Making inappropriate decisions at the expense of the participants is a serious disservice to those involved. The consequences to the participants should be considered carefully in advance of, not after, the ceremony. If you are strongly drawn to facilitate this ceremony, do not let this precaution dissuade you. Spirit knows best what each person's limits are.

THE RAINBOW CRYSTAL HEALING CEREMONY

The Rainbow Crystal Healing Ceremony has been used at many Medicine Wheel Gatherings. Until it first appeared in the book *Lightseeds* (coauthored by Wabun and by Anderson Reed), Wabun had not allowed this ceremony to be recorded. The possibility of videotaping or recording it felt all wrong. Now, however, because of the increasing danger to the earth and all of her children, Wabun feels the time has come to offer this ceremony openly. Wabun requests you use this ceremony only as an individual meditation until you are fully prepared to use it with a group of people. It is a powerful visualization technique and can cause discomfort to people in group situations if the leader does not establish the proper psychic safeguards before joining people together for this meditation. Before she found the proper safeguards, Wabun saw people become disoriented when doing this as a group visualization. She would like to spare others the experience. Done as an individual's meditation, this ceremony is a powerful healing force for the individual doing it as well as for the earth and our relations in all her kingdoms.

What you need. Smudge materials and a crystal used only for this purpose.

Estimated time. One hour for performing the ceremony and thinking about it afterward.

1. Although this ceremony can be done anywhere it is most powerful when performed near a Medicine Wheel. This is best done outside, but you may do it indoors if necessary.
2. Cleanse yourself and the crystal you will be using.
3. Set the crystal on the earth in front of you, point directed skyward. If you can do this around a Medicine Wheel, set the crystal by the Creator stone.
4. Take a few deep breaths, allowing your breath to fill as much of your body as possible.

5. Be aware of your posture. Your back should be straight but not stiff. Your knees should be bent slightly. Your stomach and jaw muscles should be as relaxed as possible. Close your eyes.

6. On your next inhalation, become aware of the sacred energy that lies at the center of your being. As you exhale, see a part of this energy form a circle around both your body and your energy or etheric field. See that circle go from above your head and down the front of your body, move through the earth, then go up the rear of your body until it reaches its beginning point. You may visualize this as a circle of white light, rainbow light, or whatever color light makes you feel safest and most loving.

7. On your next outward breath, allow the circle to spin until it becomes a sphere of light surrounding you and protecting you.

8. When you next inhale, go again to the sacred energy within you and see if there is a part of this energy you feel comfortable in sharing today. Do not be a hero and share more than is comfortable. Do not be a miser and withhold energy you might share. As you exhale, send the energy you choose to share on your breath to the crystal. Allow the energy to merge with the crystal's energy, for you know the crystal has the ability to receive, transmit, and amplify. Let the energy rest in the crystal for a moment.

9. In your mind's eye, see a beam of sunlight touch the crystal. From the crystal comes forth a perfect rainbow composed of all the colors of the spectrum from black (the absence of color), to infrared, red, orange, yellow, green, blue, indigo, violet, ultraviolet, and white (the presence of all colors). Know that each band of the rainbow contains an energy for helping and healing anything it touches.

10. See the rainbow stretch upward toward the sky, then see it bend and go into the earth. See it go through the solid layers we walk on, through the liquids beneath, through the gasses and the ethers, until the rainbow merges with the light that is at the center of the earth.

11. In whatever way is right for you, see the rainbow merging with the earth light. For some people this appears as a tapestry being woven, a painting in process, or a whirlwind of rainbow rushing through a white light. In whatever way is right for you, allow these energies to merge, knowing the earth will take from this rainbow whatever it needs now to help it and heal it. Know also that the earth will give you, through the rainbow composed of your energy and the energy of the crystal, any gifts she has for you at this time.

12. When this merging is completed, bring the rainbow up through the layers of the earth.

13. Allow the rainbow to enter through the bottom of your feet and move up your legs, spine, neck, and head. Allow the rainbow to go out through the crown of your head.

14. Send the rainbow up toward the sun and, again, in whatever way is right for you, allow the energy of the rainbow to merge with the energy of the sun. Know that the sun can take from the rainbow whatever it needs for healing, and know that it will give you any gifts it has for you at this time.

15. When this merging is completed, bring the rainbow once again to the crystal. Allow the energy of the rainbow to rest in the crystal for a time. Feel the energy there, and see how it has changed from its merging with the earth and with the sun.

16. Once again, see a beam of sunlight touch the crystal and bring the rainbow forth. This time you will send the rainbow, composed of your energy, the energy of the crystal, the earth, and the sun, over the piece of land on which you are standing. Know that as the rainbow covers this land all of the beings on it—the elements, plants, animals, and humans—can take from it whatever it is they need to heal them and to help them.

17. Now send the rainbow arcing northward until it reaches the North Pole of the planet.

18. Send the rainbow arcing southward until it reaches the South Pole of the planet. Lift up the middle so you see one arc of rainbow light stretching from North to South over whatever part of the earth you stand on. Remember that the colors, the energies of the rainbow, can give to all the earth's children whatever it is they need right now to help them and heal them.

19. Now, as though you were unrolling a carpet, send the rainbow in an eastward direction around the globe, naming each of the countries and waters the rainbow covers, until you see the whole of the earth wrapped in a rainbow of light. Know that all of your relations on the earth can take from this rainbow whatever it is they need to help them and heal them.

20. While the rainbow is covering the earth, it is a good time to send out blessings to those you know who have special needs or to those who particularly touch your heart. Remember the elements, plants, animals, and spirit forces, as well as the humans.

21. When you have finished making all your blessings, begin to roll the rainbow back into its original arc. Then bring the arc back into the crystal.

22. Become aware of your breathing and of the circle of energy that surrounds you and protects you.

23. On your next inhalation, draw your energy from the crystal back into your own sphere. Know that only energies that will help you grow can come through this sphere. Feel whether and how your energy has changed from this opportunity of sharing and merging with all of your relations.

24. Be sure you feel grounded in your body. If you do not, kneel on the earth and put your head on her until you do. When you open your eyes, look first at the sky, trees, and plants around you. See if they look different. Look closely at the beauties of nature that are always around you.

This visualization has helped many people feel a closer connection with the earth and everything on her. It is a very healing exercise for you and for the earth. It helps you become aware of your connection with all life. It is also a very powerful way to use a crystal in ceremony. Wabun has found that after a crystal has been used for this ceremony, it feels as though it does not want to be used for other things.

Because of the power and connection engendered by the Rainbow Crystal Healing Ceremony, it is a strong way in which your work with crystals, the Medicine Wheel, and ceremony can grow.

Part II

THE WHEELS

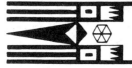

The Medicine Wheel
Mineral Reference Chart

The Center Circle

Mineral	Position	Lessons For Humans
All or Any	Creator	
Clay	Earth Mother	Healing, prayer, ceremony, strength, malleability, earth connection
Geode	Father Sun	Action, creativity, energy, healing, understanding of masculine principle
Moonstone	Grandmother Moon	Prophetic ability, wisdom, strength, romance, stability, moon connection, understand your shadow
Petrified Wood	Turtle Clan	Renewal, purpose definition, stamina, protection, health, understanding the earth changes
River Rock	Frog Clan	Soothing, cleansing, stability, change, water connection, catharsis, emotional understanding
Lava Rock	Thunderbird Clan	Purification, change, evolution, inner depth, intensity
Azurite	Butterfly Clan	Receptivity, metamorphosis, growth, psychic abilities, inspiration, prophecy, high energy

The Spirit Keepers

Mineral	Position	Lessons For Humans
Alabaster	Waboose	Gentleness and strength, paradox, purity, discrimination, high ideals, peace, the give away
Pipestone	Wabun	Peace, beginnings, wisdom, truth, communication, harmony, the collective consciousness
Serpentine	Shawnodese	Mystery, ceremony, beauty, energy and action, magnetism, trust, well-being, growth, intimacy
Soapstone	Mudjekeewis	Strength, malleability, ceremony, cleansing, purification, preparation, maturity, responsibility

The Moons and Totems

Mineral	Position	Lessons For Humans
Quartz	Earth Renewal	Amplifier, transmitter, receiver, psychic abilities, healing
Silver	Rest & Cleansing	Intuition, vision, telepathy, beauty, appreciation, mobility, emotional and spiritual healing
Turquoise	Big Winds	Protection, safety, ceremonial, rainmaking, healing, spiritual, preventative healing stone

Mineral	Position	Lessons For Humans
Fire Opal	Budding Trees	Hope, life force, visualization, spirit travel, intense energy, sexuality, power
Chrysocolla	Frogs Return	Purification, well being, strength, luck, health, peace, stability, earth connection
Moss Agate	Cornplanting	Healing, truth, courage, dreaming, spirit bridge, balance, mental/emotional integration

Mineral	Position	Lessons For Humans
Carnelian Agate	Strong Sun	Love, heart, protection, peace, healing and ease crisis, emergency healing
Garnet & Iron	Ripe Berries	Balancing, stimulant, strength, goodness, positive resolve, protection, tempering, discrimination
Amethyst	Harvest	Good judgment, justice and courage, soothes, dreaming, catharsis, spiritual attunement

Mineral	Position	Lessons For Humans
Jasper	Ducks Fly	Blessings, grounding, harmony, longevity, stimulation, clarification, balance
Copper & Malachite	Freeze Up	Purification, understanding, spirituality, power, healing, receptivity, strength, power, balance
Obsidian	Long Snows	Grounding, respect, clairvoyance, centering, stability, protection, seeing future, earth balance

The Spirit Paths

Mineral	Position	Lessons For Humans
Sodalite	Cleansing	Cleansing, focus, achievement, purification, healing, highest spiritual good, calm, courage
Peridot	Renewal	Freshness, calm, generosity, renewal, fearlessness, spiritual/physical healing, psychic abilities
Herkimer Diamond	Purity	Purity, sensitivity, kindness, serenity, gentleness, mobility, psychic abilities, recorder stone
Mica	Clarity	Clarity, calmness, peace, resolution, insight, alleviates confusion and hesitation
Jade	Wisdom	Wisdom, justice, confidence, prayer, tenderness, interpretation, courage, serenity, stamina
Calcite	Illumination	Illumination, joy, will power, love, communion, peace, grounding, protection, centering
Fluorite	Growth	Growth, perspective, communication, unity, energy, relieves anxiety and resistance to change
Lapidilite	Trust	Trust, stimulates highest good, grounding, balancing, confidence, security, hope, soothing
Rose Quartz	Love	Love, balance, heals abuse, self-worth, catharsis, emotional healing, flexibility, universal love
Hematite	Experience	Experience, recorder stone, character, fortitude, memory, resolve, resist stress, grounding
Lapis Lazuli	Introspection	Introspection, contemplation, higher consciousness, wisdom, maturity, balance, stability
Amber	Strength	Strength, persistence, ancient wisdom, harmony, beauty, longevity, abundance, perseverance

10

The Mineral Wheel

Minerals solidify the powers of the elemental forces. They aid us in harnessing and understanding the intense primitive energies that flow through everything.

Although minerals seem to be solid and unchanging, that is partly illusion. Nonetheless, they give us an anchor in life's shifting sea. Many people like to hold or sit by their totem stones in order to feel more stable and more rooted in their current position in their journey around the wheel. Others wear or carry their totem stones to bring about desired shifts in their energy field.

As you work with the Medicine Wheel you may come to realize that you feel attracted to or influenced by several of the totem stones at one time, not just by the one associated with your time of birth. That is certainly possible. Remember we all travel the wheel and, in our journey, feel drawn to the totems currently influencing us. Work with the minerals that call to you at any given time. Keep in mind while reading this chapter that although you only have one birth totem stone, all of the mineral beings described here can affect you as you travel the wheel.

THE MINERALS OF THE CENTER CIRCLE

·····

THE CREATOR—ALL OR ANY MINERALS

The Creator stone can be any stone that you wish. The Creator makes up the whole of the universe and is part of everything there is. Therefore, Creator is part of any stone you choose for this position. When building a Medicine Wheel, a buffalo skull or crystal is commonly used to honor the Creator.

THE EARTH MOTHER—CLAY

The mineral totem for the Center Circle stone honoring the Earth Mother is clay. Clay is a firm, plastic, fine-grained earth, largely composed of aluminum silicate, which becomes hardened when fired. For untold thousands of years clay has been used to make bricks and pottery and to help with healing. Clay has also been used in ceremonies and is found in most parts of the world.

Native people have used clay for pottery, bricks, pipe bowls, fetishes, and figurines. How clay is used in a culture tells so much about a culture that potsherds—pieces of old pottery found buried in the earth—are one of anthropologists' most valued tools in learning about the peoples who have come before.

The native people of the southwestern United States made, and still make, some of the finest pottery. Among their pots are ones used solely as initiation jars, fire making jars, hunting jars, and weather jars. The southwestern people make a wide variety of clay fetishes. Natives in other parts of the country also utilize clay for many of these same items.

Native people who make pottery today are very aware of the real and symbolic connection between clay and the earth from which it comes. They make prayers before beginning their work and look on their task as a ceremony.

Red clay, which contains iron, was considered a very sacred substance by many Native people. This clay was considered to have special medicine powers to help with healing and with understanding life. Sometimes it would be used to paint the face in particular ceremonies.

Clay has long been used to draw disease, infection, and toxicity from the body. Today fine clays are still used as facial masks and poultices. Particular clays are also taken internally often as a means of cleansing the colon or of adding certain minerals to the body.

Clay, part of the body of the Earth Mother, can remind you of the circle of life of which you are a part. Working with clay can help to strengthen your connection with the Earth Mother and with the circle of life. It can also help to strengthen you, cleanse you, and teach you the gifts of malleability.

FATHER SUN—GEODE

The mineral totem for the Center Circle stone honoring Father Sun is the geode. Geodes are round stones lined with a mineral, which is usually, but not exclusively, quartz or amethyst. Geodes are quite common and can be found worldwide. Geodes usually have a gray, white, or black exterior. Their interior can be blue, purple, yellow, gold, red, pink, white, or clear, depending on what mineral lines the inside cavity.

In traditional Native philosophy, the eagle is said to fly skyward toward Father Sun to bring messages from humans to the Creator. Eagles have been known to put geodes in their nests as though acknowledging the special relationship between the sun, geodes, and themselves.

Although geodes have some of the properties of the mineral that lines their interior, they also have qualities all their own. Generally, geodes are a catalyst for action, creativity, movement, and manifestation. They also bring healing, intensity, and warmth. Some Native peoples used them to bring rain.

Geodes are good for relieving lethargy. They stimulate energy and brain activity. They could be known as a *gym*stone instead of a *gem*stone because they help create energy during workouts and exercise. People who are working with geodes can learn how to act quickly and to bring more creativity and action into their lives.

Geodes teach you that if you want movement in your life, you have to move. They can help you to understand the active male principle symbolized by Father Sun.

GRANDMOTHER MOON—MOONSTONE

The mineral totem for the Center Circle stone honoring Grandmother Moon is moonstone. Moonstone is a sodium feldspar and a form of the mineral albite. Moonstone ranges from white to gray to bluish silver. It has a pearllike look to it. Moonstone is found worldwide.

Historically, moonstone has been used for ceremonies both during the waxing and the waning of the moon. In India it is considered a sacred stone. According to some myths, if a lover wants to know what the future holds in store for him, he should place moonstone in his mouth while the moon is full.

Moonstone is reflective and will mirror back the qualities of those who work with it. It is said to enhance romance, arouse loving passion, and balance the emotions. This stone is known to stimulate prophetic ability, wisdom, and inner strength. It can help you to reach higher realms of consciousness, and to see the truth of any situation. It is good for protection. Moonstone is said to bring the menstrual and other body cycles into a balance with the moon cycle.

Moonstone is reputed to be good for the sexual organs, in particular, the uterus. It is said to aid in childbirth.

People who are strongly drawn to this stone can utilize its mirroring abilities to learn the truth about themselves and to improve their connection with the moon and with the shadow energy within them.

THE TURTLE CLAN,
ELEMENT OF EARTH—PETRIFIED WOOD

The mineral totem for the Center Circle stone honoring the element of earth, the Turtle clan, is petrified wood. Petrification usually takes place when wood has its structure altered by earth changes, which preserve the original wood form in minute detail.

Petrified wood colors vary from red, beige, and brown to green, white, and yellow. Some of the most well-known examples of petrified wood are preserved in Arizona in Petrified Forest National Park. However, this mineral is found worldwide.

Petrified wood is honored by earth people because of its special connection with both the plant kingdom and the earth. It is wood made into stone by the actions of the Earth Mother. Often slices of petrified wood seem to contain scenes showing the earth and her mineral and plant children in different stages of planetary life. Consequently, petrified wood is considered to contain messages from these past ages.

Petrified wood is good for promoting long life; restoration of body, mind, and spirit; stamina; endurance; vitality; perseverance; protection; grounding;

and overall good health. Petrified wood is also helpful in linking people with both the mineral and plant kingdoms.

Petrified wood can awaken you to renewed strength, purpose, and definition. It can aid your understanding of the true stability of the earth, despite changes that might be occurring on her. It is a good stone to work with during the earth changes.

THE FROG CLAN,
ELEMENT OF WATER—RIVER ROCK

The mineral totem for the Center Circle stone honoring the element of water, the Frog clan, is river rock. River rock is any kind of basic mineral formation that is found in the bottom of a river, creek, or stream. The colors of river rocks are commonly bluish gray, white, green, black, red, blue, or brown. River rocks can be found in any waterway in the world. River rocks provide homes for frogs, magical or ordinary ones, and for many of the other forms of life found in waters. They change the course of streams and alter the flow of rivers.

Native peoples honored river rocks because they contain the energies both of the earth and of the waters on the earth. River rocks were considered to have the medicine of both these elements and to make the water medicine particularly accessible to people who need it. They were thought to aid people in singing the songs of earth and water.

River rocks can aid you with healing, cleansing, stabilizing, or changing your life. Working with river rocks can release negative patterns, particularly emotional ones. River rocks are especially potent if you work with them in their natural surroundings. These stones are soothing, calming, and healing on deep physical and emotional levels. They can evoke change that is concrete, tangible, and unshakable. River rocks are particularly helpful for problems that arise from growing up in a dysfunctional family system. They assist people in releasing the old, allowing it to flow away from them.

River rocks are known to be good for overall healing and catharsis. They work particularly well with the heart, hands, and sensory perceptions. People who are strongly drawn to this stone can learn about the kind of cleansing and change that comes with maturing.

River rocks can awaken you to a stable, grounded sense of your true purpose and to an honest evaluation of your positive and negative characteristics. They can also help you understand the waters of the earth and the emotions within you.

THE THUNDERBIRD CLAN,
ELEMENT OF FIRE—LAVA ROCK

The mineral totem for the Center Circle stone honoring the element of fire, the Thunderbird clan, is lava rock. Lava is a rock that flows in molten form from a volcano and makes its way to the surface of the earth. It usually cools and solidifies into rock forms such as rhyolite or basalt. The color of lava rock ranges from black, brown, beige, yellow, and white to red and burgundy. It is most often seen in dark shades. Lava rocks can be found in volcanic and mountainous areas worldwide.

Many Native people have stories about a mysterious woman who appears around the time of volcanic eruptions. This woman is similar to Pele, the Hawaiian goddess of the volcanoes. Once Sun Bear and Wabun flew over an erupting volcano in Hawaii and saw this woman dancing in the lava. This stone embodies both the energies of the fires that lie within the core of the Earth Mother, and the spiraling energy that brings them to the surface.

Lava rock can help you learn about depth, intensity, change, and the fire at the core of your own being. Lava rock can help to purify you at the deepest level of your being. It can also help you to connect this level to the Earth Mother.

Lava rock is said to be good for the soul. It can aid in the emotional and spiritual process that goes with terminal illness and death.

People who are strongly drawn to this stone can learn about purification, change, and evolution toward the highest good from it.

Lava rock can awaken you to a feeling of being burned free of any emotional or spiritual debris that would stand in the way of your highest level of evolution. It can help you see ways to become the phoenix rising from your own ashes.

THE BUTTERFLY CLAN, ELEMENT OF AIR—AZURITE

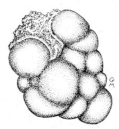

The mineral totem for the Center Circle stone honoring the air, the Butterfly clan, is azurite. Azurite is one of the basic carbonates of copper found in oxidized portions of copper-ore veins. Azurite is most frequently found as a brilliant dark azure blue or royal blue stone. In some areas the stones are light blue or even black. Azurite is found in Africa, Mexico, the Soviet Union, Italy, Greece, France, and the United States, especially in Arizona and Utah.

Historically, azurite has been used by magicians and shamans to heal the ill, increase psychic abilities, and read the future. It has been said that many prophesies were the result of working with azurite during dreamtime.

Azurite strengthens psychic and healing ability, inspiration, deep levels of meditation, good decisions, creativity, receptivity, intuition, advanced mental abilities, and higher energy levels. Working with azurite helps to bring about personal metamorphosis in much the same way as the chrysalis process transforms the caterpillar into a butterfly. If you are looking to evolve or change, work with azurite.

People who are strongly drawn to this stone can learn about transition, transformation, and rebirth. Azurite can awaken you to a feeling of leaving the darkness and coming into the light, of leaving the old and embracing the new. Azurite can draw change to you as rapidly as a wind can come on a spring day.

THE SPIRIT KEEPER MINERALS

There are many legends told about a time when the stones could speak to the two-leggeds. Because the stones have been present on the Earth Mother for many, many thousands of years longer than humans, they have many lessons to teach and stories to tell.

One story tells about a young man who lived in a part of the country that was very special, very sacred because there were cliffs that were white, red with gold, green with yellow, and black with blue, all the colors of the Spirit Keepers. There was one spot particularly sacred because there all four cliffs seemed to flow together like a river of color. Since he had been a boy the young man had loved to go to this place. When he was there he heard a special sound, a humming, that he heard in no other place.

When this young man went to seek his vision he was told he would become a powerful storyteller and a healer with a very special mission. Knowing what responsibility he was being given, the young man was happy, but also sad knowing the carefree days of his youth were over. He feared he would rarely have time to go to his special spot and listen to the humming.

This young man went to the spot to think about his vision and the training that was ahead of him. He sat down and listened for the humming. It did not begin. That made him very sad.

"Don't be sad, little brother," he heard the voice of an old woman say.

He looked around. No one was there.

"I'm here little brother," the voice said again.

He looked to where he heard the voice. Nothing was there but the white cliff.

"That's right, I am the white cliff talking to you. Your ears are open now. Before you could only hear what we said as a humming. Don't be sad. We are the ones who will train you as a storyteller. We know many more stories than any of the two-leggeds. Your vision did not make you lose us little brother. It prepared you to gain our true knowledge. Now sit down. It is time for your training to begin."

Obediently, the boy, now a man, sat. He lived in a time when people still knew that the rocks, the plants, and the animals could speak if a man could learn how to open his ears to hear them. The cliffs began to speak to the man, telling him the many stories they had to tell.

He listened, and he learned. Each day he would come with an offering, and listen to the stones. When they thought he had learned a story, they would ask him to recite it back to them. Only when his recitation was exact could he go and tell the story to his people. These were very important stories, and it was critical they be told in the proper way.

In turn his people listened and learned much from the stories.

Many many years passed. The young man was now an old man. Still each day he went to the cliffs and they told him more stories.

The man knew he was approaching the time when he would change worlds. He had no fear of dying, but he was confused because he had not yet fulfilled the second part of his vision. He did not consider himself a healer, nor did he know the special mission he was to fulfill.

As always when he had a question he went to the white cliff because this seemed to be the elder of the cliffs, the one with energy most like Waboose.

"Little brother," said the cliff when he had posed his question, "you are a healer. Your stories have healed the ills of many of your people, and prevented other ills from coming into being. And now that you approach your time of change, I will tell you your special mission.

"It is rare that we find a two-legged with ears as open as yours. It only seems to happen once in about twenty or more generations. It is good that others of your people have learned the stories you have told. These will stay with your people now. But we have many more stories to tell, and we don't know when we will find another with open ears. So we want you to learn a new skill now. When you come tomorrow, come with tools for cutting and shaping."

When the man returned the next day he found a small piece of the white cliff at the spot where he usually sat.

"Little brother," said the cliff. "Your people now have sacred pipes made of clay which they use for praying to Spirit. These are good. But we will teach you how to make pipes from us. Your special mission is to bring these pipes to your people. When the people smoke these pipes to pray to Spirit, some of their ears will be opened and, through the pipe, they will hear the truths and the stories we do not have time to tell you."

The old man learned to carve a pipe, first from the alabaster from the white cliff, then from the pipestone of the red and gold cliff, then of the serpentine from the green and yellow cliff, and finally from the soapstone of the black and blue cliff.

He took these pipes and the knowledge of how to make them to his people. From that time on, through the sacred stone pipe, people have been learning the truths of the earth, of the Spirit Keepers, and of life.

WABOOSE, SPIRIT KEEPER OF THE NORTH—ALABASTER

The mineral associated with Waboose, Spirit Keeper of the North, is alabaster. Although it is most commonly colorless to white, alabaster can also be found in translucent, white, pink, red, gray, yellow, and brown hues. Alabaster can be found in many parts of the world. There is both a soft and hard variety of this stone, in keeping with the paradoxical nature of Waboose.

Because of its malleability, the soft alabaster has for centuries been carved and polished. Some tribes as far back as the mound-building cultures have made pipes from alabaster. The Navajos carved horse fetishes from alabaster to keep their herds healthy and insure reproduction. In Babylonian mythology, alabaster was favored by a solar deity. Alabaster vases have been found in Egyptian tombs, representing the flower of youth. In biblical times alabaster represented purity, virtue, and spiritual idealism. Although soft alabaster is easily shaped, the hard form is so strong it has been used for constructing buildings.

Alabaster encourages a softness that helps guard against rigidity, while teaching one where hardness is a virtue. Alabaster is symbolic of what is meant by "In gentleness there is great strength."

Alabaster can teach you about sensitivity, strength, pureness of spirit, discrimination, high ideals, gentleness, courage, and loving convictions. Alabaster can awaken a sense of purity, serenity, peace, and gentleness. This stone can also help you to understand paradox and the true meaning of the giveaway.

WABUN, SPIRIT KEEPER OF THE EAST—PIPESTONE

The mineral totem for Wabun, Spirit Keeper of the East is pipestone, also known as catlinite. Pipestone is a red or red with white or, rarely, gold fine-grained metamorphosed clay that is easily carved. This stone is mainly found in the Minnesota and Dakota areas of the United States.

Pipestone has been used in Native ceremonies for thousands of years. The bowl of the sacred pipe is frequently carved from pipestone. So are small fetishes and figures. Several Native tribes tell a story in which, many years ago, there were two warring tribes that would not stop fighting although many, many people died. The Creator was disgusted by this killing and came to the tribes telling them they must stop their battles. To remind the people of the folly and waste of war, the Creator turned the blood of the dead into stone and told the people to make pipes from this stone. When they desired to war, the Creator instructed them to smoke the pipe instead. In this way all people had a new beginning.

Pipestone promotes peace, truth, healing, prayer, ceremony, wisdom, clear sight, and love. It can help you leave your small mental boundaries and hook into the collective consciousness. This will help with the personal healing that will help you heal the earth and work with all of nature. It also can help you develop faith, optimism, communication, harmony, and tranquility.

People who are strongly drawn to this stone can work with it to learn about new ways to help the Earth Mother and to develop deep forms of communing with her and with Spirit.

Pipestone can awaken both the peacemaker and the truth-sayer within you.

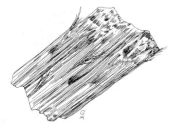

SHAWNODESE, SPIRIT KEEPER OF THE SOUTH—SERPENTINE

The Spirit Keeper of the South, Shawnodese, is represented by serpentine. Serpentine is an abundant rock that rests beneath much of North America. It has a greasy or waxy texture and varies from olive, green, yellow, black, brown, to white, and combinations of these colors. Serpentine received its name because it is thought to heal a serpent's bite and because the surface design resembles the skin of a serpent.

Serpentine has been used by Natives throughout the Americas for making both ornamental and ceremonial objects such as jewelry, carvings, fetishes, and pipe bowls. Serpentine objects have been found in ancient pueblos and villages and are still made today.

Even though it has been used for many thousands of years, serpentine is still considered a stone of mystery and is considered the perfect complement to Shawnodese, the trickster, who brings an air of mystery even to the familiar.

Serpentine, in some traditions, is used to prevent bites or stings from insects, spiders, and snakes. It is also said to stimulate energy.

The power of serpentine is like the power of the noonday sun, one of fire, heat, magnetism, energy, and action. Working with serpentine can ease fear, encourage trust and well-being, and help prepare for love. It enhances visionary abilities, growth, and the desire for intimacy. Serpentine, like Shawnodese, will help you to grow even if you are resisting such growth.

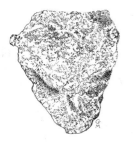

MUDJEKEEWIS, SPIRIT KEEPER OF THE WEST—SOAPSTONE

The mineral associated with Mudjekeewis, Spirit Keeper of the West is soapstone. Soapstone is also known as steatite and is composed mostly of talc. Soapstone is found in Norway, Canada, and the United States. It has a greasy, soft texture that appears dull or pearly. It got its name because it actually feels like soap.

Soapstone varies in color from pale green to black, gray, or white. Less frequently found is a reddish tint. Soapstone can range from opaque to translucent. It is a malleable stone with many attributes and uses.

Through the ages, refreshing powders and bath products have been made from its main ingredient, talc. Because of its softness, soapstone has been used for carving fetishes, jewelry, pipes, and ornamental objects. It has been said that placing this stone in the rays of the rising or setting sun will enhance and multiply its qualities.

Soapstone helps with strengthening on all levels: spiritual, emotional, mental, and physical. Fetishes carved from soapstone are powerful allies that can help keep the spirit clean and the heart true. Soapstone can be used to stay focused and wash away obstacles that stand in the way of reaching goals. It also wards off illness by cleansing away the source of disease.

Soapstone purportedly strengthens the immune system. It is good to keep other stones or medicine tools on or near soapstone as it works to strengthen and purify them. For many people this stone can make them feel washed clean of the old and made ready for the new. This sense of starting clean can prepare you for true maturity and a real readiness to take on your responsibilities as a teacher or a healer.

THE MINERALS OF
THE TWELVE TOTEM ANIMALS
·····

THE EARTH RENEWAL MOON,
SNOW GOOSE—QUARTZ

Quartz is the mineral totem associated with the Earth Renewal Moon (December 22 to January 19). Although all forms of quartz can affect people passing through this position, the greatest effect comes from clear quartz crystals.

Quartz is a power stone. It is an amplifier, transmitter, and receiver of universal energy and it is helpful for transmitting healing energy. It strengthens psychic and prophetic abilities. Quartz crystal gives knowledge of your power and teaches caution in exercising it properly. It reminds you not to be too hard or rigid in your views and philosophies.

Crystals bring clarity and renewal on the emotional, physical, mental, and spiritual levels. They energize and balance the chakras.

THE REST AND CLEANSING MOON,
OTTER—SILVER

Silver is the mineral totem associated with the Rest and Cleansing Moon (January 20 to February 18). Silver has long been considered one of earth's most precious minerals because of its luster, beauty, and sheen. Silver is malleable and has been shaped into many art forms. It has magical properties, allows proper emotional energy to flow, and helps to release any congested spiritual energy.

Silver encourages intuitive, telepathic, and visionary qualities. This mineral can help you awaken to your own highest nature, and can help to heal your highest self.

THE BIG WINDS MOON,
COUGAR—TURQUOISE

Turquoise is the mineral associated with the Big Winds Moon (February 19 to March 20). Turquoise provides excellent protection on all levels of being. Many Native people believe that turquoise can keep the wearer from injury and danger. In the past they used it on shields to ward off weapons. It has been used extensively in religious ceremonies, and has been carved into fetishes and inlaid into other objects. Turquoise has been used in rainmaking ceremonies.

The stone promotes healing, and strengthens already inherent healing abilities. Turquoise is a good preventive healing stone that creates natural medicine to help you understand some of the mysteries of life and the universe. Such understanding can help you avoid the perils of disease.

THE BUDDING TREES MOON,
RED HAWK—FIRE OPAL

Fire opal is the mineral associated with the Budding Trees Moon (March 21 to April 19). Opal is a symbol of hope. The stone can connect a person with the

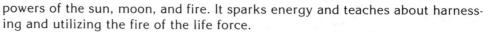

powers of the sun, moon, and fire. It sparks energy and teaches about harnessing and utilizing the fire of the life force.

Opal can be used to elicit intense mental, physical, and emotional energy so it is useful for alleviating sensations of lethargy and fatigue. It counteracts stagnation on all levels of life.

Opal enhances any existing qualities—positive or negative—within you and aids your ability to visualize or to journey into other realms of existence. Opal can assist you in understanding and healing problems having to do with your sexuality and your power.

THE FROGS RETURN MOON,
BEAVER—CHRYSOCOLLA

Chrysocolla is the mineral associated with the Frogs Return Moon (April 20 to May 20). Chrysocolla helps to balance the elements of earth and sky within you. It assists you in reaching the highest realms of consciousness while keeping a firm foundation on the earth.

Chrysocolla is a stone of good medicine that can bring luck and health to the wearer. Chrysocolla helps purify the heart, mind, and spirit. It helps to balance, ground, and have an overall sense of well-being and strength. It is a stone that promotes a feeling of peacefulness and stability, thus giving you a stronger sense of connection with the earth.

THE CORNPLANTING MOON,
DEER—MOSS AGATE

Moss agate is the mineral associated with the Cornplanting Moon (May 21 to June 20). Moss agate is an overall healing stone that brings balance to all parts of the body. It is especially beneficial to the eyes.

Moss agate has been used in rainmaking ceremonies. It is a stone that can be used to help create a bridge between the mineral, animal, and human kingdoms. It can help you to remove the boundaries between your own mental and emotional bodies.

Moss agate helps you to find truth and courage within, even in difficult circumstances. It can aid in alleviating depression, enhance your ability to dream, and ground and energize you.

THE STRONG SUN MOON,
FLICKER—CARNELIAN AGATE

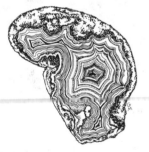

Carnelian agate is the mineral associated with the Strong Sun Moon (June 21 to July 22). Carnelian is a gift of the heart that represents love. It is good for sustaining a healthy heart and opening emotional centers.

It is said you can suspend a carnelian on a string or thong and use it pendulum-style over a wound to ease bleeding and start the healing process. Carnelian has been known to aid in emergency healing.

Carrying a carnelian will help keep your heart healthy and open, while giving you protection from any who might try to read your mind. It will also promote feelings of peace within and around you.

THE RIPE BERRIES MOON,
STURGEON—GARNET AND IRON

Garnet and iron are the minerals associated with the Ripe Berries Moon (July 23 to August 22). Garnet can help to balance your sexual energies. It is associated with the heart and blood and can stimulate the free flow of emotion in its wearer.

Garnet can help to strengthen those who carry it, can warn of danger, and can help you to lead a good and honorable life. It can also help you penetrate to the heart of any matter.

Iron is good for the blood and heart. It can remind you of the necessity of being tempered by life's experiences. It can encourage you to have a discriminating hardness that will allow you to know when no is the answer that will promote the highest good for all involved.

THE HARVEST MOON,
BROWN BEAR—AMETHYST

Amethyst is the mineral associated with the Harvest Moon (August 23 to September 22). The amethyst symbolizes good judgment, justice, and courage. It is a stone that soothes, pacifies, and teaches discrimination. Amethyst is purported to protect against black witchcraft, lightning, hailstorms, and intoxication. It can help you achieve spiritual attunement as well as a good balance between the energies of the physical and spiritual levels.

Amethyst can help you understand the sources of your anger, and thus begin to release it. It also helps to soothe and clarify the dream state. Amethyst is a stone that stimulates nobility and purity within those who carry or wear it.

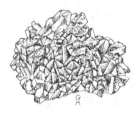

THE DUCKS FLY MOON,
RAVEN—BLOODSTONE JASPER

Jasper, particularly the bloodstone form, is the mineral associated with the Ducks Fly Moon (September 23 to October 23). Also called heliotrope, bloodstone jasper is a stone that brings many blessings. It provides a positive grounding force and helps to harmonize a person with the earth's energy.

Jasper is purported to stop bleeding; make its owner invisible; insure a safe, long life; draw poison from a snake bite; restore lost eyesight; and bring rain, if placed in water. This stone is also believed to give power over bad spirits. Jasper both stimulates and clarifies a person's mental processes, allowing him to find balance on this plane of existence.

THE FREEZE UP MOON,
SNAKE—MALACHITE AND COPPER

Malachite and Copper are the minerals associated with the Freeze Up Moon (October 24 to November 21). Copper is excellent for purifying the spirit and blood. It is a conductor of energies, spreading them evenly over a surface or person.

Copper fosters strength, power, balance, and the ability to understand your energy. It discourages weakness. It fosters healing for arthritis, rheumatism, stiffening of joints, and strengthening of the body, particularly if worn as a wrist or ankle bracelet.

Malachite has spiritual powers and raises a person's sensitivity to the voice of spirit. It increases receptivity to all forms of subtle energy and helps to cultivate your psychic powers.

THE LONG SNOWS MOON,
ELK—OBSIDIAN

Obsidian is the mineral associated with the Long Snows Moon (November 22 to December 21). Obsidian has the power to ground people to the earth energy, teaching them how to respect and use this energy within their own beings.

Obsidian reflects the thoughts of another person to the one wearing it, bestowing on the wearer a sort of clairvoyance. It also helps people to see into the future.

Obsidian is a strong protective stone and is also good for clarifying your inner state. Obsidian helps you to center your being with the earth energy, and thus provides the protection of stability.

THE SPIRIT PATH MINERALS
• • • • •

The Northern Spirit Path Minerals

CLEANSING—SODALITE

The mineral associated with the first Spirit Path stone of the North is sodalite. Sodalite is sodium aluminum silicate with chlorine, a beautiful stone with color variations of blue, white, gray, colorless, and green. It is found in Canada, the United States, India, Norway, and Italy.

Sodalite is named for its sodium content. Salt (sodium chloride) enhances any cleansing process. Sodalite helps with cleansing on all levels: mental, physical, emotional, and, especially, spiritual. Sodalite is a strong ally that can help keep the spirit clean and the heart true. Sodalite helps to cleanse away problems that stand in the way of your enlightenment and aids in warding off illness. Sodalite allows for whatever healing is necessary to align you to your highest spiritual good.

Sodalite is an excellent stone to use in conjunction with moon or water ceremonies. Sodalite invites in receptivity, calm, courage, and old knowledge. It helps release shame, humiliation, fear, and stress.

This stone is said to ease swelling from lymphatic problems and disease resulting from exposure to radiation. It assists in balancing male and female energies and strengthening chakra energies.

Working with sodalite can help cleanse and strengthen you.

RENEWAL—PERIDOT

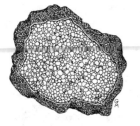

The mineral associated with renewal, the second Spirit Path stone of the North, is peridot. Peridot is a gem quality olivine, which is a reminder of a past volcanic flow. Peridot, found in several areas of the world, is clear dark green in color or a transparent yellow-green.

Historically, peridot has been called the evening emerald because in the evening light it can be easily mistaken for emerald. This stone has been revered since ancient times. It is also said to have a connection with the star Polaris, which is synchronistically called the North Star.

Peridot brings the qualities of freshness, rebirth, beauty, lightness, balance, tranquility, and fearlessness. Peridot is best used by those who have gone through a cleansing or by people who have clarity. Otherwise the startling clearness peridot brings can be overwhelming. Before seeking renewal with peridot, it is good to work with sodalite. Without cleansing, renewal is unlikely.

Peridot heals the spirit as well as the body. It is especially good for those who have fears on a spiritual level, or those who have had a negative or fearful image of the Creator taught to them as children. Peridot also promotes psychic ability, a gentle vibration, and an integration of higher knowledge. It discourages envy, anger, and negativity.

Peridot is helpful for physical problems that have evolved from spiritual sickness. Peridot can help you renew your spiritual purpose as you rebuild your physical body.

PURITY—HERKIMER DIAMOND

The mineral associated with purity, the third Spirit Path stone of the North, is Herkimer diamond.

Herkimer diamonds are an exceptionally clear quartz crystal found only in Herkimer County in upper New York State. They resemble the clear, sparkling beauty of a diamond and need very little polishing, if any, after being mined.

Herkimer diamonds promote purity of mind, body, and spirit. They aid in releasing constriction and stress and bringing you back to the softness, mobility and flexibility you had at birth. The medicine of the Herkimer diamond is a gift of restoration and balance to the spiritual body and absorption of the negative from all layers of your being.

Herkimer diamond purportedly relaxes muscle tissue, removes toxicity, balances, purifies, stabilizes, and is a general healant. Because it is a recorder stone, it has impressions of the past, the present, and the future. It encourages psychic and prophetic abilities and memories of past lives.

Herkimer diamonds can help you receive the energy and healing you need to truly purify all levels of your being then transmit this healed energy to the Earth Mother and all your relations on her.

The Eastern Spirit Path Minerals

CLARITY—MICA

The mineral totem associated with clarity, the first Spirit Path stone of the East, is mica. Micas are silicate translucent minerals arranged in layers that allow you to cleave or shave off paper-thin sheets. Large sheets of mica are said to come from "books." Mica is quite common throughout the world. The largest, most perfect books come from India. Mica ranges from clear and colorless to pale yellow, brown or dark black or green.

Both the sheets of mica and the quality of clarity are much like the layers of an onion. The onion brings tears that may initially blur your perceptions but then wash from your eyes leaving greater clarity. As sheets come off a book of mica, the remaining layers often become more transparent.

Some Native people considered mica a window to higher realms. Clarity is also like a window, a window into ourselves and all of life. Mica has been used as a scrying (future telling) stone by some Native people. It both protects and encourages psychic abilities.

Mica can teach you the powers and limitations of clarity. Working with mica can alleviate confusion and a tendency to withdraw or hesitate. It can help you feel less awkward, chaotic, or frustrated. It can help you clearly see all options in any situation.

WISDOM—JADE

The mineral totem associated with wisdom, the second Spirit Path stone of the East, is jade. Jade is a glassy mineral with color ranging from various shades of light or dark green to black and, in rarer cases, white, brown, or blue.

Jade is mined chiefly in China, Japan, Burma, Guatemala, Mexico, Australia, and the United States. It occasionally washes up along the coast of Carmel, California.

Historically, jade has played a part in many religions. Jade artifacts are found among many burial sites of early humanity. The Aztec and Mayan people, and the native Maoris of New Zealand used jade for tools: knives, axes, scrapers, and war clubs. Good-quality jade is said to be so hard that you can hit it with a hammer and not make a scratch.

Jade has been revered for centuries in the Orient, especially by the Japanese and Chinese. They feel jade is the most important stone that exists. The Chinese attribute five valued characteristics to jade: wisdom, justice, modesty, courage, and clarity. Jade is used in the Orient to draw from the wisdom of the ancestors and from any past life experiences. Jade has been strongly linked with music for centuries and is thought to enhance musical abilities.

Jade helps with prayer, ceremony, meditation, and dream interpretation. It strengthens feelings of tenderness, kindness, warmth, tranquility, strength, confidence, nurturing, and love. Jade promotes fertility and aids in birthing. It increases stamina and helps one achieve a long, strong life.

Working with jade can bring the serenity that is a catalyst for making good decisions, ones drawn from your deepest level of wisdom.

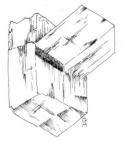

ILLUMINATION—CALCITE

The mineral totem associated with illumination, the third Spirit Path stone of the East, is calcite. Calcite is crystalline calcium carbonate. It is a main component of the shells of living sea organisms that build up over time to make limestone then, after more time, marble. The evolution of calcite is similar to the spiritual evolution that leads one to illumination. Both processes necessitate many transformations before realizing the finished state. Yet illumination is always at the core of our being as calcite is at the core of many rocks.

Calcite is considered to be the most common and varied mineral in existence. It is found worldwide. Calcite is fluorescent, often transparent or a translucent milky white or seemingly colorless. However, its association with foreign atoms and other mineral mixtures causes frequent and endless color variations.

Silver, pyrite, quartz, and other beautiful minerals can be found with calcite, just as many luminous gifts are found with illumination. As illumination can be found by a true search so calcite is readily available to those who know how to recognize it. Illumination cuts through the darkness of ignorance as the fluorescence of calcite cuts through the darkness of night. Beautiful calcite crystals can be found almost everywhere by those persons willing to dig for them.

Calcite is said to be good for healing. It also empowers and magnifies ceremony.

Working with calcite teaches about joy, receptivity, balancing male and female energies, grounding, protection, strengthening of willpower, optimism, and love. It attracts prosperity and aids in meditation, centering, and astral travel.

Calcite can awaken a feeling of closeness to spirit, opening of the heart, communion with life, and peace, calm, and happiness.

The Southern Spirit Path Minerals

TRUST—LEPIDOLITE

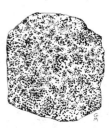

The mineral associated with trust, the first stone of the southern Spirit Path, is lepidolite. Lepidolite can be found in California, Maine, North Carolina, Connecticut, the Soviet Union, Germany, Italy, and Czechoslovakia. The color of lepidolite varies from pink, purplish, lilac, and mauve to gray, green, yellow, pale, translucent, and transparent.

In recent times, lithium, a derivative of lepidolite, has been given as a medication to persons diagnosed as manic-depressive. Lepidolite is frequently carved for wands, massage tools, eggs, and jewelry.

In addition to its own unique qualities, lepidolite has most of the properties of quartz crystal. It is used for healing, grounding, and balancing and is excellent for transmitting and receiving energy. The crucial difference between the two stones is that lepidolite discriminates between good and bad and can only be used for the highest good whereas quartz can be programmed for good or be empowered for evil. Lepidolite is totally impotent unless being used for the powers of good.

When working with shamanic journeying, astral travel, extraterrestrials, or any work of this nature, it is good to have lepidolite present. When traveling on the etheric, spiritual, or astral planes, lepidolite can be a connecting force to tie one to the physical/earth plane.

Lepidolite encourages people to faith, confidence, security, harmony, love, stability, hope, and the belief in the best interest of all involved. It encourages reliability, strengthens the fabric of being and lightens the soul. Lepidolite reduces competition, fear, insecurity, hate, emotional scars, and pain. It is good for sedating, relaxation, calming, and soothing. Lepidolite is good for the heart and helps heal all levels of being: emotional, physical, mental, and spiritual.

Lepidolite can help you to determine whether people and situations are trustworthy and can awaken a feeling of deep trust, as well as belief in yourself and the world around you.

GROWTH—FLUORITE

The mineral totem associated with growth, the second Spirit Path stone of the South, is fluorite. Fluorite belongs to the crystal family, has a glassy luster and comes in cubical and octahedral shapes. Fluorite ranges in color from colorless to purple, green, yellow, violet, blue, black, reddish pink, brown, and white as well as fluorescent.

Although fluorite is found in other countries such as Switzerland, Italy, and England, the United States is the largest producer.

Fluorite comes from the Latin word *fluere,* which means "to flow," because fluorite melts with much ease. It is commonly used as a flux in the smelting of metals. Because of its ability to change and its natural property of altering its condition, fluorite is able, through melding other minerals, to become something more than itself. If you are willing to flow with life, to allow life to alter you, there may be opportunities to grow into a stronger, more evolved version of yourself.

It has been said that fluorine, the main component of fluorite, helps determine the shape of the human body. Lack of it can result in a weak structure, tooth decay, and diseases of the bone.

Working with fluorite encourages growth, gives perspective, and aids with integrating information and thought processes. Fluorite promotes relaxation, balance, expansion, personal advancement, and universal unity. It also helps with communication and grasping of higher ideals. It relieves depression, anxiety, stagnation, anger, and resistance to change. Fluorite is said to be generally healing.

Fluorite can help you grow beyond previous limitations to new realms. It can awaken you to a feeling of trust that will allow you to stretch and grow beyond the self you now know.

LOVE—ROSE QUARTZ

The mineral totem associated with love, the third Spirit Path stone of the South, is rose quartz. Rose quartz is composed of silicon dioxide and is part of the quartz family, as crystals are. However a significant difference is that rose quartz is found in solid chunks or forms rather than in crystalline ones.

The hue of rose quartz ranges from rose to light red or pink. Rose quartz is a fairly common stone that can be found in many locations worldwide.

Rose quartz has sometimes been called the Bohemian Ruby. It has been used in both Wicca rituals and Native American ceremonies. Rose quartz is good to use with children, as well as with those adults who were neglected as children, because it engenders feelings of love both for the self and others. It is good for healing heart wounds, particularly those stemming from abuse. Rose quartz encourages emotional release, compassion, understanding, fidelity, emotional balance, warmth, positive resolution, relief from child abuse issues, beauty, appreciation, rebuilding, and renewal. This stone can help to alleviate loneliness and increase flexibility and mobility. Rose quartz is known to help release negative emotions such as anger, shame, frustration, and fear. It can assist in healing traumatized relationships and sad affairs of the heart.

Rose quartz is said to be good for all organs and body parts affected by radiation, or nuclear or hazardous waste exposure.

Working with rose quartz can teach you about unconditional, all-healing love and awaken you to a feeling of love for yourself and others.

The Western Spirit Path Minerals

EXPERIENCE—HEMATITE

The mineral totem associated with experience, the first Spirit Path stone of the West, is hematite. *Hematite* is the Greek word for bloodlike. Hematite is ferric oxide, the most significant part of iron ore, and can be found in large amounts in North America and other locations worldwide. The color range of hematite goes from steel gray and metallic silver to red and black.

Historically, gems cut from hematite have been called Alaska Diamonds. Both polish for stone and pigment for paint is made from hematite.

Hematite is a recorder stone—one that holds a memory of other times, events, persons, places, and things—and can impart these memories to humans. This stone will help one resist stress; become solidly grounded on the earth; build character; maintain fortitude; stick by decisions; ward off compulsiveness; and avoid repetition, emotional amnesia, and denial.

Hematite can help you remember past uncomfortable situations so you do not have to repeat your own mistakes. It can also teach you about drawing from humanity's collective consciousness of experience so you will not repeat other people's mistakes.

Working with hematite is good for alleviating fear and for releasing compulsive habits such as drinking, overeating, and smoking. It helps you to be firmly grounded and have strong boundaries. Hematite generally energizes, strengthens, and encourages a positive self image, confidence, and balance.

Although hematite will not prevent you from avoiding painful experiences or problems, it can help you learn and grow from them without having to repeat the same lessons over and over again.

INTROSPECTION—LAPIS LAZULI

The mineral totem associated with introspection, the second Spirit Path stone of the West, is lapis lazuli, also called lazurite. Lapis is predominantly calcite tinted blue and can be found in a variety of locations. The colors of lapis lazuli are royal blue, azure blue, violet blue, and greenish blue.

Lapis lazuli has been used throughout the centuries by magicians and holy persons to enhance receptivity to spiritual powers. Lapis is thought to be the sapphire of the ancients. The Old Testament refers to this stone as do ancient Egyptian records. All through the ages lapis has been used in powdered form as a paint pigment. During the time of the czars in Russia, lapis was used for mosaics and intricate inlaid work, especially on urns and vases. In other countries lapis has been used for jewelry, bowls, small carvings, and fetishes. More recently, lapis has been used for massage tools and wands.

Lapis aids in self-examination and contemplation. It promotes clarity, spiritual and emotional maturity, wisdom, balanced life force energies, stamina, sexual compassion, strength, and stability.

Working with lapis encourages healing in relationships as well as courage, joy, faithfulness, psychic powers, protection, spiritual growth, physical well-being, and health. Lapis is helpful for friendship, bonding, and balanced love. Lapis also helps with communication and with developing strength of character and will.

Lapis lazuli can awaken in you a feeling of respect and connection with your higher consciousness.

STRENGTH—AMBER

The mineral totem associated with strength, the third Spirit Path stone of the West, is amber. Amber is a fossilized resin that comes from prehistoric pine trees. It is not uncommon to find winged dragonflies, or other insects, completely preserved inside pieces of amber. The color of amber ranges from clear to golden yellow to transparent red to brownish yellow.

Amber is found in the Soviet Union, Denmark, Europe, Norway, Africa, and other locations and is thought to be one of the oldest stones used for adornment. It has been found in European burial sites as far back as 8000 B.C. In German amber is called *bernstein,* which means "stone of the bear." The deposits where amber is found were said by many Native peoples to be the resting place of the spirits. In recent times, soft, nonfossilized amber resin is being used as a powerful agent for aromatherapy.

Amber is said to contain the strength of maturity, the great bear, and Mudjekeewis. Amber helps activate the healing essence within a person. This stone strengthens and solidifies the body, mind, emotions, and spirit. Amber is good for working with the elemental kingdoms and with nature powers. It helps call in the elders and ancient wisdom. Amber discourages negativity, weakness, lethargy, depression, and procrastination. Amber encourages beauty, longevity, stamina, abundance, love, healing, persistence, good relationships, healthy sexuality, diligence, and perseverance. This stone makes ceremonies and ritual more powerful.

Amber can teach you about strength with wisdom, strength with calm, the strength that comes from doing something well, the harmonizing sort of strength that can help you truly understand life.

MEDICINE WHEEL MINERAL MEDITATION
(Special thanks to Sonia K. Watts)

What you need. Smudge and notebook and pen or tape recorder.

Estimated time. Forty-five minutes.

To do this meditation, one must be able to visualize the wheel itself, paying particular attention to the mineral totems.

1. Smudge, sit quietly, breathe deeply, and enter a meditative state.
2. Visualize the Medicine Wheel in any setting that feels comfortable for you.
3. Enter the rim of the wheel at one of the four directions. Greet the Spirit Keeper of that direction, acknowledge the stones for the Spirit Path, and make prayers if you wish. See if any of the minerals have lessons or messages for you.
4. When you are ready, move to the next position on the wheel, sunwise, and greet the mineral totem of this moon. For instance, if you have entered the wheel in the West and have greeted Grandfather Grizzly Bear, as well as acknowledging soapstone, then go to the next position, the Ducks Fly Moon (Raven). Greet and interact with bloodstone jasper.
5. Continue on around the wheel, greeting and interacting with each of the mineral totems of the moons, the Spirit Keepers, and the Spirit Paths.
6. When you have returned to your starting place, visualize going to the Center Circle, interacting with each of the mineral totems for these positions.
7. When you have completed your work with the mineral beings, return to normal consciousness.
8. Write or record your experience.

Variations

1. Visualize going directly to the center of the wheel then invite the minerals to come to you one by one.
2. Visualize going to the center and ask whichever mineral has a message for you to come to you.
3. Visualize going to the center. Ask a question and ask that the mineral being who has an answer for you comes to work with you.
4. Work only with the Spirit Path stones or the Center Circle to help you connect with these gifts or beings.

HERBAL STONE BATH

What you need. Smudge, herbs or herb tea, stones, notebook and pen or tape recorder, and if desired, cheesecloth, candles, and music.

Estimated time. One hour.

1. Draw a bath and put a cheesecloth bag with herbs into the water. You can also make a tea of herbs and add this to the water or just add loose herbs. It is most powerful to use the herbs that correspond to the positions of the stones with which you are working.
2. Smudge yourself, the bathtub, and the room.
3. Get in the tub then place the stones you want to work with around you in the tub.
4. Invite the energies of the stones to be with you. Ask for what it is you seek, be it healing, relaxation, or an answer to a question.
5. Close your eyes and let yourself relax and drift.
6. Be aware of any images or other signs that come to you.
7. When you are finished, write or record your experience.
8. For variations, light candles, play music, or place the stones on your belly underneath the water.

MINERALS AND DREAMING

What you need. Smudge, stones, notebook and pen or tape recorder.

Estimated time. One night.

1. Smudge yourself and the area where you sleep.
2. Choose stones that correspond with the energy, healing, or transformation you would like to work with on subconscious levels.
3. Smudge the stones, then say a prayer inviting in their powers.
4. Place them around your bed, underneath your bed, and/or under your pillow.
5. Place a notebook and pen or tape recorder by your bed. Immediately on awakening write down or record whatever comes to you or what you can remember about your dreams.
6. The stone kingdom will continue to connect, energize, heal, or transform you after you awaken. Be aware of any subtle or obvious signs from the stone kingdom. Your active participation and openness to change is a powerful factor in how much energizing, healing, and transformation will take place.
7. Repeat this process regularly until you feel there is a strong and open line of communication and receptivity between you and the mineral wheel.

WAYS TO HONOR THE MINERAL WHEEL

1. Smudge the stones regularly.
2. Give them salt, saltwater, or plain-water baths.
3. Wrap them in soft, natural cloth.
4. Handle them carefully, lovingly, and respectfully.
5. Place them in full or new moonlight.
6. Place them on an altar in a natural setting, then sing, drum, rattle, or chant for them. Sunset or sunrise is a good time to do this.
7. Give them offerings of cornmeal, tobacco, or other substances that seem appropriate.

SPECIFIC MINERAL MEDICINE WHEELS
•••••

A specific mineral Medicine Wheel is a wheel made up completely of one mineral, representing one of the positions of the wheel.

This kind of wheel is beneficial for working with specific needs for help or healing. The benefit of this type of Medicine Wheel is that its energy is very apparent and easily felt. In addition, there is a particular and strong energy set in motion when using all one totem stone in a wheel. Such a wheel generates a powerful current.

Many people have experienced the healing qualities of this type of Medicine Wheel. Although results vary greatly, depending on the specific mineral used and the help needed by the person using the wheel, everyone who has experienced a specific mineral Medicine Wheel has reported that the experience created some changes in his or her life.

A specific mineral Wheel powerfully merges the energy of the one position the stone represents with the energies of all the other positions of the wheel, thus creating a very particular energy for providing healing and help in a specific aspect of someone's life. For example, if you were using amber (strength) and placed it in the four Spirit Keeper positions, you would create a special prayer for strength in all aspects of a person's life: physical (Waboose), mental (Wabun), emotional (Shawnodese), and spiritual (Mudjekeewis). If you placed amber in all positions you would be asking for the strength of each position.

Choosing the Mineral for the Specific Medicine Wheel

What mineral is used in a wheel is determined by the problem you are addressing. For instance, if you wanted overall healing you could use moss agate. If you needed more courage, you would use amethyst; for protection, turquoise.

BUILDING A ONE-MINERAL MEDICINE WHEEL

What you need. Sixteen to thirty-six stones of one of the Medicine Wheel minerals if possible, common rock to fill in if you do not have enough stones of the mineral, smudge, offerings, enough herbs to make a circle the size of the wheel's circumference, notebook and pen or tape recorder, and, if desired, drum, rattle, chanting, blanket, pillow, pipe ceremony, and sensory medicine (see Medicine Wheel Sensory Healing Ceremony).

Estimated time. Two hours.

1. For a sixteen-stone wheel, place your stones in the places of the four Spirit Keepers and twelve totems. In this wheel you do not need stones for the interior of the wheel, because you will leave this part empty so that the person experiencing the wheel can lie down inside it. Be sure to make the Medicine Wheel large enough for the person needing the ceremony to stretch out comfortably. If you use a thirty-six-stone wheel, it needs to be large enough for the person to lie in one quadrant.
2. Follow basic guidelines for building a wheel. Carefully choose the loca-

tion. Smudge all persons involved, everything that will be touched during the ceremony, and the area where it is to be done.

3. If someone is available to drum or chant softly, instruct them to begin.

4. Make offerings to Creator, the Earth Mother, Spirit Keepers of the area, and all those that dwell in Spirit.

5. Make an herbal circle marking the location where you are about to build the wheel. If available, use the plant that corresponds with the mineral with which you are working. If not available use sage, cornmeal, or tobacco. Ask for prayers for protection, well-being, and for the highest good of all those involved.

6. Build the wheel starting with the Spirit Keeper of the North, then the East, South, and West. Follow this with the totem stones beginning with the first position of the wheel (the Earth Renewal Moon, Snow Goose). Then follow around the wheel. As you place each stone make a prayer inviting in an element or quality of the position the stone honors. Through these prayers, you let the mineral know what it is you want.

   For example, if you were using fire opal you would make a prayer like this:

   > Fire opal, this little one invites you to be here and asks that you stimulate [name of person for whom you are doing the ceremony]'s highest realm of consciousness. Fire opal, with this next stone, I pray that you bring good medicine. Fire opal, with this stone I ask for strength of body for [name of person for whom you are doing the ceremony].

   Make a prayer with each stone you place. If you are using thirty-six stones, build the wheel in the regular way, beginning with the Creator stone. Make a prayer with each stone.

7. The person requesting the ceremony then enters the wheel from the East. He should lie down and get comfortable. It is okay for him to lie on a blanket and even use a pillow if these items have been smudged.

8. This person should feel the energy of the earth beneath him and take a moment to look at the sky above. This connects him with the current of energy passing between what is below and above him.

9. The person in the center should close his eyes, breathe long, slow, deep breaths, and relax within the energy of the wheel. He should take a moment to *feel* this energy.

10. At this point he can just drift off, dozing, daydreaming, or resting so that the wheel can take effect.

11. This would be the appropriate time to do a pipe, if a pipecarrier is available, or to incorporate any of the sensory medicine from the Medicine Wheel Sensory Healing Ceremony. Such medicine could include ceremonial musical instruments, medicine objects, or aromatherapy. Carefully reread that ceremony before integrating these techniques. Do not underestimate the power of the experience by overloading the participant. Less is better with this ceremony. Much activity will be happening that appears subtle but has a profound effect. Remember, results are not up to you. They are up to Spirit.

12. It is good to stay inside the wheel for twenty minutes to an hour. If a participant begins to be agitated, restless, or suddenly becomes alert and

wide awake, then it is usually a sign that it is time for him to leave the wheel.

13. When he leaves the wheel, smudge him and the wheel to clear the energy.

14. Give the participant a chance to talk about his experience if he wants to. Have a notebook and pen or tape recorder close by so he can write down or record any images, visions, or information he received. If he does not want to talk or does not seem to have much to say, do not press him.

15. When he is ready and fully present, make another offering and prayer thanking both the mineral and the Creator for what took place.

16. Take the wheel apart.

Quartz Crystal Medicine Wheel

One person wanted to remember and understand her dreams better. She built a large crystal Medicine Wheel that she left up for an extended period of time. Whenever she had the chance she would spend time in the wheel. After working closely with the quartz mineral wheel in this manner she said not only does she remember her dreams but they are profoundly affecting her. She also says her psychic abilities and healing abilities have been magnified. Her energy flow is markedly improved, and her mental clarity has sharpened.

Lepidolite Medicine Wheel

On numerous occasions people have entered a lepidolite wheel in states of distress. One person was stressed from work, another was agitated by his relationship, yet another was dealing with difficult problems related to her disturbing childhood. All left the wheel feeling calm, balanced, and grounded. This wheel is reported to be more effective than a hot bath or sedative. Participants have unanimously agreed that a lepidolite wheel is a powerful relaxant on all levels of being.

Chrysocolla Medicine Wheel

A chrysocolla Medicine Wheel was helpful to a woman who had a very weak physical structure and was prone to injuries and illnesses. Her fragility was causing her to feel unstable, imbalanced, and distressed. After working with the energies of a chrysocolla wheel, her heath problems improved. She began to trust her body, which helped her regain her balance and sense of well-being. She attributed these physical and emotional improvements to working with the mineral wheel.

Amethyst Medicine Wheel

An amethyst Medicine Wheel can help you gain a sense of courage and good judgment. This type of wheel is particularly effective for those seeking the strength and courage to make changes in their lives.

One woman had a problem with poor judgment that led her into difficult situations in which she often felt victimized. She feels that working with the amethyst mineral wheel played a significant part in her obtaining the courage to make decisions insuring better protection and well-being. She says that the experience of the amethyst mineral wheel was a turning point for her both spiritually and in terms of her self-worth.

Other Experiences

Many people have reported direct and personal communication with Spirit Keepers, medicine animals, plants, or minerals stemming from using a specific Medicine Wheel. For some of these people, working with specific wheels has been a catalyst for deepening their understanding of the spirit kingdoms.

One woman who used an amethyst wheel told of a bear enfolding her in the warmth of his fur, allowing her to feel security and protection in her life for the first time. She reported this feeling remained with her and gave her confidence. Her new inner security carried over into her relationships. By learning to trust the bear she also learned to trust her friendships and herself, thus enriching her life.

Specific Mineral Wheels on Vision Mountain

I, Sun Bear, have been on personal terms with Snake for many years. I am now writing a book about serpent medicine. A bite on my upper calf from a rattler many years ago has given me powerful snake medicine as well as a deep level of respect for this Grandfather.

Upon my arrival at Vision Mountain in Spokane, Washington, in the summer of 1989, I noticed that my usually light-colored rattlesnake scar was deepening in color to a crimson purple. I knew this meant Grandfather Snake was in the area, and I told people to use extra caution.

Crysalis had recently built a snake totem Medicine Wheel of malachite and copper. I knew this wheel could possibly be generating powerful energy.

Normally there are a few rattlesnake sightings in the area. Our general policy at Vision Mountain is to move these highly honored messengers of Spirit to a location far away from places occupied by people. Just to be ready, we prepared a special apparatus to move any snakes that might make an appearance.

Within the week that followed, six rattlesnakes came to visit us. They were moved to other locations a safe distance away. We then unanimously decided to take down the snake totem wheel. After removing the wheel no more rattlesnakes were reported for the rest of the summer.

When Crysalis placed the Snake Wheel, she also placed ones to honor other animal totems such as the Snow Goose, the Beaver, and the Brown Bear. In the winter following the placement of the mineral Medicine Wheels, other Medicine Wheel animals not usually seen were spotted in the area—among them a mountain lion and a bear. The Medicine Wheel animals that are common on Vision Mountain—deer, geese, turtles, frogs, butterflies, eagles, coyotes, red hawks, flickers, ravens, earthworms, hummingbirds, owls, rabbits, mice, and ants—were more frequently spotted.

Working with mineral Medicine Wheels can have many positive effects on all levels: the mental, emotional, physical, and spiritual. Experiment with the different stones and see what works best for you. After you have made a strong connection with these wheels, you may then share them with others.

The Medicine Wheel
Plant Reference Chart

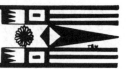

The Center Circle

Plant	Position	Lessons For Humans
All or Any	Creator	
Corn, Beans, Squash	Earth Mother	Nutritional, medicinal, ceremonial
Sunflower	Father Sun	Good for heart, kidney, bladder, skin, hair
Mugwort	Grandmother Moon	Promotes dreaming, good for smudge, female problems, stomach, joints
Cattails	Turtle Clan	Good for stimulant, energizer, stabilizer, nutritional and delicious
Algae	Frog Clan	Good food supplement, nutritional, disinfecting, rich in vitamins and minerals
Fireweed	Thunderbird Clan	Earth healer, delicious food for humans
Butterfly Weed	Butterfly Clan	Good for lungs, intestinal tract, fever, rheumatism

The Spirit Keepers

Plant	Position	Lessons For Humans
Sweetgrass	Waboose	Ceremonial, good for inviting in good energies and spirits
Tobacco	Wabun	Ceremonial, communication with spirit, offering, poultice. Brings clarity, transforms negativity
Sagebrush	Shawnodese	Ceremonial, smudge, good for cleansing and transforming energy
Cedar	Mudjekeewis	Ceremonial, good for smudge and for cleansing areas from sickness

The Moons and Totems

Plant	Position	Lessons For Humans
Birch	Earth Renewal	Good for skin, arthritis, kidney, bladder, digestion, communication, cleansing, ancient wisdom
Quaking Aspen	Rest & Cleansing	Good for congestion, allergies, asthma, toxicity, relaxing and playfulness
Plantain	Big Winds	A master healer, cools, soothes, heals, a good blood cleanser, good for skin and pain relief
Dandelion	Budding Trees	Nutritional, soothing, healing, calming, cleansing, alkalizing
Blue Camas	Frogs Return	Good for balancing, purgative, stimulation, nutritional, sustaining
Yarrow	Cornplanting	Tonic, diuretic, anesthetic, digestion, strengthener, cleansing, alleviates menstrual pain
Wild Rose	Strong Sun	Helps cure colds and flu, astringent, tonic, soothing
Raspberry	Ripe Berries	Cleansing, stimulating, astringent, balancing, helps in pregnancy, delicious fruit
Violet	Harvest	Heals toxicity, cleanses blood, relieves sore throat and breathing problems, cooling, soothing
Mullein	Ducks Fly	Strengthens lungs, heart, bladder, kidney, liver; soothes mucus membranes, earaches, skin
Thistle	Freeze Up	Nutritional, heals brain and internal organs, reduces fever, increases milk in nursing mothers
Black Spruce	Long Snows	Antiseptic, expectorant, inhalant, helps colds, strengthening

The Spirit Paths

Plant	Position	Lessons For Humans
Echinacea	Cleansing	Good for blood, lymph glands, abscesses, infections, skin, treats poison oak and animal bites
Red Clover	Renewal	Good for vagina, stomach, throat, rectum and skin, blood cleanser
Trillium	Purity	Endangered species, historically used for female problems, birthing bleeding, diarrhea
Rosemary	Clarity	Astringent, stimulant, spice, good for pain reliever, colon, indigestion, headaches, cold relief
Sage	Wisdom	Good for cooking spice, as smudge, tonic, bath or tea
Wild American Ginseng	Illumination	Endangered species, historically used for spice, sedative, strengthener, increasing vitality
Comfrey	Growth	Food, animal food, astringent, expectorant, good for sprains, bruises and for stopping bleeding
Borage	Trust	Cough suppressant, mood stabilizer, relieves pain, problems with tendons, back, sprains
Hawthorne	Love	Relieves anxiety, good for blood pressure, heart, arteries, circulation
Olive	Experience	Massage oil, good for heart, skin, pores and joints, breaks down cholesterol
Chamomile	Introspection	Good for overall healing, headaches, earaches, sedative, pain reliever, relaxant, skin care
Nettle	Strength	Food, tonic, good for anemia, gout, lower blood sugar, skin, hair, rich in vitamins and minerals

11

The Plant Wheel

Minerals solidify the powers of the elements and plants give the energies of the mineral and elemental kingdoms movement. Plants help those in the human kingdoms to understand the softly moving, healing energies in all of life.

Powerful helpers to humans and other animals since the dawn of existence, plants awaken, enliven, heal, feed, and make life better in many ways. Plants open human eyes with their beauty, enchant noses with their fragrances, touch skin with their multitudes of textures, and urge people to join them in their windblown dance. They provide shelter, transportation, music, beverages, implements, furniture, and entertainment. Plants abound in many areas of the world, reminding people of the other parts of the sacred circle of life. Sometimes their very abundance allows humans to ignore their existence, using them but not honoring them for the help they give.

As you travel the Medicine Wheel, note the plant helpers associated with the different positions you visit. Learn from them, honor them, and allow them to introduce you to their many relations.

THE PLANTS OF THE CENTER CIRCLE
•••••

THE CREATOR—ALL OR ANY PLANTS

There is no single plant that always represents the Creator because the Creator is the sacred energy that dances through all plant life. The Creator is part of every plant, but cannot be limited to merely one form.

THE EARTH MOTHER—CORN, BEANS, AND SQUASH

The plants for the Center Circle stone honoring the Earth Mother are corn, beans, and squash, the staple foods known to many Native people as the three sisters. Nimimosha of the Bear Tribe told us this story of how they got that name:

In long-ago times, the people of the Eastern Woodlands lived in abundance and in harmony with Mother Earth, and learned about life by watching and listening for her voices.

There were three girls who wanted to visit relatives in another village. It happened that they were sisters, born to the same mother. Nonetheless, the three girls had not learned to get along. They were always quarreling, disagreeing, arguing, and criticizing each other. They had very few friends, but they did have relatives, and when they began to wish for companionship and the warmth of other humans, they visited their relatives. It was a morning's walk to the village where their relatives lived.

One day they started out toward the other village. Inevitably, it was not long before the girls began finding fault with each other.

The girls walked and fought most of the morning. An hour before they reached the village of their relatives, they became so loud and angry that the people of the village could already hear them. "Oh, no," they moaned. "It's those three girls. Why do they have to come here?"

In the village, an old woman came out of her lodge. She stood in front of her lodge waiting. The girls were very involved in their quarreling, and they didn't notice the old woman until they were almost at her house. The old woman's stern look startled them.

The old grandmother took the girls inside her lodge. "Look this way," she instructed, and she led them to an opening that served as a window.

"Tell me what you see in the garden. Tell me how it is out there," urged the old woman.

"There's tall corn, Grandmother," said one of the girls. "Its roots are in the earth, but its tassels reach high toward the sun and wind, and it is growing good food for the people."

"And there are beans," said the second girl. "They are growing with the corn, and their vines wind around the tall corn stalks. I cannot tell which plant is holding the other up, but the beans are also growing good food for the people."

"And the squashes are growing there too," said the third girl. "Their beautiful big leaves shade the moist earth to keep the water in, and it helps the corn and beans to grow. And these vines are also growing good food for the people."

"You are right," the old grandmother said. "All three of you have told part of the truth, and only when each of you had spoken was the whole story told. Like the three sisters growing in the garden, the corn, the beans, and the squash, each of you has a gift for the people. Your gifts will not ripen to their fullness, though, unless you do as the plants do, and help each other, and grow together.

"And now," she said, "I have a gift for you. It is only one gift for the three of you, so you must learn to share, and you must not quarrel over this gift, for it is a reminder of the lesson you have learned today."

Out of a birch-bark basket, the old woman drew a belt of wampum beads made of pure white shell.

"Take this belt with you now, whenever you are together, or whenever people cannot find harmony with each other. It will give you strength to help them. You will not bicker with each other any more, because every time you do, one of these beads will turn black and spoil the belt. When people see that even you three girls can learn to love and help each other, they will be inspired by your example."

Many peoples on this continent of Turtle Island still grow the three sisters together in their gardens, just as their ancestors did in ancient times.

That is the story of the three sisters.

Corn, beans, and squash have tremendous culinary and nutritional value. They are the dietary staples of many cultures worldwide. Not only do these plants complement each other when they grow but they also provide a complete balanced meal when eaten together.

The three sisters are also important medicine plants. All are used ceremonially as offerings and in medicine bags. Traditionally corn is a common offering either as whole kernels or as cornmeal.

It is a wise person who remembers the story of the three sisters and the bounty of the Earth Mother they represent.

FATHER SUN—SUNFLOWER

The plant for the Center Circle stone honoring Father Sun is the sunflower. This plant is named in honor of Father Sun because of its brilliant yellow petals, which resemble the blazing star that heats our planet. Sunflowers are such kindred spirits to Father Sun that they move to face the direction of the sun from dawn to dusk.

In its effort to reach Father Sun, the sunflower grows to heights of more than fourteen feet. To strengthen its reach, the sunflower's roots run deep into the earth. The sunflower seeds nest in the middle of the sunburst of petals.

The botanical name for the sunflower is *Helianthus annuus.* The seed—delicious when roasted—provides vitamins and nutrients. The sunflower seeds and oil made from them are purported to be good for the heart, teeth, skin, fingernails, kidneys and bladder, and can help with such conditions as arthritis and diarrhea. Healthcare products made with sunflower oil are known to put luster and softness back into the skin and hair. Sunflower oil is also good as a massage oil.

Like Father Sun, the sunflower plant can enrich our lives and brighten our day.

GRANDMOTHER MOON—MUGWORT

The plant for the Center Circle stone honoring Grandmother Moon is mugwort, a member of the *Artemisia* genus that is particularly helpful for dreaming. This plant, like Grandmother Moon, balances female energies and encourages feminine strength.

The botanical name for mugwort is *Artemisia vulgaris,* which refers to the fact you can find it everywhere.

Mugwort can be used medicinally as a tea, tonic, smudge, tincture, herbal bath, oil, lotion, or poultice. It is also used in Chinese acupuncture. Mugwort's main medicinal purpose is for regulating menstruation, and alleviating painful cramps. It is known to be helpful during labor for easing pain and for dispelling the afterbirth. Mugwort, however, should be avoided during pregnancy as it may stimulate the onset of labor.

Mugwort also has been helpful in curing ailments of the stomach, the liver, the bladder, and the joints. This plant is known to improve circulation and calm rattled nerves.

Mugwort is excellent for promoting dreaming. It is often sewn in small dream pillows along with roses, lavender, and chamomile to induce dreams. Used in a smudge or when working with the powers of Grandmother Moon, mugwort is a powerful ally and protecting force, giving protection from exterior forces.

THE TURTLE CLAN,
ELEMENT OF EARTH—CATTAILS

The plant for the Center Circle stone honoring the Turtle clan, the element of earth, is the cattail, a water-growing plant that turns many ponds into swamps, which later become solid earth.

Cattails belong to the genus *Typha* and are long and reedlike plants with a brown, fuzzy, cylinder sprout at the end of the stalk. Like Turtle Island, the continent herself, this plant provided for many needs of the Native Americans. Cattails are a plant from which all parts can be used. Food made from cattails can be quite delicious. Flour was made from the roots of this plant. The top sprout, eaten young, makes a tasty cornlike dish. Shelters were created from the rushes. Boats, baskets, and mats were also made from cattails.

Medicinally cattail was used to build stamina, to strengthen, and to create sustainable physical energy. It is a stimulant that encourages the general life force.

Cattails have strong earth energy that grounds, balances, and stabilizes people.

THE FROG CLAN,
ELEMENT OF WATER—ALGAE

The plant for the Center Circle stone honoring the Frog clan, the element of water, is algae, a member of the plant people found in waters throughout the earth. Algae is a group of plants, some one celled, some many celled, that contain chlorophyll and have no true root, stem, or leaf. Algae is found in water or in damp places. Seaweeds, spirulina, and blue-green algae are all forms of this plant.

Native people in many places around the world know the value of certain types of algae. Seaweeds are used as both vegetable and spice. Edible algae are one of the most potent sources of nutrition available today. Because of their high chlorophyll content they are rich sources of vitamins and minerals and an excellent disinfectant for the system. They give people a quick energy pickup.

Today people are rediscovering the value of some forms of algae both as medicine and food. Some pond algae are being harvested and sold as a powerful food supplement, as are certain types of seaweed. Seaweeds, a rich source of iodine as well as other vitamins and minerals, are purported to help counteract the effects of radiation on the body. They also help the digestive system work more effectively.

Like the waters from which they come, algae are rich in the energy of life. They help keep the body alive and active enough for all the emotional energies to flow through it.

THE THUNDERBIRD CLAN, ELEMENT OF FIRE—FIREWEED

The plant for the Center Circle stone honoring the element of fire, the Thunderbird clan, is fireweed, one of the first plants to grow in damaged or burned areas, thus helping to bring the earth back to life. Fireweed is a common name for a variety of plants. The species associated with the Thunderbird clan is *Epilobium angustifolium,* a beautiful, tall plant with purple spikes which resemble fire. Fireweed grows up to six feet tall and is found throughout the United States and Canada.

In addition to helping heal the earth, fireweed also helps humans. The young leaves are delicious eaten raw in salads or cooked in soups and casseroles. The young shoots are similar to asparagus. The older leaves are too strong to be a vegetable, but they may be dried for tea. Like the Thunderbird, fireweed is a plant that happily serves all of its relations.

THE BUTTERFLY CLAN, ELEMENT OF AIR—BUTTERFLY WEED

The plant for the Center Circle stone honoring the Butterfly clan, the element of air, is butterfly weed. Like a big brother to dandelion, the seedpod of butterfly weed is filled with silky seeds that resemble fluffy parachutes as they sail off with the wind looking for new land to bless. Traditionally, butterfly weed was considered by Native Americans to be a lifesaver, a truly powerful healer.

The botanical name for butterfly weed is *Asclepias tuberosa.* This plant is also known as milkweed or pleurisy weed. The part of butterfly weed most commonly used for medicinal purposes is the root. Butterfly weed is most widely known for its healing qualities for pleurisy and other lung ailments, because it induces sweating and is a strong expectorant. This plant also can bring healing to the intestinal tract and helps alleviate colds, fevers, and rheumatism. Use butterfly weed root in small doses because too much can cause stomach upset and vomiting.

Butterfly weed, like the butterfly, is a catalyst for healing and transformation.

THE SPIRIT KEEPER PLANTS
· · · · ·

The animals associated with the Spirit Keepers are ones with special significance to earth peoples, as are the plants. The four Spirit Keeper plants are the plants most often used in ceremonies. These are the plants most frequently offered to the fire so that their smoke can carry the prayers of the humans to the Creator. Because they give of themselves so generously to people, people have long honored these plants as being special representatives, special messengers of the plant world.

WABOOSE, SPIRIT KEEPER
OF THE NORTH—SWEET GRASS

The Spirit Keeper of the North, Waboose, is represented by sweet grass. To show respect for the great mother from whom all plants grow, sweet grass is usually braided before it is picked. For this reason, sweet grass is also known as the "hair of the Mother."

Carrying the deep wisdom of the earth, sweet grass draws positive energies toward the person burning it or toward the place where it is burned. Its sweet smoke calls to the good spirits of a place and invites them to come join in whatever ceremony is occurring there.

Its botanical name is *Hierochloe odorata.* Sweet grass is a perennial that can be found near wet areas such as marshes or ponds. It grows long and reedlike, which enables it to be woven into thick braids. If you buy sweet grass, you will most readily find it braided. Often bits of the sweet grass are snipped or twisted off one end of the braid to blend in a smudge mixture. However the end of the braid can also be lit and used as a smudge in this form. One of the most common smudge mixtures is that of sweet grass, sage, and cedar.

The North is the place of the giveaway. The white buffalo gave all of itself so the people could live, grow, and learn about the spirit deep within them. In a similar manner all parts of sweet grass are used in ceremony, except for the roots. These are left deep within the earth so that like all things associated with Waboose they can soak up the deepest earth energy and prepare themselves, at a later point, to give away their most special of gifts to all of their relations.

WABUN, SPIRIT KEEPER OF THE EAST—TOBACCO

The Spirit Keeper of the East, Wabun, is represented by tobacco. Many Native peoples tell a story of a sacred woman who became pregnant with twin boys. Even inside the womb these boys fought. One represented all that was good in humans while the other represented the opposite. When it was time for them to be born the good son was born in the normal way. The other son was so anxious to get out of the womb that he kicked his way through the side of the woman thus mortally injuring her.

The good son remained with his mother, and with his extraordinary powers, buried her as she instructed. She told him that even with her death good things would come to the people. He remained by her grave for some days as she requested. Before he left he saw that from her body grew the three sister plants—corn, beans, and squash—which would from that time on give sustenance to all the people. From her forehead came the sacred tobacco plant.

Because it came from this part of the sacred woman, tobacco is considered to be an herb whose smoke can bring clarity. Clarity is a two-edged gift that can draw you both to good and bad: freedom or prison. So it is with tobacco. Used properly it can bring clarity, draw in energies, absorb negativity, and transform it into positive energies. Used incorrectly, it can poison you. It is a plant that must be used with respect.

Tobacco is considered one of the most sacred plants by Native Americans. When smoked in a sacred pipe it carries prayers to Spirit. It is frequently used for making offerings to the Spirit Keepers and Spirit Guides. To smoke tobacco is to call to the Spirit plane for help. If someone smokes for recreation then they are continually calling Spirit to them with a false alarm similar to the one given by "the boy who cried wolf." The tobacco leaf is six to twelve inches long, large, broad, and pointed. The leaf is the part that is used for smoking.

The tobacco plant belongs to the genus *Nicotiana.* Most store-bought tobacco is laden with chemicals. It is largely the chemicals that are hazardous to your health.

A common Native American name for a smoking mixture is kinnikinnick. Kinnikinnick can refer to just one herb, most often uva-ursi, or to tobacco and herbs in combination.

Tobacco is a strong helper plant. Used in smudge or in the sacred pipe it can, like Wabun, bring new beginnings to whoever is using it or to whatever projects or places for which it is burned.

SHAWNODESE, SPIRIT KEEPER
OF THE SOUTH—SAGEBRUSH

The Spirit Keeper of the South, Shawnodese, is represented by the sagebrush, most often referred to simply as sage. Despite its name, this prolific plant is a member of the *Artemisia* genus and is not a true sage. Artemisias are ruled by the moon. Sagebrush grows in many forms around the world. Its name sometimes causes it to be confused with culinary sage, which is a member of the mint family. How typical of the Shawnodese energy is that confusion! However sage and sagebrush look, smell, and grow very differently.

Sagebrush is a shrub with two- to four-foot-long slender branches that hold many bushy leaves. The tufflike flowers are most often purplish pink. Sagebrush grows wild in drier climates and in the desert areas such as California, Washington, Utah, and many other states. It is an earth healing plant, which helps preserve both soil and moisture in these dry areas.

The most important use of this sage is as a smudge. Along with sweet grass, it is the most common herb used for smudging today. Whereas sweet grass is considered to draw in all the good energies, sage is considered to help transform any energies that are not working for the highest good of a person, place, or ceremony. When burning, sage emits a pungent, strong, thick smoke. The sage smoke, like the rapid growth of the summer, helps bring change to everything.

MUDJEKEEWIS, SPIRIT KEEPER
OF THE WEST—CEDAR

The Spirit Keeper of the West, Mudjekeewis, is represented by the cedar tree, an evergreen that grows throughout the world. Cedar is a strong plant, one that houses, nurtures, guards, and protects many of earth's children. Both the boughs and inner bark of the cedar are used ceremonially.

Cedar is spiritual kin to sage and sweet grass. It is the third plant often used in the sacred smudge of Native American ceremony. Any of these three plants can be burned alone but are most effective when burned together. Burned as a single smudge (using the leaves or inner bark) cedar is a cleanser frequently used when there has been sickness.

Like sagebrush, cedar is a cleansing and purifying plant. Its smoke has a particularly pleasant pungent odor. Cedar is like people in western positions: strong healing agents.

In old times cedar bark was also used for parts of houses, canoes, implements, clothing, and ceremonial items.

Whether cedar is tall and stately or short and scrubby, it is a tree that commands attention and respect. Its noble look bespeaks age and wisdom. Because people of the West carry so many of the burdens of living, cedar can be particularly helpful in keeping them refreshed, cleansed and healthy.

THE PLANTS OF
THE TWELVE TOTEM ANIMALS
·····

THE EARTH RENEWAL MOON,
SNOW GOOSE—BIRCH

The birch tree is the plant associated with the Earth Renewal Moon (December 22 to January 19). Birch is one of the most ancient and abundant of trees. Native people used the bark for writing, the sap for syrup and a beverage, and the bark and leaves for teas and medicinal remedies. Placing the leaves on hot rocks in sweat baths creates a vapor that helps to cleanse the body and get rid of static electricity. Branches of the birch can be bound together and used during sweats to thrash the body helping to expel toxins. Birch makes a good tea to treat skin conditions, arthritis, rheumatism, kidney, bladder, and digestive problems. Birch brings knowledge of ancient traditions and lost wisdoms. It opens up all energies so that they flow well, thus helping your ability to transmit and receive the powers of the universe.

THE REST AND CLEANSING MOON,
OTTER—QUAKING ASPEN

Quaking aspen is the plant associated with the Rest and Cleansing Moon (January 20 to February 18). The leaves, bark, and buds of this tree can be used for a tonic or tea to help with liver or digestive disturbances. Quaking aspen has also been used as a relaxant, for faintness, for hay fever, for internal organs, and as an astringent. Used daily, quaking aspen has helped with skin conditions such as eczema, ulcers, and burns. The powder scraped from the bark can be used as a deodorant and has been said to help treat cataracts. Teas and tonics from quaking aspen can help prevent congestion in the body, hay fever, asthma, bronchitis, and toxicity. Being near quaking aspen trees, with the bell-like song of their silver leaves, increases your sense of play and belief in magic.

THE BIG WINDS MOON,
COUGAR—PLANTAIN

Plantain is the plant associated with the Big Winds Moon (February 19 to March 20). Plantain is a master-healer plant. It can be used internally as a tea or externally as a compress to cool, soothe, and heal. Plantain is known to be an excellent blood cleanser and helps to alleviate pain. In some cases, plantain is said to reverse the effects of poisons. Used as a tea, compress, or in a bath, it can help heal sores, stings, ulcers, and inflammation. It also helps heal kidney and bladder troubles. Being a harbinger of spring, plantain is a reminder of the eternal promise of new life. Its deep roots demonstrate the importance of tenacity and stability and help to ground you in the earth.

THE BUDDING TREES MOON,
RED HAWK—DANDELION

Dandelion is the plant associated with the Budding Trees Moon (March 21 to April 19). The dandelion is an herb with many uses. The root is good as a coffee substitute and herbal remedy as well as a cooking herb. The young dandelion leaves can be used in salads. Older leaves are a delicious cooked green. They are high in vitamins A, B, C, and G; calcium; phosphorus; iron; and natural sodium. Dandelion is soothing, relaxing, and mildly sedating. It can be used to cleanse all the eliminative organs of the body. Dandelion helps to purify and alkalize the bloodstream. It also helps to balance the blood sugar levels in the body. The ubiquitous dandelion can remind you of the necessity of exploration and experimentation in life. It can also show you the beauty of various stages of growth.

THE FROGS RETURN MOON,
BEAVER—BLUE CAMAS

Blue camas is the plant associated with the Frogs Return Moon (April 20 to May 20). Blue camas was an important food for many Native people. It is essential to use only camas with blue-colored flowers. Any with yellow or greenish white flowers are deadly poisonous. Blue camas is a good food staple, and can be used to make pancakes, molasses, and a sugar substitute. It is a food that has sustained people for thousands of years. Blue camas is purported to be good for balancing blood sugar levels and as a purgative and emetic. This plant is excellent for creating movement where there is stagnation, for providing sustenance, and for teaching discrimination on all levels of life.

THE CORNPLANTING MOON,
DEER—YARROW

Yarrow is the plant associated with the Cornplanting Moon (May 21 to June 20). The whole plant can be used medicinally. Yarrow is terrific as a tonic and strengthener. It has been used with good results for digestive tract disturbances and as a blood cleanser. Yarrow is an herb that helps conquer the common cold and brings relief to flu sufferers. It is a good diuretic and opens pores and helps to eliminate toxins through the skin. Yarrow is excellent for stopping bleeding and is a primary herb used to alleviate menstrual cramps. Externally, yarrow acts as a local anesthetic and disinfectant. It also helps relieve mosquito bite itch and toothache. Yarrow also aids the lungs, glands, and bronchial tubes. Being around yarrow can help you discover the healing powers that flow through you, as well as your inner strength.

THE STRONG SUN MOON,
FLICKER—WILD ROSE

Wild Rose is the plant associated with the Strong Sun Moon (June 21 to July 22). Besides its beauty, the wild rose has many other gifts. The fruits of the rose, called rose hips, are high in vitamin C and bioflavinoids. Either eating them or using them in tea helps cure sore throats, colds, and flus. Rose hip tea has been used to treat blood or liver problems. Rose petal tea is a mild astringent and tonic. Rose water has been used as an eye lotion and to relieve the discomfort of hay fever. The wild rose can refresh your spirit and aid with problems that require a gentle, cooling effect. It can also help lift your spirit and open your heart.

THE RIPE BERRIES MOON,
STURGEON—RASPBERRY

Raspberry is the plant associated with the Ripe Berries Moon (July 23 to August 22). The raspberry itself is a delicacy, and the leaves and root of the plant have medicinal properties. The berries not only delight but also cleanse the system. They can aid in breaking up and expelling gallstones and kidney stones and stimulate the action of the urinary tract. The root is an astringent and has some antibiotic and healing properties. It can be used as a gargle for sore throats. The tea as a compress has been applied to wounds and cuts to slow bleeding. A tea from the leaves can be used to cure diarrhea, cankers, uterine problems, and menstrual issues. Raspberry leaf tea is one of the best herbal teas for pregnant women, acting as a tonic. A tea from the twigs is good for colds, flus, difficulty in breathing, and for balancing blood sugar levels. Raspberry plants can teach you to find the sweetness within the thorns of life.

THE HARVEST MOON,
BROWN BEAR—VIOLET

Violet is the plant associated with the Harvest Moon (August 23 to September 22). Violet symbolizes quiet, warmth, and reserved sentimentality. The violet is also a powerful medicinal plant. Both the leaves and the flowers are good as soothing agents, particularly for irritated mucous membranes. It is also high in vitamin C. Medicinally, violet is good for penetrating the blood and lymphatic fluids, dissolving toxins in those areas. Violet can assist in healing cancer, and toxicity in stomach or bowels. It relieves sore throats, difficulty in breathing, and helps cure tumors of the throat, ear problems, and headaches. Violet is good for relieving toothaches and skin problems. It cools high temperatures. Violet can be used as a thickener in stews and for flavoring in hot dishes, salads, jams and syrups. Being around violet awakens the heart to the fullness of its feelings and helps you understand the depths of your love.

THE DUCKS FLY MOON,
RAVEN—MULLEIN

Mullein is the plant associated with the Ducks Fly Moon (September 23 to October 23). This tall plant with its velvety-looking leaves is a versatile healer. Tea made from mullein is good for soothing mucous membranes and for strengthening the lungs, heart, bladder, kidney, and liver. Mullein helps to alleviate nervous conditions and is a general astringent. Used externally, the tea helps heal hemorrhoids, ulcers, tumors, swelling of the throat, and muscle tenderness. Oil made from mullein flowers has long been used for the ears, warts, bruises, sprains, and chapped skin. Mullein can teach you to explore the smooth and healing parts of your nature.

THE FREEZE UP MOON,
SNAKE—THISTLE

Thistle is the plant associated with the Freeze Up Moon (October 24 to November 21). Thistle is both a healing and sustaining plant. All parts of the thistle are rich in minerals. The young stem or root of the thistle can be peeled and eaten raw or cooked. The fruitlike seeds can be eaten raw or roasted. Thistle tea is good for curing stomach and digestive problems, for reducing fever, expelling worms, increasing milk in nursing mothers, and strengthening internal organs. Thistle is said to increase alertness and make the brain function with more activity. Thistle can aid you in understanding and working with the many different levels of reality.

THE LONG SNOWS MOON,
ELK—BLACK SPRUCE

Black spruce is the plant associated with the Long Snows Moon (November 22 to December 21). Apart from providing beauty, wood, and oxygen, the black spruce has other uses. The tips of this tree are high in vitamin C and can be used as a tea or nibbled on. A tea made from the leaves is good as an antiseptic and helps to loosen mucus in the throat and chest. The gum can be applied to cuts and wounds to clean them and can also be used as an inhalant both in and out of the sweat lodge. The tree gum can be made into a plaster for setting bones. A tea from the twigs makes a good bath and is helpful in curing colds. Black spruce can help you explore lofty ideas, your earth connection, and your unique ways of reaching to Spirit. It can teach you about a deep inner strength that encourages softness.

THE SPIRIT PATH PLANTS
•••••

The Northern Spirit Path Plants

CLEANSING—ECHINACEA

The plant associated with cleansing, which is the first Spirit Path position of the North, is echinacea. Echinacea is also referred to as purple coneflower and, grows wild on the prairies of the United States. It is one of the most powerful cleansing herbs. In herbal traditions, echinacea is renowned as a blood purifier and cleanser. It was well known to Native Americans as a healer, used particularly for snake bites and infections.

The root of echinacea can be used for medicinal purposes—internally or externally—as a tonic, tincture, poultice, herbal bath, smudge, or mild tea. This plant is healing for the blood and lymph glands. It helps fight fevers, infections, abscesses, irritations of the mucous membranes, vaginal infections, and blood poisoning. It is good for treating poison oak or ivy as well as bites from animals and insects.

RENEWAL—RED CLOVER

The plant associated with renewal, the second Spirit Path position of the North, is red clover. This prolific herb, with its striking red flower, is found in pastures, lawns, and meadows as well as other grassy areas. It is a cleansing plant that also begins to rebuild any depleted parts of the body. This plant is so favorable to the well-being of humans that it is considered one of the Creator's greatest gifts to the two-legged ones.

The blossoms are used medicinally as a tonic, tincture, poultice, gargle, tea, smudge, salve, and herbal bath. Red clover is used for irritations of the throat, vagina, stomach, rectum, and skin. It has been known to be good for ulcers, cancer, lungs, coughs, colds, bronchial problems, burns, cuts, scrapes, and acne. It is soothing, calming, and good as a sedative. Drinking red clover as a tea or using it as a poultice on a wound can bring renewal to you internally or externally.

PURITY—TRILLIUM

The plant associated with purity, the third Spirit Path position of the North, is trillium. Trillium is a flowering herb with a root that looks similar to ginseng. Trillium thrives in rich, dark, damp woods, and rain forests. It is a delicate plant that only shyly peeks its dainty flowers around the other beings found in such pristine areas. This delicate plant is one of thousands of plant species that are casualties of the blind destruction of the planet's rain forests, one of our most valuable and irreplaceable natural resources. This shy, noble, pristine plant is an endangered species looking at a precarious future. Future herbal historians may well look on our generation as the one that brought trillium to its end, as general historians might look on this generation as the one that ended the possibility of pure earth, air, and water.

Historically, the trillium root was used in a powdered form that was then boiled to make a tincture, tea, poultice, or herbal bath. Trillium was good for bleeding, coughs, the lungs, and for stopping diarrhea. It was used as a powerful pain reliever and to clean wounds. The species *Trillium pendulum* is also known as birthroot because it was used by Native women during birthing for pain, as an astringent, and as an antiseptic. It was also used if hemorrhaging occurred. This species was known to be healing for the female organs, especially for heavy menstrual bleeding and for problems of the vagina and uterus.

Drinking trillium tea has been said to purify the mind, body, and spirit. However, given its endangered status, trillium should not be used at all until it has had an opportunity to regenerate its own species.

The Eastern Spirit Path Plants

CLARITY—ROSEMARY

Rosemary is the plant associated with clarity, the first Spirit Path position of the East. Its botanical name is *Rosmarinus officinalis*. The flowers of rosemary are light to deep blue. The leaf is slim and leathery, highly scented, and slightly oily to the touch. Using rosemary as a tea helps to strengthen your mental clarity.

The leaves and flowers are used medicinally as a pain reliever and are especially good for headaches. Rosemary is used to relieve stomach and colon problems such as gas, indigestion, nausea, and stomach pain. It can be used as an astringent, a stimulant, or for fevers and is particularly renowned as an aid for colds and lung problems. It is a powerful herb to use for healing female problems.

When used as a mouth wash, in an herbal bath, or as a smudge, it is an effective healer as well as refreshing and calming. Rosemary can be used as an oil for aromatherapy; in teas, tinctures, and tonics, and in dream pillows and sachets. As a cooking herb it brings a savory flavor to dishes prepared with it. Rosemary used in cooking, healing, or for ceremonial purposes will bring you clarity and reason.

WISDOM—SAGE

The plant associated with wisdom, the second Spirit Path position of the East, is sage. The botanical name for sage is *Salvia officinalis.* Sage grows well in a garden. It is a perennial with light whitish or a grayish green leaves and numerous blue flowers. True sage is a member of the mint family. Sage has been associated with wisdom for such a long time that it has become a synonym for it.

Traditionally, it is said, "For both flavor and health use sage." Indeed, both as a culinary spice and medicinal aid, sage is a very essential herb.

The leaves of this plant can be used as a cooking herb; medicinally (both internally and externally) as a tonic, tincture, poultice, or herbal bath; as a tea; or as a smudge.

This plant is healing for the stomach, colon, sinuses and nasal passages, lungs, liver, kidneys, skin, pores, joints, bones, mucous membranes, throat, and sex organs. Sage can be used as an astringent, disinfectant, hair conditioner and dandruff remover, antiseptic, body oil, expectorant, and agent in aromatherapy. It is good for colds, fevers, allergies, sinuses, arthritis, sexual problems, pain, ulcers, cuts, scrapes, and burns.

Used as a gargle, it can help sore throats. To calm your nerves drink sage tea. For skin disorders, insect bites, wounds, or for sedation soak in an herbal sage bath.

It is a wise cook or healer that uses this diverse herb for culinary delight or medicinal aid.

ILLUMINATION—WILD AMERICAN GINSENG

The plant associated with illumination, the third Spirit Path position of the East, is wild American ginseng. Wild American ginseng's botanical name is *Panax quinquefolius.* The whole plant reaches heights from eight to more than eighteen feet tall. The root is gnarled, with thick protrusions. Ginseng root grows in lengths from two to four inches and up to one inch in width. This elusive plant is as sought after as the quality it represents. One way of finding ginseng is to look at night for the slight fluorescence that it gives off. The inner light of ginseng can draw you to it in much the same way the inner light of an illuminated being draws others. However, once you find ginseng you can demonstrate your degree of illumination by leaving it alone. The plant will be extinct within a few years if people continue to harvest it.

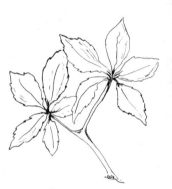

The ginseng plant takes as much as four to eight years to reach a state of being in which it is deemed fit to use medicinally. Although it is possible to find plants that are fifty years old or more, it is rare. Wild American ginseng is so sought after by those familiar with its powerful qualities that few of this plant exist past the eight-year mark.

The root of wild American ginseng has been used for cooking as well as medicinally. Although we discuss the historical uses here, we do not feel the plant should be harvested at all today. It was used as a spice or tea. It was also dried and ground into powder to use as a spice, tincture, or tonic or put in a capsule to be taken orally. It was renowned as one of nature's most delectable culinary gifts, a reputation that led to its overuse. It was considered a preventive against poor health and an overall healer, sedative, and strengthener, particularly effective for ailments of the stomach and for regenerating sexual and general vitality.

Ginseng was good for the lymphatic glands, the heart, the brain, the urinary tract, and nervous system. It helped ease rheumatism and calmed most forms of spasms, coughs, or asthma. It helped increase the appetite.

You will show the depth of your illumination by not using this plant at all. Instead, use cultivated American ginseng. Doing so not only gives life to an almost extinct species, but also supports the farmers growing this plant.

The Southern Spirit Path Plants

TRUST—BORAGE

The plant associated with trust, the first Spirit Path stone of the South, is borage. Its botanical name is *Borago officinalis*. This plant has numerous broad leaves that come to a point, with flowers that look like lovely, purple starbursts. The parts that are used are the seeds, leaves, and flowers. Borage is a plant that has long been associated with the energy of the heart. Borage is connected with trust because of its ability to open up your heart and to enable you to work with heart energies.

Borage can be used medicinally, internally and externally, as a gargle, eye wash, tea, poultice, tincture, tonic, herbal bath, or smudge. For best results, take it internally and externally simultaneously.

The flowers of borage are used for culinary purposes and to flavor already-made white wine. The leaves of borage have a cucumberlike taste.

Medicinally, the seeds, flower, and leaves are effective as a cough suppressant and mood stabilizer. Borage can be used to increase milk in nursing mothers.

This plant is excellent for washing away inflammations of the skin or eyes. It is particularly effective for insect bites, lung ailments, flus, colds, animal bites, wounds, and rashes as well as any kind of infections or sores that cause itchiness. Borage is good for releasing poisons, lowering fevers, inducing sweat, purifying the blood, and cleansing the body's systems. This plant is helpful for stopping jaundice, breaking up mucus, and healing ulcers and herpes. A little goes a long way so excessive usage should be curtailed.

Using borage encourages you to trust the healing process and the natural order of life.

GROWTH—COMFREY

Comfrey is the plant associated with growth, the second Spirit Path position of the South. Comfrey is a good example of the power of growth. Once the root of the plant is in the earth, comfrey grows prolifically, spreading in all directions. Used either as food or medicine comfrey strengthens the being taking it just as growth strengthens individuals.

Comfrey is an everything-in-one, serious plant that can be used internally or externally, as a cooked green, tea, tincture, tonic, poultice, herbal bath, or powder. It is also a good animal food for our grazing four-legged friends.

Comfrey was used by Native Americans to stop internal bleeding and blood in the stools, nose, lungs, or urine. It is reputed to be effective in the treatment of cancer. It is a powerful astringent, expectorant, cough syrup, pain reliever, stimulant, and purifier. Comfrey is known to charge through a person's system, cleansing disease and making way for the growth of healthy new tissue as well as general good health and well-being.

This plant is good for the respiratory organs, lungs, stomach, female organs, sore breasts, gallstones, throat, kidneys, tendons, bones, back aches, joints, as well as sexual excess, burns, internal or external ulcers, sprains, bruises, sores, and swelling.

Comfrey is a powerful healing agent that promotes regeneration and growth on all levels—physical, spiritual, emotional, and mental.

LOVE—HAWTHORNE

The plant associated with love, the third Spirit Path position of the South, is hawthorne. Hawthorne's botanical name is *Crataegus oxyacantha.* Hawthorne shrubs and trees have scalloped leaves, small round-petaled flowers, and oval-shaped berries. Hawthorne trees can grow to thirty feet in height. Like love, hawthorne strengthens your heart helping it to be healthy and open. Borage may draw love to you by teaching you to trust, but hawthorne gives you the strength to be vulnerable enough to maintain loving relationships on a consistent basis in your life. Hawthorne brings love into your life by giving you the strength to take risks and engage in friendships and love relationships that may appear to be beyond your means and capabilities. Hawthorne represents heart strength. This plant also helps you to have the strength and courage to deal with love rejected or affairs of the heart that have cooled or taken a negative turn.

Hawthorne is effective internally or externally, as a tonic, tincture, tea, poultice, herbal bath, or gargle. It has been used for stabilizing both high and low blood pressure. This plant is considered one of the most significant aids for healing the heart, for relieving hardening of the arteries, for kidney disease, and for circulation problems. It relieves sleeplessness and anxiety. The berries are most frequently used for assisting the heart, digestive system, and circulation.

This plant is good as a diuretic, astringent, and calmant. Native Americans have used hawthorne for sore throats and arthritis.

Hawthorne's greatest ability is that of creating love and strengthening every aspect of the heart be it in the physical body or on the emotional or spiritual plane.

The Western Spirit Path Plants

EXPERIENCE—OLIVE

The plant associated with experience, the first Spirit Path position of the West, is the olive tree. Olive is among the oldest trees now found on the earth. It is a tree that has experienced many millennia of history. This ancient tree has much to teach us about the value and insights of experience.

Olive trees are a medium-size tree. The fruit of the tree, the olive, has been a delicacy for many thousands of years and has provided humans with one of the healthiest oils known.

Internally and externally olive oil can promote health. Externally, in the form of massage oil, olive oil can aid the skin, pores, and joints.

In cooking, olive oil can be used to enhance most recipes using oil. Although any oil in excess can be harmful, olive oil is said to help break down cholesterol rather than produce it.

Working with an olive tree, branches, or leaves can open you up to new experiences beneficial especially on the spiritual plane. It is helpful for encouraging maturity, perspective, peace, and understanding.

Because of its age and experience of life the olive tree has the ability to teach us about patience, and the value of being without doing.

INTROSPECTION—CHAMOMILE

The plant associated with introspection, the second Spirit Path position of the

West, is chamomile. Chamomile's botanical name is *Matricaria chamomilla*. This delicate, sweet-smelling plant can be made into a tea that will help you to relax to the point where you are capable of making the inward journey that allows you to look deep within your being.

Chamomile is known to be a remedy for various maladies of life that afflict humans from birth to adulthood. Chamomile helps to ease pain both of body and spirit.

As a preventive medicinal plant there are few better. If chamomile tea was a regular staple of childhood diets, many ailments and later accumulative health problems could be deterred. It can be used as a tea, tonic, tincture, salve, aromatherapy oil, poultice, herbal bath, and gargle. It is excellent for adults and children for colds, flus, measles, mumps, earaches, headaches, and any manner of illness. It brings comfort, relieves pain, is a calmant, and soothes distress. It is highly recommended for any stomach problems.

Chamomile is known to ease heavy menstrual bleeding and uterine discomfort related to nursing. An oil or salve made from this plant is good for skin care. Chamomile makes a refreshing and invigorating herbal bath.

A cup of chamomile tea can help you to relax, go within, and find solutions to pains or problems.

STRENGTH—NETTLE

The plant associated with strength, the third Spirit Path position of the West, is nettle. The botanical name for nettle is *Urtica dioica.* The common name is stinging nettle. Nettle grows wild, and its stems reach out to entangle and sting the person not conscious of its presence. While nettle can be an irritant it is also a giver of health and healing.

It is best to use the leaves of young plants. The leaves can be used internally and externally as a tea, tonic, tincture, shampoo, and hair rinse, poultice, oil, lotion, or herbal bath. It is rich in vitamins and minerals including chlorophyll, potassium, manganese, and iron.

Nettle is a very valuable food plant once cooked. When fresh it will sting. It is particularly rich in iron and vitamin C. As a food it can be used in soups, cooked salads, as a tea, or cooked like spinach. Medicinally it is effective for relief from arthritis, particularly when used as a poultice. Nettle can help cure skin disorders, blood disorders, anemia, and gout and can lower blood sugar levels. Nettle is effective for dealing with female problems, rashes, and dandruff. Many body care products—such as lotions, hair conditioners, and shampoos—contain nettle.

Nettle teaches strength through attention. If you are not prepared to deal with nettle, it stings you to remind you that discrimination is an important element of strength. If, however, you are centered in your own strength and power, you can pick this plant without receiving any of its prickly, burning welts.

WORKING WITH THE
MEDICINE WHEEL PLANT HELPERS
▪▪▪▪▪

FINDING YOUR CURRENT PLANT HELPER

To determine which Medicine Wheel plant you should work with at any given time you can use the following exercise, which will help you work both intellectually and intuitively with the plant wheel.

What you need. Smudge materials, a Medicine Wheel, paper and pen or tape recorder, and, if desired, an offering.

Estimated time. Thirty minutes.

1. Smudge yourself and the area. Go to your Medicine Wheel, either in visualization or reality. If you know which position you wish to work with, sit near that stone. If you do not know where you are in your travels, circle the wheel either physically or mentally and sit in the position where you feel the most draw.
2. Quiet and center yourself. Ask the plant of the position you occupy to help you. Ask whether this is the plant you need to work with now to strengthen and heal yourself.
3. If you receive an affirmative answer ask the spirit of this plant to help you learn about the plant.
4. If you receive a negative answer, ask the spirit of this plant to guide you to the plant being you need now. Keep asking until you receive an affirmative answer about a plant with which you should be working. When you have received an answer, thank the spirits of the plants that have helped you.
5. Record your experience.

When you have ascertained the Medicine Wheel plant that can help you now, read about it in this chapter. If you feel you need more information, refer to other books. Study the plant until you feel you know enough about it to enable you to find it. If you know the plant might grow in an area around you, go to that area and ask the spirit of the plant to guide you. When you find your plant helper, make an offering and prayer, then sit with it using the techniques described in the Hug a Tree exercise on page 170.

If (and only if) there is an abundance of the plant and you are not on someone else's property, ask the plant whether you may pick one of its relations. If you receive an affirmative answer, ask the plant to guide you in doing so.

If you know the plant that draws you does not grow in your area, see if you can obtain some of the dried plant. Even this will be impossible with some of the Medicine Wheel plants that are rare or endangered or do not have a normally recognized medicinal value. In this instance obtain a photograph of the plant calling to you, or work with the illustrations in this book. You can photocopy the drawing of a particular plant so you can work with it.

If you have been gifted with a plant—whether fresh or dried—keep it near you as you would a stone that had just become one of your helpers. Do the same with a plant photograph. Experience the plant with as many of your senses as possible. With a photograph, you can look, study, visualize, meditate, and dream. With a dried plant you can also smell, feel, and taste. With a fresh plant you can study it in nature, learn how to dry the plant, then observe the sensory differences between the fresh and dried plant.

If the plant with which you are working is appropriate for a variety of uses, and is an abundant plant, you can work with it in any of the ways described in this chapter: tea, smudge, bath, candles, dream pillows, smoking mixtures, offerings. Observe the differences in the plant and in you as you work with it in whatever ways you choose.

Keep a small photo or a pinch of the plant with you, particularly as you dream, meditate, or do ceremony. See how the plant affects you during these times. Particularly observe whether the plant has any healing help for you. Watch your dreams, quiet times, and meditations. Listen to your plant helper and follow the suggestions it gives you.

When you feel you really know one plant—which could take anywhere from several days to several years—then you are ready to move to another position and repeat the procedure.

The following sections serve as a beginning manual to help you commence your work with the Plant Wheel. After you work with these exercises you might wish to continue your association with the plant kingdom by studying some good herb books or working with a competent herbalist.

How to Pick, Dry, and Mix the Medicine Wheel Plants

The most important aspect of picking any plant is showing awareness and respect. *Do not pick any plant if for any reason it seems endangered.* This means that if there is a lot less of a plant this year than there was last year do not pick it but, rather, make prayers that it might regenerate. Never "clear-cut" an area of any plant. Never pick a plant without first asking the spirit of that plant whether it wants to help you and then making prayers and offerings to the plant for its help.

There are many ways to pray over a plant and talk with its spirit. What is common to all of them is that you must approach the plant with respect. You are not deifying the plant by praying to it; rather, you are acknowledging that the same Great Spirit that is within you and around you is also within the plants you need. Some people pray to every plant they must pick. They might first thank the plant for the gift it is giving them and then ask the plant spirit to leave before they actually cut into the body of the plant. They might tell the plant why they need it then ask the plant to give its help and blessing to their task.

Other people find what seems to be the oldest plant of the species in the area—the grandfather or grandmother plant—and make their prayers to this elder. They explain their need to the elder and ask for her blessing in picking some of her children.

Before beginning to pick plants, most people leave an offering of either cornmeal or tobacco. If you do not have one of these available, you can leave a hair from your head or a coin. The purpose of the offering is to give something back for the gift this species of plant is giving you.

You must also be very careful about the human interference when picking wild plants. Never pick a plant unless you are sure that the area has not been sprayed with any kind of herbicide or other chemical. Never pick a plant by the side of the highway. Exhaust fumes contain quite a number of chemical residues that could be dangerous for you.

Never pick a plant unless you are absolutely sure of its identification. There are look-alike plants that have very different properties. The most glaring example in the Medicine Wheel plants is blue camas and white camas. Blue camas is an important food. White camas contains an often deadly poison. However, there are many other look-alikes that can cause problems. For example, dog fennel looks very much like chamomile. Even somewhat experienced herbalists can be fooled. Chamomile relaxes you, but dog fennel can make you feel sick as a dog.

If you need a plant and are not absolutely sure of its identification, the best thing to do is check with an experienced herbalist. If that is not possible and your need for the plant is greater than the risk you are taking, you can ask the plant which it is. (*Never do this with blue camas! The other camas is deadly.*) If you have been practicing the visualizations in the first section of the book, you will know how to sense the answer. For some people the plant will emit a subtle light, an aura. For others, they will hear the answer with their inner ear. Others yet will feel a shift in energy in the midpoint of their body, or a tingling in their hands or warmth or cold. If you have worked with your own feelings enough you will know what the plant is communicating to you.

Some people would determine whether they have the correct plant by using a pendulum. If it swings in the direction that means yes to them, they would know the plant was okay. If the pendulum swings in the no direction, they would not pick that plant.

When you have picked the plants you will be using you should also exercise care in drying them. You should not dry most plants in direct sunlight. The sun can rob them of the essential ingredients that make them most helpful. You should dry most plants slowly, but not so slowly they have time to mold. Hang plants either singly or in bunches on strings, and then string them from nails in the rafters of the roof. Some people dry herbs in food dryers and that is fine if you carefully follow directions provided with the dryer. Others dry them in the oven with the oven on very low heat. That is also okay, if your oven doesn't get too hot, but can make your house pretty warm in the summer.

In mixing herbs you should first be sure that the herbs you are mixing complement each other. Some herbs work well together. Others do not. Consult an herbalist or herbal book for good combinations.

Herbs for Healing

Some of the Medicine Wheel herbs are excellent helpers in healing a variety of problems. To utilize them in this way you can use them as teas, in capsules, or in tinctures. If you will drink herb tea, that is the best way to take herbs. The tea allows you to feel the herb as you prepare it, smell its natural scent, taste its flavor, and see how it looks before and after preparation. Generally, to make a medicinal tea of leaves or flowers you use one tablespoon of herb to one cup of boiling water. You add the water to the herb, cover it and let it steep about ten minutes before straining and drinking. For roots, barks, and branches you use the same amounts but you bring water to a boil, reduce to a simmer, add the herbs, cover and simmer for ten to fifteen minutes. Strain and drink. The amount of herb to water does vary, so be sure to check the proportions with an herbalist or good herbal book.

Some people do not like to drink herb tea in amounts great enough for the tea to be effective. For them, encapsulating the herbs or buying or making an herbal tincture will work better. If you do take herbs in capsules, be sure to follow them with a cup of hot water as this activates the herb. Tinctures also work better if you take them with warm water. If you don't like the taste of one of your plant helpers you are wiser to take it in capsules or as a tincture. No herb can work well if it is not taken in the correct amount.

Some herbs are used externally as compresses, salves, or ointments. The instructions for preparing various herbs in these ways varies enough that you should check this with an herbalist or good herbal book. Most health food stores now carry a variety of herbal salves and ointments. You will find several of the Medicine Wheel plants—notably plantain, comfrey, sunflower, olive, nettle—present in many of these preparations.

Smoking Mixtures

Although many herbs can be used for smoking, some cannot. Of the Medicine Wheel herbs, we would only recommend using the following in smoking mixes: plantain, raspberry, mullein, red clover, tobacco, sage, sagebrush, and rosemary.

To make a smoking mixture you thoroughly dry all herbs then blend them together by hand. As you use the smoking mixture you will come to see that some herbs smoke better than others. You can then use a greater amount of these herbs in future mixtures. Given the state of the earth today, and all the pollutants we inhale, smoking anything is a questionable activity. We do not recommend any smoking for recreation. However, we believe that sacred smoking in the pipe, with the smoke just taken into the mouth then blown out for Spirit, is not harmful, if done with great moderation and proper intent.

Offerings

All of the herbs of the Medicine Wheel can be used to make offerings to Spirit. Most herbal offerings are of dried herbs that are carried with you then offered whenever it is time to make a special prayer.

By using herbs that have a specific meaning you can communicate with Spirit. A traditional way to make an offering is to extend a pinch of the herb to the Creator, the Earth Mother, and the four cardinal directions, then sprinkle it onto a plant, the Earth Mother, or whatever you are thanking.

MEDICINE WHEEL DREAM PILLOWS

Dream pillows can be very effective helpers in connecting you with your subconscious as well as in allowing Spirit to communicate with you during your sleeping hours.

Many people have excellent dream medicine that merely needs encouragement. Dream pillows can provide this and also be an excellent catalyst for connecting you with your dreams. Dream pillows can also encourage stronger dreams and allow you to remember them better. Used in conjunction with the meditation to remember dreams in chapter 6, they can help anyone to be able to recall dreams.

Making a dream pillow is a good way to connect with the plant kingdom as well as with your dreams. You can fill the dream pillow with plants that will help with whatever specific healing you need or with whatever energies you are working with at the time. For example, yarrow could be used as an overall tonic, mullein could be used to call in the powerful forces of the universe, or rose petals to beckon the power of love. Mugwort is excellent for dreaming medicine, as is chamomile.

MAKING A DREAM PILLOW

What you need. Smudge materials, cloth, scissors, needle, thread, dried herbs, and, if desired, herbal oils.

Estimated time. Time for gathering herbs, plus one hour to make the pillow.

1. Smudge yourself and all materials to be used.
2. Choose your cloth. Soft cottons, calico, or velvet are all nice materials for dream pillows.
3. Fold the material in half. Measure and mark a square about eight by five inches. Cut out this square. If the material is not too thick cut through both layers together.
4. Turn the material inside out. Pin together.
5. Sew three sides together: Sew across the top, down one side, and then across the bottom, leaving the last side open.
6. Mix the Medicine Wheel plants you want to place in your dream pillow. You can add herbal oils if you wish, although the natural plant scent can be very powerful alone. If you add oil, use enough drops so that the scent is strong but be careful not to drench the herbs. Give the oil a chance to dry before putting the herbs in the pillow. Otherwise they may mold.
7. Fill the pillow with herbs until it is quite fluffy.
8. Sew the remaining side closed.
9. Before going to sleep smudge yourself and your dream pillow then place it under your regular pillow. Consciously ask to remember your dreams. Place a notebook next to your bed so that you can write dreams down, first thing, when you wake up. Keep this dream journal over a period of time, at least one to three months. Using a journal with the dream pillow will help you grow to remember and understand dreams better as well as to see patterns of growth in yourself and your dreams.

HERBAL MEDICINE WHEEL CANDLES

▪▪▪▪▪

Burning a candle that has herbs of the Medicine Wheel rolled inside will invite in the qualities of the herb as well as the qualities of the color of the candle. When you light the candle you are also inviting the powers of the element of fire. If the candle is scented with oil then you can open your sense of smell as well as sight.

MAKING AN HERBAL MEDICINE WHEEL CANDLE

What you need. Smudging materials, flat sheets of beeswax in the color of your choice, candle wicks an inch longer than the length of the beeswax, herbs corresponding with the Medicine Wheel position represented by the color of the wax or that are affecting you now, and, if desired, herbal oils or scents.

Estimated time. Thirty minutes.

1. Smudge yourself and anything that you will be touching while making the candles.
2. Lay a sheet of beeswax on a flat surface in front of you.
3. Make an offering with a small pinch of the herb that you wish to roll inside the sheet of beeswax. Spread the herb evenly over the whole sheet of beeswax. Use only a small amount of herb or later, when you light the candle, you may end up with a fast-burning torch instead of the pleasant candle experience you had anticipated. If you are using flower petals such as rose petals use four to six of them. Place the petals closer to the side that will be rolled last.
4. Place the wick close to an edge with about ¾ of an inch laying over the edge. Gently roll just enough of the beeswax so that the wick is covered. Press this into place. Then roll the candle until it is complete. Apply pressure evenly as you roll the squared beeswax into a cylinder.
5. Next gently press and blend the seam of the beeswax so that there is a smoother edge.
6. Slightly dampen your fingertips with the oil or scent of your choice and lightly press this onto the exterior of the candle.

A MEDICINE WHEEL CANDLE CEREMONY

Candle ceremonies are very powerful aids for manifestation and actualization. Consequently, don't underestimate the power of this ceremony or treat it lightly. Be careful of what you ask for as you most likely will get it. Keep in mind your responsibility to only work for the highest good of all those involved.

What you need. Smudging utensils, candles, candle holders, a piece of paper and pen.

Estimated time. Thirty minutes to two hours.

1. Smudge yourself and everything you will touch during the ceremony, including the area in which the ceremony will occur and anyone else involved.
2. Write down what it is that you want.
3. Light a candle and invite in the energies you want to be there. Acknowledge the element of fire and the powers of the color, herb, and scent of the candle. Give thanks for their presence.
4. Take a moment to gaze at the candle and connect with its energies. Breathe at least four long, slow, deep, breaths while you are connecting with these energies. Be aware of the life force in you, around you, and through you.
5. Use the candle to light the piece of paper that has your prayer on it. When it is burning well, place it into the smudge bowl. Keep praying for what it is you want while the paper burns. If it goes out and it is not a hazard to pick up and relight, do so until it has burned to ashes. If it is difficult to burn, leave it lying in the smudge bowl after it has made contact with the flame at least once.
6. Now stay with the candle and continue praying until it burns down completely.
7. Give thanks to the element of fire and the energies of the color, scent, and herb of the candle for their presence and gifts.

8. When the candle burns down completely the ceremony is done. Take any remains of the candle or ashes and bury them.

BURNING CANDLES DURING OTHER CEREMONIES

It can be powerful to burn candles during other ceremonies, such as a Medicine Wheel Healing, a pipe ceremony, or when you are doing something of a ceremonial nature such as grinding corn or bundling sage. However, there are guidelines to honor because candle burning is in itself a ceremony.

1. Smudge yourself and the candle before lighting it.
2. Acknowledge the element of fire and the energies of the color, herb, and scent of the candle.
3. When the candle burns down, give thanks to these energies for their presence and gifts.
4. Bury any remnants of the candle.

If it is not appropriate to let the candle burn down due to time constraints or circumstances, then you may put the candle out. Do not, however, use this candle for any purpose other than a similar ceremony. If it was a highly charged, intensely emotional, or specific healing ceremony, then it is best to bury the candle in its partially burned state immediately after the ceremony.

WORKING WITH THE MEDICINE WHEEL TREES
·····

All trees can be a limitless source of answers and wisdom. They are the keepers of much spirit knowledge. Like all nature spirits, tree spirits will answer if you call to them asking for help or medicine.

Trees' inherent medicine is one of prophecy and wisdom. They are sacred monuments bearing knowledge of the past, present, and future. Trees are the keepers of ancient teachings and old ways. They are all planetary elders. Some of the most revered are now living tenuously at best in the rain forests. The seeds that fall from their branches are recorders that carry on the sacred lineage of these ancient beings.

Never pull live branches from a tree nor use nails, saws, or force when working with tree medicine. It is inappropriate and harmful for the tree as well as detrimental to any ceremony you might be doing.

If you are harvesting leaves or bark from a tree or cutting down a dead tree to recycle for wood, always make prayers to release the tree spirit then make an offering of gratitude. A tree gives completely. Its fruits and nuts are a food source, the leaves give shade and oxygen. Even in death, trees give us wood for our homes, fuel for our hearth, and a means to cook our food. If trees fall to their end in the forests they give life to hardworking grubs and homes to busy bees.

Trees are a truly great example to us of how to give fully. You can use fallen branches from trees in many different ways. They can be the framework for medicine hoops, dream nets, staffs, medicine wands, or other medicine objects.

Working with the colored blossoms and leaves of trees can help you experience both aroma and color therapies. Hanging from a sturdy branch of a stout tree is great exercise that also can stretch and adjust a sore back.

You can also work intuitively with trees by taking time to be with them. This is particularly powerful medicine if you take time to be with one of the Medicine Wheel trees when you are working with the energy of the position it represents.

HUG A TREE EXERCISE

What you need. A tree.

Estimated time. Thirty minutes.

1. To really experience a tree, hug it.
2. Just hug it for fifteen minutes or more and feel the flow of life energy in the tree, in yourself, and between you and the tree. Be willing to take the time necessary to slow yourself down to a rhythm closer to the tree's.
3. You should be aware of what you are feeling in your body while you are hugging the tree. Let your awareness flow up and down through your body as you are doing this exercise. Remember the life energy can feel the same as sexual energy.
4. Keep hugging the tree until you feel a difference in your energy. Note what the difference in feeling is.
5. Turn your back to the tree and lean against it until you feel an energy shift. Be aware of how the shift feels.
6. Thank the tree and leave an offering.

It is a gift both to and from Spirit to embrace a tree. Another great gift to a tree is to dance and frolic around its base letting the earth energy flow from the tree's roots into your being and letting your joy and energy flow up and into the branches of the tree. This cycle of joy can renew both you and the tree spirit. If a tree is very strong and you are a climber you can climb the tree and cuddle up into the branches.

Once you have experienced the energy of one tree you might try the same exercises with other trees, with bushes, shrubs, and herbs! Try all the Medicine Wheel trees then other trees as well. You have your whole life to finish doing these exercises. Notice that different trees evoke different feelings in you. You can begin to learn some of the healing properties of trees and other plants if you can sincerely focus on these feelings.

12

The Animal Wheel

Minerals solidify the elemental powers and plants bring movement to the minerals. Without the elements, minerals, and plants, animals could not exist. By watching how naturally the animals relate to each other and all their relations in the sacred circle of life, we two-leggeds can learn how to honor and express the instinctual, heartfelt energies that move through us.

Animals give so many gifts to the human kingdom that it is difficult to speak about them in generalities. From the crawlers we learn to look down, to keep our sight on the Earth Mother. From the swimmers, we learn the joy both of moving in water and of seeing the beautiful, totally different world contained within water. From the winged ones we learn about the miracle of flight and of the difference in perception when we rise above our usual view. From the four-leggeds we learn about movement, grace, and balance. From all the animals we can learn about different ways of structuring life, community, and world view. We can also learn about the beauty of song, dance, and motion.

Some of the elements, minerals, and plants offer themselves to the animals, and some animals offer themselves to the humans to provide food, clothing, shelter, implements, and medicine, completing the connection of all the kingdoms.

171

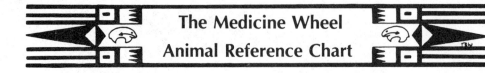

The Medicine Wheel
Animal Reference Chart

The Center

Animal	Physical Descripiton	Where Found	Distinguishing Habits
All or Any			
Tortoise	Amphibious, shell-covered reptile	Worldwide. Giant: Galapagos, zoos	Lives on land
Lizard	Small, scaly, leathery reptile with bulging eyes	N. America, Norway, New Zealand	Can attach to any surface, even ceilings
Loon	Gregarious birds that swim and dive	Asia, N. America, N. Europe	Strong swimmers who make eerie music
Turtle	Amphibious, shell-covered reptile	Worldwide. Endangered in S. Amer.	Withdraws into protective shell, lives in water
Frog	Green, leaping, four-legged amphibian	Water and woods, worldwide	Metamorphosis from tadpole to frog, song
Thunderbird	Big, singing hawk	Spirit plane	Serves Thunder beings
Butterfly	Resembles beautiful, colored moth	Worldwide	Changes from caterpillar to butterfly

The Spirit

Animal	Physical Descripiton	Where Found	Distinguishing Habits
White Buffalo	Large, brawny, horned, and magnificent	Africa, America, Europe	Roam and graze
Golden Eagle	Highest flying, most regal winged one	Europe, Asia, North America	Aerial acrobat
Coyote	Sharp, swift, dog/wolf like	North America	Trickster, survivor with an eerie song
Grizzly Bear	Large, furry, thick bodied bear with grizzly coat	Alaska, Yellowstone, Yukon B.C.	Hibernates

The Moons

Animal	Physical Descripiton	Where Found	Distinguishing Habits
Snow Goose	Beautiful, large, white bird	South in winter. North in spring	Fly in V, migrate, honk
Otter	Medium sized water weasel with webbed feet	Lakes, riverways. N. California coast	Play, utilize tools
Cougar	Largest member of feline family on this continent	U.S., Canada, Mexico	Swift runners and climbers

Animal	Physical Descripiton	Where Found	Distinguishing Habits
Red Hawk	Large, red tailed hawk	U.S., Mexico, Canada	Magnificent flyers
Beaver	Largest U.S. rodent, big front teeth, broad tail	U.S., Canada	Build dams
Deer	2-4 feet tall, 50-400 lbs., leggy, some horned	U.S.	Graceful and alert, shy and lovely

Animal	Physical Descripiton	Where Found	Distinguishing Habits
Flicker	Red or yellow shafted woodpecker	Woods, farms, and suburbs	Drum out songs with beak
Sturgeon	Known as king of fish	Northern Temperate Zone	Swim upstream to spawn, reach large sizes
Brown Bear	200-400 lbs., 2-3 feet at shoulder, brown, furry	Worldwide in remote areas	Curious, hibernate, can walk on two legs

Animal	Physical Descripiton	Where Found	Distinguishing Habits
Raven	Large, all black bird with wedge-shaped tail	Worldwide	Loud croak and caw
Snake	A limbless reptile with expandable jaws	Worldwide	Shed their skins
Elk	Largest, most regal member of deer family	Woodlands	Males shed antlers annually; all trumpet

The Spirit

Animal	Physical Descripiton	Where Found	Distinguishing Habits
Raccoon	Small animal with rings around tail and eyes	U.S. and Canada	Cleans food
Earthworm	Wet, soft, worm, size and shape of small finger	Worldwide. In dirt or after a rain	Squirmy, tenacious
Dolphin	Cetacean, pronounced grooved beak and white belly	Warm and mild waters	Warns of danger, social, playful
Hummingbird	Tiny bird that hovers	North & Central America	High wing beat rate, speed, agility
Owl	Large headed, big eyed, feathered bird	Worldwide	Emits an eerie question of: Who?
Firefly	Small, illuminating, winged insect	Worldwide	Emits light
Rabbit	Small, furry, long-eared, with strong hindquarters	Worldwide	Extremely prolific
Salmon	Bare-headed, finned fish	Atlantic, Pacific	Powerful, swims upstream to spawn
Wolf	Regal, lean, bushy tailed, long snouted, dog-like	N. America, Europe, N. Africa	Runs in pack, has complex social structure
Whale	Largest, most ancient mammal on earth	Oceans worldwide	Sprays water from blow hole
Mouse	Tiny rodent with whiskers and long, thin tail	Worldwide	Twitches nose, keeps in small territory
Ant	Strong, tiny insect	Worldwide	Live in colonies, build hills, lifts 4x its weight

The Medicine Wheel
Animal Reference Chart

Circle

How Humans Relate To Them	Lessons For Humans
Some honor, others hunt	Patience, experience, endurance, ancient wisdom, sacrifice, service, rewards of work and integrity
Revere them, make them pets, hunt them	Good omen, cheer, warmth, optimism, adaptability
Hunt them, or honor them	Transformation, maneuverability, mystery, fidelity
Some honor, others hunt	Honor, ancient wisdom, stability, endurance, protection
Enjoy their song, honor them, hunt them	Transformation, evolution, mystery, joy, humor, communication
Love and respect them	Messenger, goodness, kindness, service, cleansing, healing, humility
Love them, have endangered them with pollution	Transformation, growth, evolution, beauty, regeneration, change, fearlessness, joy

Keepers

How Humans Relate To Them	Lessons For Humans
Hunted to near extinction. Native Americans love	Spirituality, selflessness, service, generosity, ancient wisdom, hope
Inspired by them. Endangered species by hunting	Clarity, spiritual messenger, greatness, vision, inspiration, new beginnings
Love them or hate them	Trickster energy, humor, wildness, endurance, trust, adaptability, survival, creativity, mystery
Revered, but hunted to near extinction	Stability, durability, healing, introspection, awareness, maturity, leadership, teaching

and Totems

How Humans Relate To Them	Lessons For Humans
Hunt them, delight in their flight	Beauty, gregariousness, tradition, transmitting, receiving, keen visionary, personal evolution, ceremony
Sea otters almost extinct	Playfulness, nurturing, prophetic, intuitive, inventiveness, originality, humanitarian, noble, curious
Respected but misunderstood and feared	Initiative, speed, grace, mystery, stalking, territoriality

How Humans Relate To Them	Lessons For Humans
Native people: very special. Whites: misunderstood	Aware, insight, truth, adaptability, survival, deliberation, optimism, prayer, intensity, openness
Greatly valued for pelts and musk glands	Security, contentment, industry, balance, comfort, affection, fidelity, orderly, self-reliant, patient, grounded
Very fond, but hunt them	Sensitivity, grace, alertness, protection, adaptability, clever, nimble, creative, heart and spirit connection

How Humans Relate To Them	Lessons For Humans
Special to Native Americans, pests to others	Protection, courage, joy, relentlessness, nurturing, loving, communication, harmony, relationship
Over-fished for their roe, caviar	Determination, teaching, leadership, consistency, knowledge, depth, strength, generous, sexual
Very special to Natives, hunted by others	Caution, fortitude, bravery, fairness, good decisions, pleasure, leadership, organization, grounding, curiosity

How Humans Relate To Them	Lessons For Humans
Good omen to some, bad omen to others	Messenger, spiritual, intelligence, community, assistance, encouragement, wary, balance, duality, mystery
Avoid. Some peoples respect them others kill them	Mystery, adaptability, the feminine, transformation, healing, life force, sensitivity, sensuality, psychic
Hunted, but respected as elder teacher	Confidence, strength, joy, agility, speed, protection, justice, wisdom, responsibility

Paths

How Humans Relate To Them	Lessons For Humans
Indulgent and amused, or consider a nuisance	Merriment, openness, boldness, cleansing, intelligence, contentment, wiliness, survival, tenacity, humor
Play with them. Use them for bait	Regeneration, stamina, self-healing, renewal, earth healing, transformation
Net, kill, capture for marine shows or love dearly	Purity, lightness of being, communication, love, intelligence, playfulness, kindness, spiritual attunements
Delight in their presence, or consider a nuisance	Precision, lucidity, energy, vibrancy, tenacity, grace, clarity, mystery, healing
Respect them or fear them	Old wisdom, knowledge, mystery, paradox, the shadow, the feminine, listening, the unknown
Like to catch them, watch them, wonder at them	Illumination, understanding, mating, the life force, continuity, wonder, awe, appreciation, light and darkness
Hunt them, raise for food, like them	Dealing with fear, productivity, growth, cunning, agility, innocence, creativity, self-actualization
Eat them, respect them	Trust, strength, perseverance, willpower, determination, courage, loyalty, tradition, sustenance
Love or fear them	Love, healing relationships, fidelity, forgiveness, intimacy, community, generosity, compatibility, cunning
Hunted to brink of extinction or loved an respected	Experience, strength, widom, stamina, ancient knowledge, observation, harmony with the environment
Squeamish or really like them, often trap and kill	Introspection, perception, innocence, observation, trust, resting, acceptance, content, satisfaction
Avoid	Strength, endurance, efficiency, persistence, productivity, courage, forethought, community

During your travels around the Medicine Wheel, observe the animal totems of the different positions. Watch them, dance and sing with them, and from them learn how positive the animal within you can be.

THE ANIMALS OF THE CENTER CIRCLE
·····

THE CREATOR—ALL OR ANY ANIMAL

There is no single animal that always represents the Creator. The Creator dances through all the animals. The Creator is part of every animal, yet not limited to merely one.

In our Medicine Wheel Gatherings we often use the buffalo skull to represent the Creator. That is because grandmother/grandfather buffalo was so sacred to the Native peoples. She gave all of herself so that the people could live. From her flesh came food; from her hide, shelter and clothes; from her bones, tools and medicine. We owe a lot of thanks to the buffalo so we honor her in this way. But the buffalo is not the only animal associated with the Creator. All are.

THE EARTH MOTHER—TORTOISE

The animal honoring the Center Circle stone representing the Earth Mother is the tortoise. Although tortoise and turtle are interchangeable terms, tortoise most often refers to a turtle that lives on land. Giant tortoises are now an endangered species and are most often found in the Galapagos Islands and in zoos. These tortoises can reach five feet in length and weigh up to a quarter of a ton. This large reptile has the lumbering grace, the patience, the experience, and the endurance of the earth herself. The tortoise is one of the longest-living earth beings, often reaching 100 to 150 years. All turtles and tortoises are honored by Native peoples because of the actions of a giant tortoise who lived many, many years ago.

That was a time, in many ways similar to today, when humans had forgotten the law of unity by which they were to live. They were fighting with each other over the smallest idea or action. They were showing jealousy, hatred, and greed. The Creator tried to send messages to tell earth's children to live in a better way, but the humans acted as if they were deaf. So Creator called all the spirits of water together and covered all of the lands. Only the minerals and a few plants and animals survived.

The Creator was sad because humans were needed to fulfill her vision. A spirit woman who lived in the clouds was sad also. She asked Creator for a spirit man so she could bring forth life. One appeared and they mated.

On earth the remaining animals were also lonely for the sort of companionship humans had given them in early days when humans observed the law of unity. The animals saw the spirit woman and decided to invite her to bring forth life on earth. But they knew she and her children would need land on which to walk. While they sat in council a giant turtle—a tortoise—came and volunteered his back as a place on which the spirit woman could live.

The spirit woman accepted this sacrifice of the tortoise. She and the animals crawled onto turtle's back and saw it was a large and fine home. The spirit woman instructed the water animals to dive into the water and find a morsel of earth. When the small but tenacious muskrat succeeded, the spirit woman dropped the earth all around the edge of the tortoise's back.

"Turtle," said the spirit woman, "you may now return to your life. But, in honor of the sacrifice you made, this land shall be called Turtle Island. Even though you tend to be a creature of the water you will also be thought of as the creature of this land, this part of the earth."[1]

That is how the tortoise came to represent the Earth Mother, and how turtle became the totem of the Earth clan.

Working with the tortoise will teach you about ancient wisdom, about sacrifice, about the joy of service, and the rewards of working well and being who you truly are. It will also teach you patience, endurance, stability, dependability, and the value of experience.

FATHER SUN—LIZARD

The animal associated with the Center Circle stone honoring Father Sun is the lizard, a truly sun-loving member of the reptilian family. The sun sometimes hides from view behind the clouds. The lizard often slips out of sight behind some rocks or shrubbery. Most often, the lizard is only in full sight when the sun is also out in all his glory.

There are almost 4,000 species of lizards living all over the world. These reptiles live in trees, burrows, semiaquatic, and terrestrial dwellings. Lizards appear to have mastered gravity as they dart up and down walls and even walk upside down on ceilings, attaching onto any surface with their gripping toes. Their colors vary from green, brown, gray, and black to some bright colors. Their most distinguishing features are their scaly, leathery skin and bulging eyes. Certain lizards are known to live for more than fifty years.

Lizards are revered in some Native cultures because of their ability to blend with the earth. Other Natives keep them in homes because of their expertise as fly catchers. Lizards avoid human contact, a good survival mechanism because some lizards are killed for their leathery skins, or stuffed as novelty tourist items.

Lizards are a good omen and should be smiled on just as you would smile about a sun-filled day. When the lizard appears it is a sign that Father Sun is shining warmly on you. Lizard comes to remind you that life can be as warm and cheerful as sunbeams caressing you on a warm day. Working with lizard can help you be more optimistic and adaptable.

GRANDMOTHER MOON—LOON

The animal associated with the Center Circle stone honoring Grandmother Moon is the loon, that wild member of the duck world whose eerie sound has inspired some to art and others to madness. In English a synonym for *madness* is *loony,* and *loony* is also a word used to describe the state to which the full moon brings some people.

Loons have strong aquatic capabilities. These gregarious birds are great swimmers and divers but are not terrific flyers. The loon has three separate calls: a wail, a yodel, and a tremulous laugh. It is the latter that is most eerie.

Because loons mate for life some Native people used them to symbolize fidelity. In the sacred art of the Ojibwa people, mating loons are depicted as creating the transformation from which all life comes. Through being faithful to the mystery of life, as well as to each other, loons create something that did not exist before.

---

1. This legend appears in its entirety in *The Medicine Wheel.*

Through the loon and the eerie mystery evoked by this bird, you can come to know some of the magic aspects of Grandmother Moon, weaver of dreams, leader of feminine life, and controller of the waters on the earth, as well as within all of earth's children.

THE TURTLE CLAN,
ELEMENT OF EARTH—TURTLE

The animal associated with the Center Circle stone honoring the element of earth is the turtle. This small member of the reptile class, like the tortoise who represents the Earth Mother herself, is one of the most ancient and longest-living animals on the earth today. As a smaller sister to the tortoise who gave the people a home on the earth, the turtle is honored by many Native peoples. The North American continent is often called Turtle Island to show respect for this animal and the service its giant ancestor gave to the people.

The body of the turtle is covered with a sturdy shell from which only the head, four legs, and a pointed, leathery tail emerge. Turtles lay eggs in holes covered with sand so that the heat from the sun incubates them, much as the earth herself needs the heat of the sun for life to come forth.

When antagonized or pestered, turtles withdraw within their protective shell. They have great reason to withdraw these days. They are becoming endangered in some countries because people hunt them for food. Turtles are also frequent casualties of the garbage and pollution that is dumped into the waters of the world. The endangering of this strong ancient animal is a sad reminder of the danger in which human irresponsibility is putting the element of earth and the earth herself.

Working with turtle will help you connect with and honor the powerful element of earth. Turtle can teach you how to care for yourself and all of life as you would your closest loved one.

THE FROG CLAN,
ELEMENT OF WATER—FROG

The animal associated with the stone honoring the element of water is the frog. While Ripid-do, a frog chief, caused some of the frog people to live out of the water most of the time, the majority of frogs are happy in their watery world.[2]

Ripid-do became dissatisfied with all the Creator gave to him. He was convinced that if he could live on the mountain he saw in the distance he would have all the good things of life and the biggest, most delicious bugs in existence. He talked about his unhappiness until all the other frogs also became dissatisfied. One day Ripid-do decided to lead the other frogs to the mountain, even though a voice inside told him this was not the right thing to do.

As Ripid-do and the frogs who followed him climbed the mountain they noticed most of the other animals coming down, and they noticed steam and melting waters. Ripid-do told himself this was all a trick of the Creator to keep him and the frogs from life's good things. As things became worse, Ripid-do realized he had put all who came with him in danger.

He prayed to the Creator offering to sacrifice himself if the other animals could be saved. Creator answered the prayer by letting all the other frogs jump into a waterfall that carried them back to their ponds and rivers. As Ripid-do prepared to die, a gust of wind carried him into a tree so high on the mountain he was safe from the volcanic eruption.

2. This legend appears in its entirety in *The Medicine Wheel.*

"Little brother," said the Creator, "since you so much wanted to live on the mountain, this is where you'll be from now on. You'll be smaller than you were before, and you'll no longer live in the water. The trees will be your home and the home of your children for all generations to come."

That is how the tree frog, that land-locked relative of the water-happy frogs, came to be.

A distinguishing trait of the frog is their metamorphosis from tadpole to adult frog. The frog is one of the few four-limbed animals capable of such transformation. In this process they are like the element they honor—water—which can transform from vapor to liquid to solid—from steam to rain to hail, snow, and ice.

The green, slick-skinned frog is characterized by his ability to leap and hop, springing from danger and captivity. His voice is also distinctive. Frogs do love to serenade all who will listen. As the song of the loon stirs people, so does the song of the frog. It seems amazing that such a small creature can have such a big voice. So it is with water. From many tiny drops coming together, the ocean is formed.

Frog can teach you about transformation, communication, mystery, joy, humor, and evolution.

THE THUNDERBIRD CLAN, ELEMENT OF FIRE—THUNDERBIRD

The animal associated with the stone honoring the element of fire is the thunderbird. The Big Hawk Who Hides Behind the Clouds is a very important symbol to Native people. To some, thunderbird calls the Thunder Beings; to others, they are one and the same; to others still the thunderbird is the servant of the thunderers, the symbol and messenger of these beings of fire.[3]

The thunderbird is said to be the biggest hawk to have ever lived on earth. This magnificent hawk was not only good and kindly but very powerful as well. He could sing beautiful songs that would gather others to counsel. He could also sing a song that would draw the rain clouds near. His songs made small game surrender to his mighty talons.

Alas, this mighty bird fell prey to his own ego. He got swept up in his own greatness and became awed with himself. In his dance of arrogance during his last time on earth he was raised to Spirit in a burst of fire from a thunderbolt. Creator gave him another chance by making him a servant to the Thunder Beings, where he gained pleasure by serving others and learning his place in the universe.

Thunderbird lives in Spirit now but comes sometimes to teach us about goodness, kindness, cleansing, and healing. He also reminds us of the fiery pain of displaying too much arrogance. Thunderbird teaches us to rise out of our arrogance and go to serve and heal the people.

THE BUTTERFLY CLAN, ELEMENT OF AIR—BUTTERFLY

The animal associated with the stone honoring the element of air is the butterfly, that symbol of regeneration. Because of its ability to change itself so thoroughly—going from caterpillar, to chrysalis to butterfly—the butterfly is a universal symbol of change, life, and hope.

3. The legend appears in its entirety in *The Medicine Wheel*.

Butterflies came to the people many years ago when a healer named She Who Weaves Rainbows in the Air passed into the spirit world. While she lived she was always helped in her healing by beautiful colored crawlers who would sit near her or crawl up on her shoulder adding the energy of their colors, and their power, to hers. These crawlers were afraid that, with her death, they would no longer be able to help the people. But one crawler knew better. This one asked to be buried with She Who Weaves Rainbows in the Air, knowing that when his body died, his spirit would merge with hers and, together, they would continue bringing healing to the people.[4]

After her burial, a beautiful colored flyer came out of the grave of She Who Weaves Rainbows in the Air. It had all the colors of the rainbow spread over its wings. From that time on butterflies have always been with the people brightening the air and bringing healing to all who will accept it.

Butterflies resemble moths but are distinguished by the beautiful hues of their delicate wings. Butterflies are found worldwide. They are often fearless, fluttering close by humans, gently spreading joy and beauty wherever they go.

The butterfly teaches us to not be afraid of change and transformation for, as warm and fuzzy as a caterpillar may be, it is the butterfly that lives fully and beautifully after having endured the fear and darkness of the unknown to reach the light outside of the cocoon.

THE SPIRIT KEEPER ANIMALS

.....

The four animals connected with the powers of the directions are all strong members of the animal kingdom who, at one time, wanted to be chief of all the animals. Through the intervention of One Greater they each chose instead to merge their power with that of one of the cardinal winds and thus make the circle of life stronger for all of the people. Because of their service to their own kingdom, and to that of the two-leggeds, Native people have long honored the Spirit Keeper animals.

WABOOSE, SPIRIT KEEPER OF THE
NORTH—WHITE BUFFALO

The Spirit Keeper of the North, Waboose, is represented by the white buffalo. The white buffalo is the most honored member of this revered animal family. In the stories of many Native people it is White Buffalo Woman who brings the gift of the pipe, the gift of Spirit to the people.

White Buffalo Woman is a spirit woman who goes by many names in many tribes. To the Ojibwa people, she is Daybreak Star Woman. To the Lakota, she is White Buffalo Calf Woman. To the Navajo she is Spider Woman. To the Nootka people she is Copper Woman. This spirit woman is part of the sacred feminine principle and aspect of the Creator, perhaps best described as She Who Brings Forth All Things. White Buffalo Woman brings all the important medicines to the people: the knowledge of life, birth, and death; the practice of healing; understanding of the feminine cycles; the first medicine; the sacred pipe; the sweat lodge; and many of the most sacred of ceremonies.

In a similar way, the buffalo gave all of its physical being to help the people

4. This legend appears in its entirety in *The Medicine Wheel*.

to live. The buffalo was greatly respected by Native people. Then the Europeans came.

It is estimated there were 50 million buffalo killed on the Great Plains of the United States after the arrival of the Europeans. So many buffalo were killed they almost became extinct. This carnage happened because the Europeans used the buffalo for sport. Hunters rode the railroads as they were being built, to see how many buffalo they could shoot as the train sped across the land. They would kill them and leave them to rot. Other hunters killed them and only removed the tongue, which was sold as a delicacy in Europe.

No longer roaming free, American domestic buffalo now graze peacefully in areas where they are being raised for meat, hide, or regeneration of the species. These large, brawny animals stand nearly six feet tall, weigh close to a ton and a half, and are magnificent to behold.

When the buffalo serves with Waboose, she wears the white coat of snow, the white coat of age and wisdom, the white coat that reminds us to look for the light despite the darkness surrounding us.

WABUN, SPIRIT KEEPER OF THE EAST—EAGLE

Wabun the Spirit Keeper of the East is represented by the golden eagle, the messenger bird to the Great Spirit, one of the winged ones who flies highest and sees life most clearly. The eagle is sacred to most Native people because of its ability to take messages to the Creator. The eagle feather provided the badge of honor for medicine people, for chiefs, and for warriors because the eagle has gifts and lessons for all of these areas of life. Like medicine people, the eagle can soar to the Creator. Like chiefs, they earn the respect of all of the other winged ones. Like warriors, they fight fiercely to protect their territory and their young.

This mighty bird of prey is an inspiring aerial acrobat. Although eagles have long touched men's imaginations, humans have hunted the eagle to the point of endangering the species. The remaining eagles can be found widely scattered in Europe, Asia, and North America.

Although Eagle the Spirit Keeper befriends the two-leggeds, guiding us toward Spirit, the majestic bird that lives on the earth plane avoids humans in order to protect his young and his life.

When serving with Wabun, the eagle wears the golden feathers of the dawn, the golden light of wisdom that reminds us each moment is a new beginning.

SHAWNODESE, SPIRIT KEEPER OF THE SOUTH—COYOTE

Shawnodese, the Spirit Keeper of the South, is represented by the coyote, that wild and wily teacher of the animal kingdom. There is a whole body of Native mythology dealing with the coyote, the old trickster who is sometimes Creator and sometimes sacred clown. The coyote is the most sacred and most profane of animals. Like loon and frog he is a powerful singer whose song can move humans to freedom or to fear. Coyote brings growth to everyone, but to those who love life he gives the gift of trust. It is trust in life that teaches true survival and real endurance.

Coyote can be found in many rural settings in North America. Smaller than a wolf, the coyote has proven adaptable to the onslaught of civilization. Coyote's most distinguishing attributes are his swiftness, sharp senses, doglike features, and song. On many evenings in the country, the yipping and howling of coyote pierces the quiet night, reminding all the two-leggeds who can hear that although they now predominate on earth, they are not the only species in existence.

How people react to coyote teaches a lot about them. Those who love life and the earth are inspired by coyote's song and his ability to outsmart the civilization that has tried to destroy him. Those who fear all that is natural also fear coyote and try to destroy him by shooting, poison, or traps. Fearful ones depict coyote as a thief, one who eats domestic livestock, like chickens. Coyote prefers to eat natural, free-roaming animals like mice or rabbits but he will lunch on an occasional chicken or small domestic animal in areas where civilization has killed all of his natural prey.

When he serves with Shawnodese, the coyote's coat is the mottled color of the sun at midday shining on the earth. Sometimes when serving with Shawnodese the coyote's coat is so mottled he seems to disappear. It is then he does his most powerful work.

MUDJEKEEWIS, SPIRIT KEEPER OF THE WEST—GRIZZLY BEAR

The animal associated with Mudjekeewis, the Spirit Keeper of the West, is the grizzly bear, a powerful member of the bear family. All bears are able to go within, to make the long sleep, and to use that time to look at life and dream. When he awakens the bear knows what to eat to bring back his power and to heal himself. The bear moves slowly, with determination. He is strong but always just. For these reasons he is a very sacred animal to Native peoples. The Bear clan was usually the clan of teachers, healers, or leaders.

Grizzly bears can stand up, and their front paws have good grasping abilities. They have acute hearing and a great sense of smell. They are covered with a thick, grizzly fur coat (hence the name), can weigh more than 900 pounds, and stand taller than eight feet. No wonder they strike awe—and sometimes fear—in human hearts.

When not hibernating, grizzly bears like to hunt, eat, and bathe. They are solitary beings except during the mating season.

Bear will not attack man unless attacked first. Grizzlies have become largely extinct in North America, exterminated by hunters, except in restricted areas such as Yellowstone National Park, Alaska, the Yukon, and British Columbia.

When the bear serves with Mudjekeewis he wears a coat the color of night to remind us of the void out of which all things come. Among this black are silver hairs. These remind us that if we reach maturity we will always realize that, even in the darkest void, light shines if we know how to look for it.

THE TWELVE TOTEM ANIMALS
· · · · ·

THE EARTH RENEWAL MOON—SNOW GOOSE

Snow goose is the animal totem associated with the Earth Renewal Moon (December 22 to January 19). The snow goose, a beautiful white bird, has been called the "goose from beyond the north wind" because of the direction these geese go when they migrate in the spring.

Some species of snow goose travel 5,000 miles each year, flying in a loose V pattern. The snow geese are very gregarious. It is not unusual to see 20,000 or 30,000 birds all stopping to eat at the same location. At their nesting grounds they show respect for tradition by allowing the experienced nesters to have the first choice of sites. Both goose and gander stay with the eggs.

Snow geese are nitpickers. They will spend hours picking mosquitoes or other insects off each other. Geese have much keener vision than humans. The snow goose honks but when several thousand geese are approaching, the sound can be mistaken for anything from a pack of wild dogs to yapping coyotes.

Working with the snow goose can teach you about the creative mystery, the universal powers, tradition, perfection, stability, community, ceremony, vision, and evolution.

THE REST AND
CLEANSING MOON—OTTER

Otter is the animal totem associated with the Rest and Cleansing Moon (January 20 to February 18). The otter is one of the most playful animals in the wild. Both river and sea otters exist in the United States.

Otters are members of the weasel family who depend on water for their existence. River otters are found in most of the large lakes, marshes, and rivers of the western United States. Sea otters are larger than those of the rivers. They are now only found off the northern California coast. The sea otter almost became extinct early in this century because hunters massacred most of them for their fur. The sea otter now spends most of its time in the ocean eating, sleeping, sunning, playing, giving birth, and raising its young.

All otters have large appetites. One of the few animals who can utilize tools, they use rocks to open up their shellfish dinners. Otters have a wide vocal range consisting of chips, squeals, screeches, hiccups, chuckles, and hisses when they are angry. Some of their calls carry for as far as a mile. When otters are not eating, hunting, or sunning they are most often playing.

Otters have warm and active home lives. Both parents assist in raising the young who stay with them longer than the young of most wild animals. Otters are ardent companions to each other. A mate will mourn the death of his or her companion.

Because of the otters' exemplary home life, nobility, curiosity, inventiveness, and playfulness, Native people recognized the power of the otter. Some of the most powerful medicine bags in certain tribes were made from the fur of otters. Otter medicine is so strong to some tribes that it is secret until you reach a certain degree of initiation.

Working with otter can teach you about playfulness, nurturing, originality, inventiveness, nobility, curiosity, humanitarianism, companionship, and child rearing.

THE BIG WINDS MOON—COUGAR

Cougar is the animal totem associated with the Big Winds Moon (February 19 to March 20). The cougar, the lion of this continent, has not been given the same respect as its African counterpart. The cougar has been misunderstood and feared, often resulting in its wanton slaughter. The cougar—also known as the mountain lion, puma, panther, screamer, painter, and ghost cat—is the largest member of the feline family on this continent. Cougars measure between seven and nine feet, and weigh 150 to 300 pounds. Their black or brown-tipped tails and ear tufts never seem to stay still. Cougars were found all across the United States before the spread of this current civilization. Now they are found in the western United States, Florida, Canada, and Mexico.

Cougars are the best climbers of all felines. They are swift runners who have large individual territories. Their social structure does not allow these territories to overlap.

Cougars are hunters. They like the chase and will often join efforts with their mates or relations to obtain better results. They do not hunt for more food than they eat. They only hunt livestock when their natural food supplies have been depleted. Female cougars are better hunters than the males.

When cougars mate, the female frequently is the aggressor. Most litters are born in the spring and consist of only two kits. Although the mother cougar is very loving and devoted to her kits, male cougars do not have much to do with them.

Cougars can teach you about speed, grace, territoriality, sensitivity, mystery, communicating without words, stalking, and initiative.

THE BUDDING TREES MOON—RED HAWK

Red hawk is the animal totem associated with the Budding Trees Moon (March 21 to April 19). The red-tailed hawk is the only hawk with a broad wing span and a fan-shaped red tail. It is a large hawk, which has been called the chicken hawk by farmers who incorrectly feared the birds were stealing their poultry.

Red-tailed hawks are sometimes attacked by crows, magpies, owls, other hawks, and songbirds in territorial disputes. These attacks rarely end in injury. Red-tailed hawks can live to fourteen years of age. They usually nest in tall trees, cacti, yuccas, or on the faces of cliffs. Both parents help raise the young. Red-tailed hawks often return year after year to the same nest. Hawks used to be found all over the United States. Now they live mainly in the western states, Mexico, and Canada. Red-tailed hawks are very adaptable and can survive almost anywhere man leaves them alone. Their voice in flight can sound like steam escaping from a kettle. Red-tailed hawks are magnificent fliers, especially during their mating dances.

Red-tailed hawks are very special to Native people. Pueblo peoples referred to them as "red eagles" and felt that red-tailed hawks, like the eagle, had a special connection with the sky and the sun. Because hawks are high fliers who can see the earth clearly from their heights, their feathers were often used ceremonially to carry prayers to the sun and the Creator. Hawk feathers, as well as eagle, were also used in healing ceremonies. Southwestern people used them in ceremonies to pray for rain. To the Ojibwa, the Red-Tailed Hawk clan was one of the leadership clans. Its members have the gifts of deliberation and foresight.

Working with the red hawk can teach you about adaptability, flying, survival, far- and clear-sightedness, prayer, leadership, deliberation, optimism, intensity, and openness.

THE FROGS RETURN MOON—BEAVER

Beaver is the animal totem associated with the Frogs Return Moon (April 20 to May 20). The beaver is, apart from man, the only animal capable of changing its environment drastically to provide for its own peace, security, and contentment. The beaver is the largest rodent in the United States. Adult beavers weigh between thirty and seventy pounds. Beavers never stop growing, and can grow to three to four feet in length.

Beavers do not make many sounds. Occasionally they bark, hiss, or squeal, but usually they only make a soft mew in the privacy of their lodge. They slap the water with their tails to warn of danger. Beavers mate for life. They are affectionate parents who keep their children around for two years, or until the next litter comes. Old males who lose their mates sometimes become surly.

The beaver is a land mammal that spends a lot of time in the water. Its body is amazingly engineered to suit its habits and habitat. Beavers' adaptable bodies could have made them the dominant animal on earth except that beavers have two things that men desired: beaver fur (long used for making gentlemen's hats) and a gland that secretes castoreum. Castoreum was regarded as a cure-all from the time of the early Greeks until the eighteenth century. Beavers were in such demand that the search for them probably did as much to motivate European exploration of the Americas as anything else. Because humans wanted their parts, beavers were almost driven to extinction by the 1800s. Finally humans discovered that beavers helped maintain the water table and were of great value to fishing, wildlife, vegetation, and aesthetics, so they let the species live.

Native people had also valued beaver fur and meat and had used the castoreum to effect healing, but they had hunted beaver with moderation and respect. When the Europeans came they encouraged the Natives to hunt more beavers and offered the most prized trade goods in exchange for beaver fur. These practices helped to erode the traditional Native culture in some areas.

Working with the beaver can teach you about stability, balance, tradition, true value, adaptability with the environment, healing, affection, tenacity, hard work, and self-reliance.

THE CORNPLANTING MOON—DEER

Deer is the animal totem associated with the Cornplanting Moon (May 21 to June 20). The deer is a sensitive, graceful, and alert creature. His beauty brings joy to all who see him.

Despite some differences in size and habit among different species of deer, they all tend to range between two and four feet at the shoulder and between 50 and 400 pounds. Deer have a bleating voice but snort when excited, squeal when under attack or in pain, and sometimes have a special bleat with which to call their fawns. The fawns of all deer are spotted when they are born, to camouflage them. Fawns are also born without a scent to afford them greater protection. Bucks have sets of antlers they lose and regenerate every year.

Deer live in herds, or in small groups with others of their own sex, except during the mating season when otherwise friendly bucks will fight using their now fully grown antlers. After mating season an older doe usually leads the herd for the winter. In the spring the does give birth, often to twins or even triplets. Multiple births sometimes cause overpopulation. Cougars, coyotes, dogs, bears, bobcats, forest fires, humans, and automobiles are the killers of deer. It is estimated that more than 400,000 deer are killed annually in the United States on highways and other roads.

Deer were a very important part of the circle of life for many Native peoples. They provided staple food for a number of tribes who would honor the deer's gift through ceremonies, dances, and prayers.

To some tribes, notably the Huichol in Mexico, the deer was the most important of animals. The Huichol believe the deer represents the heart and is the gatekeeper to the spirit world. The Deer Dance is the most sacred dance for the Huichol, one that helps them pierce the veil between worlds.

Working with the deer can teach you about adaptability, camouflage, grace, beauty, speed, healing, sensitivity, alertness, creativity, your heart energy, and your connection with Spirit.

THE STRONG SUN MOON—FLICKER

Flicker is the animal totem associated with the Strong Sun Moon (June 21 to July 22). Flickers are woodpeckers. There are two kinds in the United States: the yellow-shafted flicker, found east of the Great Plains, and the red-shafted

flicker, found west of the Great Plains. Both types can be found in a variety of places: woods, farms, and even suburbs. Flickers are drummers. They play their song on dead limbs, tin roofs, and wooden houses, sometimes to extract insects and sometimes for the sheer joy of playing. During mating, flickers present an especially magnificent display of their musical talents.

Flickers dig a gourd-shaped hole in a tree trunk for their nest. Often other birds use it later. Like most birds, flickers are good and caring parents. They nurture their young until it is time to allow them to fly on their own.

The flicker is a special bird to many Native people. Some legends say he has red wings because he went too close to a fire set by the Earthquake Spirit to try to put it out. The flames from this fire colored his wings and tail red. Native people particularly value flickers because they drum so well. Red flicker feathers are associated with blood and are often presented to war spirits. Red feathers on prayer sticks are considered war offerings, against either human or spiritual enemies. Members of some medicine societies wore flicker feathers in their hair to identify their affiliation.

Working with flicker can teach you about communicating, music, joy, nurturing, courage, protection, tenacity, and your connection with the universal.

THE RIPE BERRIES MOON—STURGEON

Sturgeon is the animal totem associated with the Ripe Berries Moon (July 23 to August 22). The sturgeon is known as the king of fishes. A primitive fish that has probably existed on the earth since around the time the dinosaurs disappeared, the sturgeon comes in a variety of sizes, but can reach twelve-foot lengths and at least 300-pound weights.

Sturgeons were considered the royalty of fishes among the Native people who lived in the Great Lakes area. In the Ojibwa nation there is a Sturgeon clan that is one of the teaching clans. To the Ojibwa people the sturgeon represents depth and strength.

The European people who came to North America did not have the same respect for this fish. At first they considered it a nuisance when sturgeons got in their nets. Later they almost fished it to extinction when they discovered the value of its roe, which is better known as caviar. The sturgeon is rarely found now.

Working with the sturgeon can teach you about your determination, perseverance, depth, knowledge, generosity, strength, and sexuality.

THE HARVEST MOON—BROWN BEAR

Brown bear is the animal totem associated with the Harvest Moon (August 23 to September 22). The brown bear is the same species as the black bear. In fact, some females will have one brown and one black cub in the same litter. Brown bears make their dens in holes, in caves, beneath fallen trees, in deserted buildings, or beneath waterfalls. They are generally careful and quiet creatures. Brown bears are omnivorous, eating anything they can get their paws on. Among their favorite foods are honey and berries. Their only enemies are humans and forest fires.

Bears are curious just like their cousin the raccoon. Bears are slow, deliberate, and pleasure oriented. They take time to watch and learn from the things around them. They only hurry in the fall when they must eat enough to sustain them through their long winter sleep. The bear's hibernation is not a complete one. During the latter time of hibernation females have their cubs, so they have to be awake enough to nurse them.

Bears have a cheerful and good nature and share many abilities with humans. They can stand on two legs and walk for a short distance. They can climb trees; remove honey from bee trees; and spear fish, using their claws as spears.

To Native peoples, the bear was a very special animal. In many legends of the animal world, such as the one telling how the Spirit Keeper animals were designated, the bear is acknowledged as the head of the council of the animals. In that legend bear had long been chief of the animal council but his leadership was being challenged by buffalo, eagle, and coyote, all of whom felt they had attributes that would make them good leaders. As the debate between advocates of these different animals threatened the unity of the council of animals, Mudjekeewis, Spirit Keeper of the West, came into the council and told the four debating animals that because of the special qualities each had, each one would serve with one of the Spirit Keepers. In this way all of their gifts would be utilized, and the animal council would stay united, with bear, who would also serve with Mudjekeewis, as the chief. Bear is council chief because of his fairness, his strength, and his courage. In most tribes the Bear clan was either the medicine, leadership, or defense clan.[5]

From working with bear you can learn about deliberation, pleasure, observation, slow and steady movement, fairness, courage, strength, healing, and teaching.

THE DUCKS FLY MOON—RAVEN

Raven is the animal totem associated with the Ducks Fly Moon (September 23 to October 23). The raven is usually an all-black bird with a wedge-shaped tail that is often mistaken for the smaller crow. The raven is as large as a red hawk. Although ravens are found all over the world, in the United States they are most often found in the west. Their song is a loud croak.

Sometimes aggressive, ravens are most often wary. They are intelligent birds who know how to drop shellfish from the air in order to break the shells. They are omnivorous and capable of riding the winds with as much enjoyment as their hawk brothers. Ravens are both group oriented and very defensive of their territory. Some ravens pair for life. It is said these birds have tribal councils.

To Native peoples, ravens are considered birds of balance between man and nature. Almost all tribes have a legend about the raven explaining why he is black. In all of these legends the raven begins as a white bird whose color was changed either as a punishment for wrongdoing or because of danger undertaken in an effort to help man. This duality in the legends indicates the duality Native people feel about the raven. To some, the raven is a bad omen; to others, a good one. The Pueblo peoples connect the raven with the kachina spirits. Ravens have been given credit both with bringing the dark clouds that yield the rain and with holding them away.

THE FREEZE UP MOON—SNAKE

Snake is the animal totem associated with the Freeze Up Moon (October 24 to November 21). The snake, or serpent, is that old, mysterious, maligned, and misunderstood member of the vertebrate family. In the world there are close to 2,500 species of snakes. In the United States there are 114.

Snakes are a carnivorous, limbless reptile with expandable jaws. They mostly eat small animals such as rats and frogs. They will also eat insects. Because of their dietary preferences, snakes are an essential part of the balance

---

5. The legend appears in its entirety in *The Medicine Wheel*.

of nature. When man has wantonly murdered snakes he has usually been overrun by rats and mice.

Snakes are very adaptable to their environment and are exquisitely sensitive to touch and vibrations. They are cold-blooded so depend on their environment for warmth and hibernate in winter. They can change their color to blend with the land that surrounds them, and shed their skins. Snakes have no voice, but some hiss. Rattlesnakes buzz their rattles. Despite their reputation for being emotionless, the courtship of snakes can be a very warm affair. Most snakes, even those of the poisonous varieties, avoid humans and strike only in self-defense.

The snake was respected in most Native cultures. The feathered serpent, an ancient symbol to South and Central American tribes, represented justice and transformation. The Hopi people believe the snake is a messenger to and from other realms and has the power to bring the life-giving rains. The Ojibwa people have a Snake clan, which is a medicine clan. They believe the snake represents patience, because he is so slow to anger. Many Native peoples used the snake to represent the life energy that flows through humans. Snake is also a symbol of the feminine powers, and of healing.

Working with the snake can teach you about mystery, the realms of creation, deep transformation, the balance of nature, adaptability, sensitivity, communication, sexuality, regeneration, patience, self-defense, justice, healing, the feminine within you, and your own life force.

THE LONG SNOWS MOON—ELK

Elk is the animal totem associated with the Long Snows Moon (November 22 to December 21). The elk, also known as wapiti, is the largest and most regal member of the deer family. Elk antlers can resemble tree branches.

Elk live in the woodlands and seem to have a sense of responsibility for one another. When snows are heavy they will take turns breaking the trail. Sometimes elk form a big circle; prance around, sometimes breaking into a gallop of joy; and seem to dance together. Elk are fast: able to go at thirty miles an hour for short distances. They are also able to leap fences as high as ten feet.

Elk have few natural enemies. Cougars, bears, and wolves will sometimes succeed in bringing down a calf, or a weak or sick animal. None of them are a match for the bull in his prime. Before 1900, however, most of the elk in the United States were slaughtered by hunters. Often the only reason for the killing was to make two of their teeth into jewelry valued by a fraternal organization.

Most of the year elk, like deer, live in same-gender herds. When the mating season is about to begin, bull elk try to get as many cows as they can into their harem, and they will fervently defend their harem from the approach of any other bulls.

In the spring, when it is time to calf, the cows go to the valleys. Calves are hidden for the first part of their lives while their mothers go out to browse. Like fawns, calves are born without a smell to afford them protection.

Native people had great respect for the elk: for her speed, her beauty, her strength, and concern for her people. In some tribes if a man dreamed of an elk, or saw one in vision, it made him one who could attend and speak in the council of women.

From working with elk you can learn about strength, responsibility, joy, speed, agility, possessiveness, protection, regality, justice, and wisdom.

THE SPIRIT PATH ANIMALS
.....
The Northern Spirit Path Animals

CLEANSING—RACCOON

The animal associated with cleansing, the first Spirit Path position of the North, is the raccoon. The raccoon is a clean animal, one that values hygiene enough to wash off its food in water whenever possible. The raccoon, like the coyote, is a good survivor. He can often be found having a midnight dinner from a garbage can in some of the better parts of many urban areas.

Raccoon is recognized mostly by the black circles on his tail and the dark band across the eyes and face that give him the appearance of a little bandit. This intelligent animal is happy on land or water but is most at home in the trees.

Raccoons will occasionally feast from an orchard or chicken coop when fishing in streams or foraging in the wild is unsuccessful. Although farmers and trappers readily hunt raccoons, they are still abundant in many areas in the United States and Canada. Variations of the raccoon family can be found in most parts of the world.

Native people thought of the raccoon as a sacred clown and trickster, rather like the little brother of coyote. Raccoons do seem to have a sense of humor and a mischievousness that can allow them to outwit humans in many situations. If you have ever tried to stop a raccoon from sorting through your garbage, you will understand what this means. If you are looking for cleansing, raccoon can teach you to peel off your mask that you may be hiding behind. Working with raccoon can also teach you about merriment, contentment, boldness, wiliness, humor, intelligence, survival, and tenacity.

RENEWAL—EARTHWORM

The animal associated with renewal, the second Spirit Path position of the North, is the earthworm. This small creature has a great purpose, for it is the earthworm that creates and renews the very soil of the Earth Mother. Both they and the earth are rejuvenated by this activity.

Earthworms are never thicker than one's finger, although they can be very long. Earthworms, which can be found worldwide, not only renew the earth but also regenerate their own bodies. They can replace missing parts whether head or tail, forming a new organ to replace one that has been broken away.

Native people respected these tiny crawlers because of their important work with the Earth Mother and because of their own power to regenerate themselves. Earthworms were considered an essential part of the circle of life.

If you want to learn about renewal, repair, healing, transformation, and regeneration in your life, work with the earthworm for he has much to share.

PURITY—DOLPHIN

The animal associated with the third Spirit Path position of the North, purity, is the dolphin. This ancient sea mammal has the purity of a child and intelligence beyond our comprehension. Always playful, the dolphin has been known to communicate with fellow dolphins, with other sea creatures, and even with those humans who are threatening his existence.

Dolphins are a cetacean found in all warm and mild waters. They love to eat fish—such as herring and sardines—in massive amounts. While chasing after these delicacies in recent times they have too often found themselves caught in the nets of fishermen trapping tuna. Sadly, large numbers of dolphins have been brutally killed in this way, then cast aside. There has been much protest against this inhumane practice and slowly the tide is turning in favor of the dolphin. But the fight for their lives is not over yet. Before you buy tuna be sure to check that it is caught in a way that does not endanger dolphins.

Dolphins are kind to and indulgent of humans. There are numerous accounts of these intelligent beings communicating warnings of danger to sailors and ships. Frequent are the tales of dolphins guiding a boat through storms and hazardous coral reefs. Native people have stories of dolphins saving humans from drowning and of guiding fishermen to good places to fish.

Dolphins are sea mammals. They must surface and breath air at times. They bear their young in the water, then keep them close to teach them. Dolphins are gregarious and social beings. There are many reports today of dolphins trying to communicate psychically with humans in an effort to help save the planet.

Dolphin teaches you how to live a path of purity even in the midst of persecution by ignorant forces. Dolphin also teaches about goodness, spiritual attunement, connecting with spirit, communication, social conduct, playfulness, and love.

The Eastern Spirit Path Animals

CLARITY—HUMMINGBIRD

The animal for the first Spirit Path position of the East, clarity, is the hummingbird. Hummingbirds vary from two to eight inches long, although the most common ones are usually very tiny. Hummingbirds eat small insects and nectar found in flowers by thrusting their long beak deep within the blossom. Their little feet are not much use to them but their outstanding wing structure compensates, allowing them to hover and beat out a vibrant hum.

Although contact between human and hummingbird is rare on the physical level, both delight in aspects of each other's presence. Humans love the hummingbird's vibrant, tenacious spirit and graceful, mysterious flight. Consequently they frequently place special hummingbird feeders in their yards for these effervescent birds. The hummingbirds love to hover in front of the feeders and eat. It is mutually gratifying.

The hummingbird is a sacred bird to many Native peoples. They see it as a symbol of getting to the heart of a matter, of clarifying an issue as the tiny hummingbird so quickly gets to the nectar within a flower.

The hummingbird is perceived by some Native people as a doctoring bird, one who can clean out old wounds and old impurities and bring new clarity to any situation. The hummingbird is also considered capable of sewing up wounds, of drawing together the torn aspects of an injury or problem. Working with hummingbird can teach you about clear sight, tenacity, grace, mystery, healing, drawing out the old, and drawing together aspects of your life.

WISDOM—OWL

The animal for the second Spirit Path position of the East, wisdom, is the owl. Distinguishing characteristics of owls are their large heads and big round eyes. Owls are nocturnal and fly silently, which gives them a strong advantage when hunting their prey. Their hearing is impeccable, and it is thought by many that they hunt by sound not sight.

The owl symbolizes many things to different peoples. To some the owl represents all that is wise and good; to others, all that is dark and bad. Owls have been thought to be wise messengers, sometimes the bringer of news of death, frequently the transmitter of old wisdom and knowledge. Owl medicine is thought to be so strong that it should not be mixed with other energies, or worked with lightly or irresponsibly. Some people of Native paths wrap any form of owl medicine in red. It is said that red cloth will help contain the power and keep it separate from other energies. Others will not touch an owl feather. Although much owl medicine is secret, it is said to relate to ancient knowledge of the feminine.

The spotted owl has recently come into the public eye because it has been put on the endangered species list in the United States, with much protest by loggers. The problem comes about because the logging companies are so heavily stripping the woods of the trees in which the spotted owl lives. By destroying the owls' habitat they are also destroying the owls. By placing the owl on the endangered species list, the trees in which they live will now also be protected. Because the trees can no longer be cut down thousands of loggers' jobs are at risk. There are no easy decisions to be made but a few things are certain. The owl was there before the loggers, and the trees protect our planet from acid rain and the greenhouse effect. In effect the spotted owl is bringing a warning for the future. This battle that will indirectly save trees will also assist in forestalling the destruction of the Earth Mother.

If you are looking for answers, ask owl who is all wise. But don't ask unless you're willing to get an answer that may lead you on journeys to unknown territories whether on the spiritual, mental, emotional, or physical plane.

Working with owl teaches about mystery, paradox, life, death, wisdom, the shadow, listening, the feminine, the unknown.

ILLUMINATION—FIREFLY

The animal for illumination, the third Spirit Path position of the East, is the firefly, also known as the lightning bug. This is the insect that punctures the twilight and night sky with its tiny flickering light. The firefly is like illumination: tiny, elusive spots of light within the darkness.

Fireflies are small beetles that emit light. The most radiant ones are found in the tropics. Fireflies have an organ in which the light-producing chemical luciferin is stored. Behind the luciferin is a layer of thick tissue that is thought to work as a reflector.

Adult fireflies have a short life span. They spend their evenings displaying their yellowish, greenish, or reddish lights at regular intervals to signal to the opposite sex. Most females are flightless and attach to plants, where they flash signals that will draw a mate to them. It is the firefly's mating dance that illuminates the night.

Although some people try to capture fireflies, captivity means death to these small beings. It is best simply to watch their beauty and allow their mating dance and their lives to continue.

Native people were as entranced by these small spots of flying night light as children and open adults are today. Because of their ability to light up the night sky some Native peoples considered them to be related to the Thunder Beings.

Fireflies produce a feeling of wonder, of awe, and of appreciation for all the small but miraculous parts of the circle of life. Such awe and appreciation is critical to illumination.

Working with the firefly can teach you about light and darkness, about illumination, about intensity, awe, appreciation, wonder, mating, the life force, the continuation, and continuity of life.

The Southern Spirit Path Animals

GROWTH—RABBIT

The animal that represents growth, the first Spirit Path position of the South, is the rabbit. The rabbit is known as a very prolific animal, one that is expert in growing more of its own kind. Individual rabbits also grow up rapidly, often reaching full size within a relatively short period of time. With their air of innocence, and their instinctual propensity both for individual and species growth, rabbits teach us of the reality of the quality of growth, always there whether or not we ask for it.

There are more than seventy species of rabbits that can be found all over the world. All of them are small, furry, have long ears, and strong hindquarters. Rabbits are fast and cunning and have excellent hearing. They run, they jump, and they will eat just about any vegetation. They are extremely prolific. It has been estimated that one rabbit couple can have more than 13 million descendants within three years.

Most rabbits are not keen on captivity, but some have been known to make good pets. Most frequently they are hunted or raised for food.

Native people respected the rabbit as a symbol of fertility and as a stable provider of sustenance for the human kingdom. The rabbit was also considered to symbolize innocence.

Through working with rabbit you can learn not to fear growing beyond your present boundaries. You can learn to stretch to become more than you are. Rabbit also teaches cunning, listening, speed, fertility on all levels, sustenance, and innocence.

TRUST—SALMON

The animal that represents trust, the second Spirit Path position of the South, is the salmon. Salmon is a powerful swimmer who is born with the knowledge and trust to return each year to the same territory where untold salmon before him have come to spawn and then to die.

Salmon will do anything to swim back up stream to their spawning grounds, sometimes against great odds. This may mean throwing themselves over falls or accelerating swiftly with much of their bodies out of water.

Different members of the large salmon family can be found in the Atlantic, the Pacific, the Great Lakes, Siberia, and other areas of the world. All salmon have bare heads, a forked caudal fin, and a dorsal fin of medium length.

Traditionally, salmon was a main staple for Natives of the Pacific Northwest. Salmon was also highly respected by these people for its courage, loyalty, strength, and respect for tradition. Salmon is one of the most important totems to Northwest Coast peoples, commanding the same reverence as eagle and bear.

Salmon can teach you to trust whatever your life calling is, to listen to your inner voice, and to follow where it leads you. Salmon also teaches determination, the power of instinct, sustenance, strength, intuition, and the ability to follow your vision.

LOVE—WOLF

The animal that represents love, the third Spirit Path position of the South, is the wolf. The wolf, often portrayed by man as a loner, is far from it. The wolf is a loving family and community animal who often places the welfare of the pack above its own. Wolves mate for life and are loving and generous partners and parents.

The wolf is a beautiful, regal animal, lean flanked but powerfully built. Wolf has a long nose; bright oblong eyes; a strong jaw; erect ears; a long, bushy tail; and a coat that is brownish gray with slight black overtones.

Wolves are cunning and known to work as a team to bring down animals much more powerful than themselves. Wolves live in packs with a fascinating and complex social system. Although once found worldwide with large numbers in North America, Europe, and North Africa, they have been brought to near extinction. Wolves are now slowly making a comeback. Ecologists feel that wolves should be allowed to exist in remaining wilderness areas to thin the diseased or weak among herds of animals such as deer or caribou. Wolves try to avoid humans.

Native people had great respect for the wolf because of his care for his people, because of his love for family, because of his protective instincts, and because of his discrimination in hunting the weak or sick animals in a herd. The wolf, in some tribes, was considered a guardian totem and a symbol of perseverance.

Wolf can teach you about compassion and loyalty to family, friends, and children. She is a particularly good animal to work with if you have not been taught trust, kinship, and love in your family of origin. If you come from an abusive or dysfunctional background the wolf can teach you to replace your painful, negative patterns with qualities that can help you become a loving adult.

Work with wolf to learn about healthy love, forgiveness, intimacy, trust, functional relationships, community, selflessness, and generosity.

The Western Spirit Path Animals

EXPERIENCE—WHALE

The animal that represents experience, the first Spirit Path position of the West, is the whale. The whale is one of the most ancient mammals on the earth. Some whale species are among the largest animals in the world. They have experienced their watery territory as an unspoiled environment, and they experience it now with all the poisons that the dominant culture has added to the waters.

Whales are cetaceans, mammals adapted to aquatic life. Whales can be as long as ninety feet, and are found worldwide, especially in the North Pacific, North Atlantic, European coasts, and the north coast of Norway.

Man has often shown himself to be whale's enemy. The whaling industry has long profited from their wholesale destruction. The number of whales alive in the world is alarmingly lower than it has been in the past. The fight to save the whale from extinction is far from over.

Like the salmon, the whale was one of the most important animals to Northwest Coast and Alaskan Native people. Its totem is often found next to that of eagle, salmon, and bear. The whale was respected as an important source of the sustenance for Native people, but was also honored as a special messenger from the Creator.

Today many people share this belief. They feel that the whale, like the dolphin, is attempting to develop psychic links with humans in an attempt to help save their waters and the whole of the Earth Mother.

Working with the whale can help teach you about the value of observation; about knowledge based on experience; about harmony with the environment; and about strength, patience, magnificence, and the most ancient of wisdoms.

INTROSPECTION—MOUSE

The animal associated with the second Spirit Path position of the West, introspection, is the mouse. This small animal, with its limited vision and territory, is an expert in looking within. Although the mouse does not see far, it sees clearly what is right beneath its little, twitching nose. This close-up view is often missed by far-seeing individuals who rarely take time to look within and see that what is around them is also within them.

Mice can be found worldwide in abundance. They are small furry rodents with long, pointy, hairless tails. They have beady eyes and little, round ears. They are inward creatures, sleeping much of the time even when they are not officially hibernating. The mouse is a foraging vegetarian that will eat anything it can find. Mice live within a small territory but one they know well.

To some Native people the mouse symbolizes trust and innocence. Because of its small size and limited territory the mouse has few defenses against any who would attack it. It must trust in its own knowledge and routine to keep it safe from danger. Its tiny boundaries also keep mouse innocent about much of what happens in the outside world. Native people, who often spent time enjoying the small miracles or nature, had a keen appreciation for the wonders within the the limited view of the mouse.

The mouse can teach you to appreciate the obvious and to enjoy the wonders of everyday life. Mouse can teach you to see your faults truthfully as well as your gifts. She shows you how your corner of the universe is special, and demonstrates that size has no bearing on the beauty of life.

Through working with mouse you can learn to look within, to have acceptance and satisfaction, to see the small picture clearly, to rest and relax, to regain your innocence, and to trust that life is unfolding as it should. From such observation can come an awareness that will lead to true inner growth.

STRENGTH—ANT

The animal associated with strength, the third Spirit Path position of the West, is the ant. This small insect is capable of lifting and carrying something that weighs four times as much as it does. That is a feat of strength that most other animals, including man, would find hard to duplicate. As a species, ants are also strong. They can survive. They can endure. According to the Hopi prophesies it was the ant people who sheltered humans during some of the previous earth cleansings, and it will be the ant people who inherit the earth if the humans do not get back on the path laid down for them by the Creator.

Ants accomplish their amazing deeds because of their social structure in which the individual's needs are definitely secondary to those of the colony of ants. There is much to be learned from observing the individual and group feats of ants who manage to flourish beneath the feet of most other animals. Ants give an example of strength that comes from forethought, persistence, and courage rather than brute force.

Working with ant can teach you to use your strength for the good of the community of humans, to use it to form lasting relationships that can benefit all involved. Ant teaches about dependability, trust, inner and outer strength, persistence, and balance with all that is around you.

ANIMAL UNDERSTANDING EXERCISE

(We thank Shawnodese for permission to use this exercise.)

What you need. Smudge materials and notebook and pen or tape recorder.

Estimated time. Thirty minutes.

1. Smudge or use whatever cleansing method works best for you.
2. Sit comfortably or lie down. Take a few deep breaths and relax as much as possible.
3. Tell the animal kingdom you wish to learn more about one of the Medicine Wheel animals. Ask an animal that would like to teach you to come into your mind now.
4. Take the first image that comes to mind.
5. Watch the animal that has appeared to you. Observe how it moves, how it sounds.
6. Ask the animal if you can see the world through its eyes for a moment. Only proceed if the animal says yes. Otherwise just observe the animal, then return to usual waking consciousness.
7. If the animal has given you permission, see yourself as that animal. Notice how the world looks. Notice what draws your attention. What would you like to eat? How would you hunt? How do you communicate? What is your dream? What is your purpose? Who eats you? How do you protect yourself? How large is your territory? Do you have a mate? Are you interested in mating? Allow the animal to show you as much of its world as it is comfortable sharing and you are comfortable seeing.
8. Now ask the animal if it can help you to move for a while. If so, return some of your consciousness to your body so that you can move it without having problems. Allow your body to move as the animal moves. Notice how this movement feels.
9. If you have heard sounds the animal makes, begin to make these now.
10. Move and make the noise of the animal that has contacted you for a few minutes, being careful to keep enough awareness of your body and surroundings that you know what is safe and possible for you to do. If you have been contacted by a bird, for example, realize you can flap your wings but you can't fly.
11. Lie down and go back to your original relaxed state.
12. Thank the animal for its gifts to you. Then take a few minutes to contemplate your experience and what it has taught you.
13. Come back to normal awareness.
14. Write or record your experience.

WAYS TO CONNECT
WITH THE ANIMAL KINGDOM

1. Go to a park or wilderness zoo. Do not bother the animals but sit quietly and observe.
2. Find a place in nature. Sit comfortably. Settle in, then do not move. Wait patiently until the area around you resumes the activity that was happening before you interrupted it with your arrival. This may take some time.

Be patient, and perhaps you will observe some of the Medicine Wheel animals in their natural setting.

3. Cut out pictures in books about animals. Place them under your pillow and ask to dream about them.

4. Take guided imagery adventures with Medicine Wheel animals you want to work with, using the framework of the Animal Understanding Exercise. You can study the pictures you cut out first. Imagine everything you can about the animal before you begin your guided imagery journey.

5. Carve or purchase animal fetishes made from wood or stone.

6. Shape animals out of clay. Ask them for guidance, direction, or knowledge.

7. Draw or paint the Medicine Wheel animals with which you want to connect.

8. Smudge, sit quietly, and ask the animal you want to work with for the best way to build a relationship.

9. Keep in mind that most human relationships do not happen instantaneously but must be nurtured with responsibility and regularity. The same applies to building relationships with the animal kingdom. Be willing to let your relationship with the Animal Wheel evolve, grow, and blossom.

The Medicine Wheel
Color Reference Chart

The Center Circle

Color	Position	Lessons For Humans
All or Any	Creator	
Forest Green	Earth Mother	Harvest, growth, energy, warmth, healing, nurturing, bonding, stability
Sky Blue	Father Sun	Spirituality, ceremony, purity, wisdom, healing the soul, energy systems and psyche
Silver/White	Grandmother Moon	Purity of spirit, magical properties, innocence, intuition, balance, truth
Green/Brown	Turtle Clan	Growth, stability, permanence, dependability, strength, courage, structure
Blue/Green	Frog Clan	Cleansing, purifying, balance, soothing, happiness, contentment, healing
Red	Thunderbird Clan	Power, physical strength, fearlessness, action, change, warrior/leader energy
Translucent with Blue	Butterfly Clan	Gentleness, inner child work, faith, tenderness, love, peace, spiritual healing

The Spirit Keepers

Color	Position	Lessons For Humans
White	Waboose	Cleansing, renewal, purity, reflection, inner growth, transformation, purification
Gold & Red	Wabun	Clarity, wisdom, illumination, rebirth, life force, enlightenment, communication
Yellow & Green	Shawnodese	Trust, growth, love, feelings, sexual, relationship, overall healing, rejuvenation
Blue & Black	Mudjekeewis	Experience, introspection, strength, responsibility, achieving goals, maturity

The Moons and Totems

Color	Position	Lessons For Humans
White	Earth Renewal	Enlightenment, perfection, compassion, evolution protection, tranquility, peace
Silver	Rest & Cleansing	Intuition, properly flowing emotions, connection with the moon, psychic abilities, prosperity
Turquoise	Big Winds	Strengthens artistic and healing abilities, connects you with earth and sky, balancing

Color	Position	Lessons For Humans
Yellow	Budding Trees	Good nature, cheer, intelligence, happiness, energy, receptivity, inspiration, well being
Blue	Frogs Return	Peace, happiness satisfaction, contentment, harmony, uplifting, relaxing
White & Green	Cornplanting	Deep healing, restoration, purity, innocence, physical, spiritual, mental and emotional health

Color	Position	Lessons For Humans
Pink	Strong Sun	All-healing, unconditional love, healthy relationships, inner-child healing, sensitivity
Red	Ripe Berries	Energy, power, life force, sexuality, strong will, tempered actions, pride
Purple	Harvest	Ceremony, wisdom, good judgment, spiritual insight, idealism, love of humanity

Color	Position	Lessons For Humans
Brown	Ducks Fly	Earth awareness, environmental consciousness, stability, grounding
Orange	Freeze Up	Ambition, integration of knowledge, self-control, intelligence, vitality, awareness
Black	Long Snows	Mystery, promise, introspection, awareness, surrender, intuition, rebirth

The Spirit Paths

Color	Position	Lessons For Humans
Pale Green	Cleansing	Cleansing, preparation, discharging, releasing, detoxifying, detachment, purifying
Dark Green	Renewal	Renewal, optimism, love, trust, new perspective, positive turning point, serious healing
Translucent White	Purity	Purification, harmony, balance, faith, peace, inspiration, honesty, sweetness, healing, unity
Clear	Clarity	Clarity, purpose, strength, travel, release, confidence, movement, bravery, gumption
Jade Green	Wisdom	Wisdom, maturity, knowledge, respect, joy, stability, comprehension, boundaries, compassion
Fluorescent Blue	Illumination	Transcendence, sacredness, faith, heals soul, mind, heart and energy systems
Violet	Growth	Growth, evolution, expansion, learning, responsibility, healing, development, opening up
Lavender	Trust	Trust, security, faith, honesty, innocence, healing the inner child, compassion
Rose	Love	Love, all-healing, appreciation, understanding, compassion, joy, fidelity, romance, passion
Steel Grey	Experience	Experience, honor, purpose, comprehension, service, efficiency, values, results, perspective
Royal Blue	Introspection	Introspection, contemplation, attunement, calm, thoughtfulness, appropriate behavior, healing
Golden Yellow	Strength	Strength, responsible power, discipline, stamina, leadership, encouragement, courage

13

The Color Wheel

Every color has its own energy, frequency, and vibration. Consequently each color has its own special power for healing and helping people. Most cultures have considered the rainbow to be a special message from Spirit, a manifestation that links this world with other realms.

There is a legend about how butterflies learned to fly[1] that can help you understand the importance of color to healing and to the different positions on the Medicine Wheel. It is a story about a young woman named Spring Flower who had amazing powers of healing. When she reached the time of womanhood and went out to seek her vision of what she would do in life, strange and beautiful flying creatures came to her and gave her the power of the rainbow they carried with them. They told her each color of the rainbow had a special quality of healing. These colorful creatures told her that during her life she would have great powers to heal and, at the time of her death, she would release healing powers that would stay with the people for all times. The name given to her in vision was She Who Weaves Rainbows in the Air.

True to her vision, She Who Weaves Rainbows in the Air became a great and kindly healer. Whenever she went to heal someone she noticed that crawl-

---

1. This legend appears in its entirety in *The Medicine Wheel*.

ers of different beautiful colors would come near her as she sat on the earth. They would come close to her and try to rub themselves against her hand. Sometimes one would crawl up her arm, perch near her ear and tell her ways to help with the healing. One day, after a long and fulfilling life of healing and of love for her family and people, she spoke to one of these crawlers and asked how she could be of service to it and its people.

The crawler acknowledged his people had always been there to help her with healing. He told her that they brought the magic of the rainbow to her by the colors of their bodies. This crawler told She Who Weaves Rainbows in the Air that soon she would pass into Spirit. His people were concerned about how to continue to bring the healing of the colors to the two-leggeds.

The crawler said that because his people were earthbound they feared that humans would not look down and notice them and thus receive the blessing of the color each crawler wore.

"If we could fly," the crawler said, "the people would notice us and smile at the beautiful colors they see. And we could fly around those who need special healing and let the powers of our colors give them whatever healing they can accept. Can you help us to fly?"

She Who Weaves Rainbows in the Air said she would try. Soon she died. Before her death she had told her husband about her conversation. When it was time to bury She Who Weaves Rainbows in the Air, her husband looked for one of the colored crawlers. A crawler was waiting and instructed the husband to bury him with She Who Weaves Rainbows in the Air.

The crawler told the husband that when the earth was over him he too would die but that his spirit would merge with the spirit of She Who Weaves Rainbows in the Air.

"Together we will fly out of the earth," said the crawler. "Then we will go back to my people and teach them how to fly so the work your wife began can continue. She is waiting for me. Bury me with her now."

The man did, and his wife's burial proceeded. When all the others had left, the man stayed by the grave of the woman he had loved so dearly. Suddenly from the grave came a flying one with all the colors of the rainbow spread over its wings. It flew to him and landed on his shoulder.

"Do not be sad my husband. Now my vision is totally fulfilled, and those who I'll help to teach will always bring the goodness, healing, and happiness of the rainbow to the people. When your time comes to pass into Spirit, I'll be waiting to rejoin you."

When the man died several years later his children stayed at his grave after all the other people had left. They noticed one of the beautiful new creatures called butterflies hovering near the grave. In a few minutes another butterfly of equal beauty flew up out of their father's grave and joined the one who was waiting. Together they flew North to the place of renewal. Since that time butterflies have always been with the people brightening the air with their color and beauty.

Most cultures have considered the rainbow to be a special message from Spirit, a manifestation that links this world with other realms. The gifts of the rainbow, of color, have long been known to people in many cultures, including the dominant one today. Think how many sayings equate emotional states with colors: "I'm blue." "He was seeing red." "She's got a yellow streak." "He's in a purple funk." "Everything looked black." Think how many times you have chosen an outfit, an automobile, or a room color because the color made you feel better.

As you travel around the Medicine Wheel, note the various colors and how they affect you. A change in color preference may be one of the first clues you are preparing to travel, or have traveled, to a different position on the wheel.

When working with the Medicine Wheel colors it is appropriate to mix and match according to what positions are affecting you or what energies you desire. By wearing the color associated with one position you attract the energy of that place on the wheel to you. You can do the same thing by being in a room or car of that color or by looking at a card or candle or light of that hue. You can visualize the color, use it in a meditation, carry a stone of the proper shade, or watch for butterflies to fly near you. Do not underestimate the power and beauty of working with colors. These sparkling rays of light and motion contain the very essence both of who we are and who we can become. Our bodies are dense energy, made up of particles of light in a condensed form. When people refer to humans as part of the light, they literally mean our light particles connect us with all that is. Humans tend to limit their existence so as to make it seem secure and concrete. Look farther than your flesh and you will see and feel your connection with color. Through working with the colors associated with the different positions on the Medicine Wheel you can also strengthen your understanding of each aspect of the wheel and of the wheel as a whole.

THE COLORS OF THE CENTER CIRCLE

THE CREATOR—ALL OR ANY COLORS

There is no single color that always represents the Creator. The Creator is part of all colors, the totality both of the rainbow and of its absence.

THE EARTH MOTHER—FOREST GREEN

The color honoring the Center Circle stone representing the Earth Mother is forest green. This is the green of all growing plants when they are sparkling with aliveness: full of life, full of energy, full of water. Although this green varies from light to dark, it is a green we most often name forest green, with little yellow or brown mixed with it.

Working with forest green encourages the warmth and growth stimulated by the Earth Mother resulting in deep healing, nurturing, bonding, and stability. This color is good for manifestation, abundance, and reaping a bountiful harvest.

FATHER SUN—DARK SKY BLUE

The color associated with the Center Circle stone honoring Father Sun is a dark sky blue. This color both honors the sky home of Father Sun and reminds us that blue is one of the colors of fire burning hot, without impurities. Any of you who use gas fires in your homes for heating or cooking know the elusive blue flame.

This dark blue encourages spirituality and connecting with your deepest levels of consciousness. This color is excellent for meditation, ceremony, or connecting with your highest level of purity and wisdom. Dark sky blue is good to work with for healing the soul, psyche, emotional body, and the body's energy systems.

GRANDMOTHER MOON—SILVER-WHITE

The color associated with the Center Circle stone honoring Grandmother Moon is the silver-white we see when the moon shows herself against the darkness of the night sky.

Working with silver-white can deepen your connection with Grandmother Moon as well as encourage a purity of spirit and purpose. These colors invite the magical properties of the moon into your life while helping you maintain a pure innocence that can bring you to the highest level of planetary and personal good. Silver-white can help your ability to recognize deceit or decipher inaccurate information. This color encourages high principles and a finely honed intuition. It is also powerful for working with female problems, and for balancing male/female energies.

THE TURTLE CLAN,
ELEMENT OF EARTH—GREEN-BROWN

The color associated with the Center circle stone honoring the element of earth is the green of growing plants mottled with the brown of the soil from which they grow.

Working with green-brown encourages growth, stability, permanence, dependability, a strong belief system, strength, courage, structure, and a firm grasp of reality. These colors are good to use for healing male/female energies, for completing a difficult task, and for restoring health to a weakened system.

THE FROG CLAN,
ELEMENT OF WATER—BLUE-GREEN

The color associated with the stone honoring the element of water is the blue-green of the ocean on a clear, sunlit day. These colors can aid you in strengthening your relationship with the waters within you and around you. The Frog clan colors provide powerful help during times of water shortage or of flooding. These colors are also useful when there is a need for thorough cleansing of the body, mind, or spirit.

Blue and green are excellent colors to work with for cleansing and purifying the spiritual, emotional, or physical bodies. These colors stimulate a balance between your inner consciousness and the exterior world around you. Blue and green can soothe "troubled waters" thereby awaking a deep sense of happiness and contentment. These colors aid in healing.

THE THUNDERBIRD CLAN,
ELEMENT OF FIRE—VIVID RED

The color associated with the stone honoring the element of fire is the vivid red of the flame visible between the orange and yellow that draw its boundary.

This color represents the "fire of Life" and encourages physical strength, power, fearlessness, sensuality, and heat. Vivid red is the color of action, movement, change, and transformation. If you want to take charge, to be a leader, to encourage your warrior energy, or to embrace your "path of power" work with vivid red.

When working with this color or with the power and forces of the element of fire keep in mind the fact that the same fire that heats you can also painfully burn you. This is not the color to use when you need to moderate your actions.

THE BUTTERFLY CLAN, ELEMENT OF AIR—
CLEAR TRANSLUCENT WITH A HINT OF BLUE

The color associated with the stone honoring the element of air is a clear translucent with a hint of blue. This is the color of some fine goblets made from sand that bespeaks the blue of the water that has washed over it. It is what you see when looking through the wings of butterflies or through frost on a windowpane on a clear, crisp winter morning.

This color allows you to see the physical plane with eyes coated with the gentle veil of Spirit. This translucent blue can soften the harshness of life's lessons by reminding you of the Creator's all-encompassing love.

Clear translucent with a hint of blue helps heal the soul, the heart, and the emotions and is excellent for working with your inner child and healing childhood hurts. These colors encourage faith, tenderness, innocence, love, and peace. Clear translucent with a hint of blue is especially good for healing the spirit.

THE SPIRIT KEEPER COLORS
#####

The seven colors connected with the powers of the directions are the three primary colors—red, yellow, and blue; black, the absence of all color; white, the presence of all color; gold; and green, the color of the living earth. These are the most powerful manifestations of the color spectrum.

These are also the colors that predominate during the seasons and the times of day associated with each of the Spirit Keepers.

WABOOSE, SPIRIT KEEPER OF
THE NORTH—WHITE

The Spirit Keeper of the North, Waboose, is associated with the white of winter snow, the white of the stars in the night sky, and the white of the hair that tops the heads of the most respected elders.

This white can assist you in cleansing, renewing, and purifying your mind, body, and soul. This color encourages you to reflect on yourself and your connection with spirit. It aids inner growth and profound transformation. It can help you achieve a deepened state of consciousness and knowledge about the wisdom of the elders. White helps with the purification necessary for continued rejuvenation.

WABUN, SPIRIT KEEPER OF
THE EAST—GOLD AND RED

Wabun, the Spirit Keeper of the East, is represented by the gold and red of the sun rising over the horizon, heralding the dawn and the start of a new day. This is also the golden light that comes with spring sunshine and the golden light of wisdom that can light our path through life, reminding us each moment is a new beginning. The red of Wabun is the red of vitality, the red of blood.

Gold and red assist you in finding clarity, wisdom, and illumination. These colors encourage rebirth, rejuvenation, strong life force, enlightenment, and courage. Red alone can stimulate aggressiveness and fearlessness, so it is important to temper its energy with gold, which adds balance and sensitivity. Gold and red help you work with things of the earth as well as other planes. These colors will ground you, and help you communicate your true thoughts and feelings.

SHAWNODESE, SPIRIT KEEPER OF THE SOUTH—GREEN AND LIGHT YELLOW

Shawnodese, the Spirit Keeper of the South, is represented by the green of growing things mixed with the yellow of the sunlight that helps them to grow. This is a clear, pure light yellow, and it lightens all of the green it touches. Green alone is the color of growth, trust, restoration, and healing, whereas yellow is the color of intelligence, mental receptivity, and natural wisdom.

Green and light yellow can help you learn about trust, growth, and love. These colors encourage maturity, the ability to draw from universal wisdom, and a strengthening of feelings and intuition. Green and light yellow help you to find your purpose in life, make necessary changes, and enable you to make good decisions. These colors stimulate the energies of reproduction, and mating. Green and light yellow can be used for healing of the sexual organs and adrenal glands and for blood purification. These colors are also good for general, all over healing and rejuvenation.

MUDJEKEEWIS, SPIRIT KEEPER OF THE WEST—BRILLIANT BLUE AND BLACK

The colors associated with Mudjekeewis, the Spirit Keeper of the West, are the brilliant blue of the sky as twilight begins its approach and the black of the clouds that signal the end of blue sky for another day. Blue alone is the color of spiritual strength, idealism, and selflessness. Black is the color of a person looking within and purposely blinding herself to the things of earth to experience the formlessness from which all things can come.

These colors can help you understand your life experience. They encourage introspection and inner strength. Brilliant blue and black teaches you how to slow down, work hard, handle responsibilities, achieve sought-after goals, and act from a place of maturity. These colors teach you what you can learn from your mistakes, as well as what your strengths and weaknesses are. Brilliant blue and black can be healing for the arteries, blood vessels, and the nervous system.

THE COLORS OF THE TWELVE TOTEM ANIMALS
·····

THE EARTH RENEWAL MOON, SNOW GOOSE—WHITE

White is the color associated with the snow goose and the Earth Renewal Moon (December 22 to January 19). This is the white of the snow that comes with winter: the white that makes everything appear new and sparkling. White is the presence of all colors, the sum of all colors. Although it appears to be no color it is, in fact, all color. White is considered to be the color of enlightenment, perfection, and advanced evolution. Many people invoke white light to cover and shield themselves from any negative energies that might be around them. Although white can protect, it can also blind you to the fact that you must work to know yourself, in order to have the truest protection from anything that could be harmful. Having white around you encourages feelings of purity, tranquility, peace, balance, serenity, compassion, protection, and altruism.

THE REST AND CLEANSING MOON,
OTTER—SILVER

Silver is the color associated with otter and the Rest and Cleansing Moon (January 20 to February 18). Silver has long been considered a magical color. Some religious philosophies teach that it is a silver cord that holds soul to body; others that there are silver heavens above those of gold. Silver is the color of wealth, prosperity, and richness of spirit. Silver is associated with the moon and consequently is a color that enhances your connection to the Grandmother. Having silver around you promotes psychic abilities and feelings of improved perception, intuition, and properly flowing emotions. It also helps you to have an improved attitude toward money and your own prosperity.

THE BIG WINDS MOON,
COUGAR—TURQUOISE (BLUE-GREEN)

Turquoise (blue-green) is the color associated with cougar and the Big Winds Moon (February 19 to March 20). The blue of turquoise is a sky blue, similar to the sky blue representing Father Sun. This blue can indicate either idealistic, selfless, artistic, and spiritual feelings or melancholy feelings and self-imposed struggles. The green of the turquoise helps to balance these two tendencies with the serenity of a true connection with nature. Having turquoise around you helps to strengthen any latent artistic or healing abilities. It also helps you to feel the connection you have between the sky and the earth.

THE BUDDING TREES MOON,
RED HAWK—DANDELION YELLOW

Yellow is the color of the red hawk and Budding Trees Moon (March 21 to April 19). This is the yellow of the spring sun shining from the sky, the color of the dandelion flower in full bloom. This yellow is a cheerful color, one that stimulates good nature and native intelligence. It is a color that reminds you of sunshine, happiness, and energy. Having yellow in your surroundings can help you to have greater intellectual acuity, more receptivity to inspiration, a feeling of overall well-being and happiness with other people.

THE FROGS RETURN MOON,
BEAVER—BLUE

Blue is the color of beaver and the Frogs Return Moon (April 20 to May 20). This is the brilliant blue found in the camas flower or in chrysocolla that has no impurities. This color radiates feelings of peace, happiness, and subtle energy. This blue can lighten dark moods and remind one of the more subtle realms. Having this blue around you will help you to be satisfied with your surroundings, emotionally content, harmonious, and happy with life as it is unfolding for you.

THE CORNPLANTING MOON,
DEER—WHITE AND GREEN

White and green are the colors of deer and the Cornplanting Moon (May 21 to June 20). The white of this position is translucent, like that seen in many moss agates. It is a white that bespeaks formlessness and the perfect purity and innocence with which we all enter the world. The green is the dark, waxy shade found in plants growing in deep forests or in areas where water abounds. It is a green of deep healing and of restoration on the deepest levels. Having this green and white combination in your environment will stimulate the purity and innocence necessary for true healing to take place on physical, mental, emotional, or spiritual levels.

THE STRONG SUN MOON,
FLICKER—PINK

The color associated with flicker and the Strong Sun Moon (June 21 to July 22) is pink. This is the pure pink of the finest pink roses, neither too red nor too purple in shade. It is a pink associated with little girls and thus immaturity. But it is also the pink of all-healing love often invoked by those who work with color. Having this color around you will help to open your heart to love, sensitivity and your own fast-flowing emotions. It will also illuminate any areas of feeling in which you need to mature.

THE RIPE BERRIES MOON,
STURGEON—RED

The color associated with sturgeon and the Ripe Berries Moon (July 23 to August 22) is red. This is the red of the ripe raspberry, the red of the most prized of garnets. It is the red of the life force, the red of strong will. This is a red that can signify pride, greed, unthinking sexuality, and erratic actions. Having this color around you will increase your energy and power. It will also challenge you to temper your actions with thought.

THE HARVEST MOON,
BROWN BEAR—PURPLE

The color associated with brown bear and the Harvest Moon (August 23 to September 22) is purple. This is the purple of the shy violet whose flowers can so easily be missed growing on the forest floor. It is also the color of deep amethyst crystals. This purple is the color of ceremony, ritual, spiritual insight, idealism, and love of humanity. Some gradations of purple indicate someone using spiritual power for personal gain. Purple is a color of wisdom, but it can be used in either positive or negative ways. Having purple around you will inspire you, bring you spiritual insights, increase your love of ceremony, and make you examine how you are using your power.

THE DUCKS FLY MOON,
RAVEN—BROWN

The color associated with raven and the Ducks Fly Moon (September 23 to October 23) is the brown of the earth in autumn, a rich brown with tones of red. It is a brown that draws your attention to the earth, a brown that helps you to realize your connection with the Great Mother. It is a color with many shades that evoke many moods. Having brown around you can help you to increase your earth connection and your stability to the point that allows you to safely reach to the realms beyond. It can also increase your environmental consciousness.

THE FREEZE UP MOON,
SNAKE—ORANGE

The color associated with snake and the Freeze Up Moon (October 24 to November 21) is orange. This is a clear orange you can see in the sunset sky, or in the squash and pumpkins ripening in the field. This orange signifies both an ambitious and proud person and one capable of synthesizing and applying knowledge he gains from life. Having this color around you will stimulate your intellect, your vitality, and your self-control. It will help you observe life more keenly and use the information gained both for your own good and for the good of others.

THE LONG SNOWS MOON,
ELK—BLACK

The color associated with elk and the Long Snows Moon (November 22 to December 21) is black. This is the dusky black of the deep, dark evening sky. It is a black of formlessness, of mystery, of void from which anything can come. It is the dark that holds both promise and threat. Having black around you will help you to look within, to know yourself and life more deeply. Black can teach you about surrender, intuition, perception, and rebirth. It is a sacred color to many Native people.

THE SPIRIT PATH COLORS
• • • • •

The Northern Spirit Path Colors

CLEANSING—PALE GREEN

The color associated with cleansing, the first Spirit Path position of the North, is pale green, the color of lime. Pale green is a powerful color for connecting the physical and etheric planes. This color can help you to prepare, cleanse, and purify yourself for working on more refined levels of growth and transformation. Pale green helps you to release the old and allow room for the new.

Pale green is helpful for detoxifying and for removing impurities from the body, mind, and spirit. Pale green can aid in discharging emotion and releasing misconceptions. If you are preparing for a difficult ordeal or any form of transformation, having this color around you can be helpful. It also is good for stamina, releasing, cleansing, stimulating, and purifying. Pale green is healing for the whole body.

RENEWAL—DARK GREEN

The color associated with renewal, the second Spirit Path position of the North, is dark green. This is another green of the Earth Mother, the lush deep green of rain forests. This color is helpful for serious healing; rejuvenation; and renewal on the physical, mental, emotional, and spiritual levels. The dark green of renewal can help you have a healthy attitude, new perspective, and an optimistic outlook on life. This color encourages unconditional love and trust of your intuition. Dark green can help herald a turning point from illness to wellness. This color encourages healing and feelings of self-worth, prosperity, and abundance. Dark green is a powerful healing color.

PURITY—TRANSLUCENT WHITE

The color associated with the third Spirit Path position of the North, purity, is translucent white. This is the pure, opaque white of tiny clouds seemingly buoyed in space by a blue, blue sky. This color is helpful for purifying the physical body of disease and for cleansing the mental, emotional, and spiritual bodies of disharmony and imbalance.

Translucent white can alleviate dissension and quiet traumatic emotional upheaval. This color dissipates disruptive energies and chaos. Translucent white is good for working with groups or organizations because it encourages unity for a common good. Working with this white releases tendencies toward bitterness, sarcasm, and meanness. It is calming, and teaches about truth, innocence, and honesty. It is an agent of spirit that encourages the highest good. Translucent white brings faith, peace, inspiration, honesty, and hope.

The Eastern Spirit Path Colors

CLARITY—TRANSLUCENT CLEAR

The color for the first Spirit Path position of the East, clarity, is the translucent clearness of the hummingbird wing. It is the color of rain drops falling in spring and heat waves rising on a searing hot summer day.

This color will bring you clarity of purpose and strength to follow your path of power when you journey into unknown realms. It is a powerful ally and lends support at times when your intuition and heart tell you it is safe to travel to new spiritual frontiers. It is particularly helpful for releasing obsolete belief systems that hold you back from your highest good. Translucent clear is good to work with for spiritual support when your brain says no but your heart and spirit say yes. This color encourages confidence, movement, bravery, and gumption.

WISDOM—JADE GREEN

The color for the second Spirit Path position of the East, wisdom, is jade green. This color encourages a deepened maturity and the ability to utilize accumulated knowledge and experience in a positive manner. Jade green invites in the wisdom of all times. It deepens your own knowledge, respect, and understanding of what your personal limits and depths are. Jade green helps you to distinguish your appropriate boundaries clearly. Work with jade green if you want to draw compassion and joy to your life rather than pain and numbness. Jade green is good for stability, grounding, and self-awareness.

ILLUMINATION—FLUORESCENT BLUE

The color for illumination, the third Spirit Path position of the East, is fluorescent blue. Fluorescent blue can light the fire of life within you. This color can teach you how to ride the winds and travel among the stars. If you want to communicate with the essence of life work with fluorescent blue. This color teaches you about Creator force, the sacredness of being, and the blessedness of life. Fluorescent blue reminds you of the joy of life's most special moments. The energy of this color encourages you to reach beyond your perimeters. This color encourages a leap in faith that allows you to go beyond yourself. Fluorescent blue stimulates you to rise above the mundane to the godlike aspects that burn within each human. If you do not have belief in Creator, self, or Spirit, work with this color. Fluorescent blue is good for the soul, mind, heart, and energy systems.

The Southern Spirit Path Colors

GROWTH—VIOLET

The color that represents growth, the first Spirit Path position of the South, is violet. Violet, a gentle shade of purple, encourages growth and evolution from adolescence to adulthood. It is an aspect of the ultraviolet ray critical to the health and development of plants and animals. It is the color of lamps used to coax seeds to become sprouts. Working with violet encourages development and a maturing process especially in regard to the emotions and relationships. Violet is a color that encourages expansion on the physical, mental, emotional, and spiritual levels. If you want to open up, learn, take responsibility, heal, or reach beyond your present capacity then have violet around you.

TRUST—LAVENDER

The color that represents trust, the second Spirit Path position of the South, is lavender. Lavender promotes the security stemming from a sense of natural order such as that found in the changing of the seasons, or the sun rising with each dawn. Lavender fosters complete, absolute faith; the truth; and innocence usually distinctive of children. Lavender encourages explicit honesty. Working with lavender brings healing that only the commitment to truth can bring. Lavender can help you stop denying, disassociating, and being secretive. Lavender is healing for the inner child, spirit, and emotions.

LOVE—ROSE

The color that represents love, the inner Spirit Path position of the South, is rose. Rose is the color of romance and passion born of true, committed love. Rose, a deep shade of pink, represents a love that is deep, solid, dependable, and durable. It is the kind of love that mature individuals find. It is the love Spirit has for all life and that parents have for children. Working with rose promotes fidelity, compassion, understanding, appreciation, and joy. Rose is an overall healer, balancer, stabilizer, and relaxant.

The Western Spirit Path Colors

EXPERIENCE—STEEL GRAY

The color that represents experience, the first Spirit Path position of the West, is steel gray. Gray can help teach you what you truly honor in your life and the universe. Gray is also the color that brings knowledge of how to serve the people and the Earth Mother. Working with this color promotes enhanced comprehension and efficiency and brings valuable, necessary information that can help you plan your life. The color gray helps you to take action and learn from the results of that action. Gray brings you lessons that teach you perspective and help you to integrate and utilize what you have learned. Gray is grounding, focusing, and rejuvenating. It also helps you to find purpose.

INTROSPECTION—ROYAL BLUE

The color associated with the second Spirit Path position of the West, introspection, is royal blue. Royal blue is a color that can help you look inward and draw from your own inner strength. It encourages contemplation, reserve, and internalization. Royal blue can help you hold your tongue and think before you speak. This color can assist you in stopping inappropriate behavior and tendencies. Royal blue can teach you about your relationship with the world around you. This color fosters calm, mature decisions born of serious thought and care. Royal blue connects you with the sacred life force and attunes you to the wisest good. Royal blue is good for overall healing, spiritual attunement, and grounding.

STRENGTH—GOLDEN YELLOW

The color associated with strength, the third Spirit Path position of the West, is golden yellow. It is the color of amber resin that has aged for thousands of years. It teaches you about the responsibility of power. Golden yellow encourages the devotion and discipline needed to fairly, compassionately, and appropriately exercise power and leadership with people, places, and things. Working with this color can assist you in knowing how to make just decisions for the highest good of all involved. It also helps you learn to teach others how to take their own power. Golden yellow not only gives you personal strength but also teaches you how to encourage others to build the same strength within themselves. This color encourages you to follow your own evolutionary path. Golden yellow is good for endurance, courage, stamina, strength, faith, and discipline. Golden yellow is healing for the energy field and mind.

WORKING WITH
THE MEDICINE WHEEL COLORS

Working with the Medicine Wheel colors can effect very powerful healing change on all levels of your being—physical, mental, emotional, and spiritual—and it can be a lot of fun. Life is color and motion. Using colors can bring healing, love, laughter, and harmony into your life. It can literally brighten up your life and make it much more colorful. Working with these colors is like dancing with the rainbow. This rainbow can be integrated into your life in endless ways. Working with the Color Wheel is a wonderful way to stimulate your creativity and let your imagination flow.

Whether you choose to work with colors in a serious way or in a lighthearted, experimental mode, the healing energies of the rainbow will come through. Working with the Color Wheel is a great way to begin to generate your own ceremonies for healing yourself and the Earth Mother.

In dancing with the rainbow you will learn how to make a variety of colorful medicine tools part of your everyday life. You can work with anything that has color involved such as a rainbow macaw feather (universal perspective), green leaves (healing), white seashells (purity, enlightenment), fresh or dried multicolored spring flowers (laughter, all-healing, well-being). You can find rocks or pebbles in creek beds or streams or buy beautiful colored gemstones and minerals. You can use color cards, colored lights, colored light filters, candles, fans, fabric, or paints.

Begin by collecting and doing a bonding ceremony with the different color-oriented medicine tools you want to integrate into your life. Then begin working with them on a regular basis. Here are some suggestions on how to make them a part of your day-to-day existence.

In the Home

It is good to surround yourself with colorful healing medicine objects by placing them in strategic places such as by your bed or as a centerpiece on the dining table. Choose colors corresponding either with your current Medicine Wheel position or with energies you wish to incorporate into your life.

You can place colored stones in your shower, or outside your door or window during a warm rain, because colored stones mix well with the water energy. The two elements blend like playful lovers or friends and being near them can leave you with the same type of warm glow that comes from spending quality time with someone you love.

Decorating Your Home

Before painting or decorating your home, look carefully at the color chart to determine what colors and energies you want to draw into your life. Remember these colors will also draw the other energies associated with that Medicine Wheel position. Make a conscious choice to embrace what you are seeking by bringing the colors that will support your needs into your life.

Sleeping

Surround yourself with medicine tools in the colors with which you are working. Choose your sheets, blankets, bed covers, and pajamas based on these colors.

Eating

Choose some of the foods you eat by the colors you are working with. For example, if you want healing, eat a lot of green foods. If you want passion, eat red foods. See the color chart for other ideas. Be sure to mix these colored foods with the other foods necessary for a balanced diet.

Bathing

Float the appropriately colored flower petals in your bath water or place stones in the bottom of the tub. Be sure the stones are around you, not beneath you. Take a long, relaxing bath then note afterward the different sensations you receive by using these colored objects.

Massage

You can use any of your color medicine objects as massage tools. A gentle massage with a rainbow-colored macaw feather can cure many a woe and enlarge new perspective. Colored stones with rounded edges can be powerful massage tools. Use these to work on pressure points. Colored stones and feathers both can be used for balancing energies. You can also place colored stones under the massage table, have colored lights in the room, or drape the person in colored material. Choosing the right color to bring balance can help any massage be much more powerful.

Finger Painting

Finger painting is a lovely way of interacting with the color kingdom. You can easily mix and match whatever colors you wish to work with. You can draw symbols or pictures of what you would like to create, heal, or transform in your life.

You can write out affirmations in different colors. Hang these in different locations of your home, such as on refrigerators, mirrors, or frequented rooms.

Dance

Put on music that you like. Dance, holding colored feathers in each hand. Allow them to guide you, following the movements they evoke. Hold colored stones in each hand as you dance. Feel the energy flow and expand. Keep note of the different sensations evoked when you hold a variety of colors of stones or feathers while you dance. See if you feel different when you hold two feathers or stones of the same color from when you hold two differently colored objects.

FLOATING FLOWER PETAL CEREMONY

This ceremony is to help you work more deeply with natural colors and aromas. It is a good ceremony to integrate into the Medicine Wheel Sensory Healing Ceremony.

What you need. Smudge materials, large bowl, water, offerings, and notebook and pen or tape recorder.

Estimated time. Thirty minutes.

1. Smudge yourself and everything you will be touching during this ceremony.
2. Fill a large bowl about halfway full with water.
3. Gather fresh, colorful, highly scented flowers, with proper thanks and offerings. You may purchase the flowers from a florist if you do not have a garden available. Choose the flowers whose color corresponds with the type of healing or transformation you are looking for. This exercise is very effective either using one color of petals or many colors that draw in the rainbow of healing qualities.
4. Make another offering to the plants that gave of themselves so you could do this ceremony.
5. Place the petals of the flowers in the bowl, allowing them to float on the water.
6. Sit comfortably. Hold the bowl close in front of you. Gaze into the floating flowers. Bring the bowl up to your face, so that the blaze of color fills your vision. Breathe deeply of the sweet aroma and fragrance of the petals. Let the aroma and colors of the flowers really permeate your senses. Do this for at least five minutes. Note whether you feel any energy shifts.
7. When you are done with the ceremony, be sure to give thanks and honor the flowers for their gift to you. After working with the flowers you can dry them and use the petals in a smudge.
8. Write or record your experience.

GREEN LEAF THERAPY CEREMONY

Green will encourage serenity, healing, and balance. It also brings forth the powers and healing qualities of nature. Green is a powerful ally for bringing abundance into one's life. This is a good, healing, stabilizing ceremony, best done before sleeping.

What you need. Smudge materials, a special offering, green leaves, cheesecloth or a medicine pouch, notebook and pen or tape recorder.

Estimated time. Thirty minutes to collect leaves, a full night of sleeping, thirty minutes in the morning.

1. Smudge yourself and where you sleep.
2. Choose a tree that has very green leaves you would like to work with. Bury something that is precious to you (a stone, feather, fetish, or jewelry) at the base of the tree.
3. Pick a good handful of green leaves. Never overpick or harvest a plant that does not grow or reproduce in a plentiful way.
4. Smudge the leaves then place them in cheesecloth or a medicine pouch. Put this bundle under your pillow and ask for the powers of the color green to surround and heal you. Also call on the medicine of the type of tree, bush, or plant they are from.
5. Before you fall asleep that night, hold the pouch close to your nose and deeply breathe in the fragrance and essence of the green leaves.
6. In the morning bring the leaves back outside and spread them on the ground in a natural setting, allowing them to flow to the ground in their own lovely pattern. Make a prayer of thanks while you do this.
7. Look closely at this green foliage to see what message the leaves might have for you in the form of an image, design, or pattern.
8. Write or record your experience.

A WHITE SEASHELL CIRCLE

What you need. Smudge materials, enough white seashells to make a circle, notebook and pen or tape recorder.

Estimated time. One hour.

1. After smudging an area, make a circle of white seashells large enough to lie in. Lie down in the circle, inviting in the healing, cleansing powers of the ocean, water elements, and the powers of white that are purity, enlightenment, perfection, balance, peace, tranquility, and evolution.
2. Allow yourself to doze off. Be aware of your dreams. They can bring a message to you.
3. After twenty minutes, or when it feels appropriate to you, slowly get up and dismantle the circle with a prayer of thanks to the different elements that were there for you. You can do this exercise at the ocean with the additional healing elements of wind and the sound of the rolling waves.
4. Write or record your impressions.

SPRING FLOWER CEREMONY

What you need. Smudge materials, a blanket, offering, spring flowers, and notebook and pen or tape recorder.

Estimated time. One hour.

1. Either do this exercise in the spring in an area with prolific flowers or purchase spring flowers. In either case make an offering to the flowers you will use, and do not use flowers from plants that are endangered. Remove the petals from the flowers.
2. Smudge yourself and the area. Place a blanket on a grassy spot. (This exercise can be done inside if necessary.)
3. Center yourself and say a prayer calling in the healing energies or elements of change you desire. Ask for what you want.
4. Make an offering to the six directions, then take handfuls of colorful spring flower petals, letting them gently fall through the air onto the blanket. This will draw in the powers of the colors you are using, and of the plant kingdom. The flowers will also act as aromatherapy.
5. Lower yourself onto the blanket, then gently roll around in the petals, raising them and letting them fall lovingly on your body, making a thin blanket of them over yourself. Continue to focus on the color healing that you want and how each of the different colors can heal you. Think about how the petals looked floating down to the earth. Acknowledge the plants that are there with you, helping, healing, and giving to you. Feel their energy, allow it into your being.
6. Feel the nurturing power of the earth underneath you. After about twenty to thirty minutes (or whenever you feel it is appropriate) slowly raise yourself up. Make a prayer of thanks and honor to the spirits and elements that helped you. This can be a very gentle, loving, and healing ceremony.
7. Write or record your experience.

RED ROSE PASSION CEREMONY

This exercise is for working with and healing sexual energy. You can do this in your bed alone or with an intimate partner in the seclusion and privacy of your home.

What you need. Smudge materials, blanket or bed, offering, red rose petals, and notebook and pen or tape recorder.

Estimated time. Thirty minutes.

1. Do the same basic ceremony as the Spring Flower Ceremony, however, use all red roses. Red draws in the healing powers of passion and sexuality.
2. Using the soft petals, gently massage yourself. Open up to all your senses. Truly feel the softness of the petals.
3. If they are from a natural source, eat some of them. Feel the texture in your mouth.
4. Let yourself quietly lie with the petals, allowing yourself to soak up and feel the healing energy.
5. Breathe long, slow, deep breaths. Be aware of the healing energies of aromatherapy taking place.
6. If doing this with a partner, focus on the initial ceremony for at least thirty minutes. Afterward it is okay to be intimate with each other, being thankful for the blessed sexual energies with which Spirit has gifted you.
7. Afterward, offer a prayer of honor and thanks for the healing energies and elements that were there for you.

8. Write or record your experience.

Remember, this is a healing, loving ceremony for the highest good for all involved. It is not to be used as a romantic technique or as a means to woo someone to bed. If you do this with a partner, be clear about you and your partner's motives before you begin. Thoroughly talk about it so the highest good, healing, and happiness may occur for all involved.

Finding Help from the Medicine Wheel

Everyone has times when he feels he needs help quickly. Knowledge of the Medicine Wheel can provide such help if you know where to find it. In this chapter are listed some common mental, emotional, and spiritual problems you might encounter, along with the Medicine Wheel position that can best help you. All the positions will give some insight on any problem. Listed here are the ones that will give the easiest help.

To get this help quickly you can go and be with a Medicine Wheel physically or be with one through visualization.

You can hold the stone representing the Medicine Wheel position that will help you, wear jewelry containing the stone, find the stone in a natural setting then sit or stand by it, or meditate on its picture.

You can use the plant of this position to aid you by looking at its picture, holding it, drinking tea made from it, or finding it in a natural setting then being with it.

The animal totem can aid you if you visualize it, look at its photo, or hold a fetish that reminds you of the animal.

The color of the correct position can help you if you surround yourself with it by putting on some clothing of the color or going into a room or automobile of the color. You can also use colored lights or filters, or candles in the correct shade.

Help will come fastest if you go outside to the Earth Mother and work with the Medicine Wheel, or some element of the wheel in as natural a setting as possible. May you find the help and healing you need through this sacred circle.

Nature of Problem	Where to Find Help
Accomplishing little	*Father Sun, Thunderbird clan, Red Hawk*
Adaptability, lack of	*Frog clan*
Adaptability, too much	*Turtle clan, Snow Goose*
Afraid	*Red Hawk, Sturgeon, Brown Bear*
Aloof	*Frog clan, Thunderbird clan*
Ambition, lack of	*Father Sun, Red Hawk, Sturgeon, Snake*
Antisocial	*Butterfly clan, Otter, Deer, Raven*
Anxiety	*Creator, Earth Mother, Turtle clan*
Asexual	*Grandmother Moon, Snake, Sturgeon*
Assertiveness, lack of	*Sturgeon*
Assessment, lack of	*Mudjekeewis, Brown Bear*
Balance male and female	*Creator, Shawnodese, Illumination*
Belief, lack of	*Snow Goose, Flicker, Raven, Trust*
Believing other's ideas about how you should be	*Brown Bear, Purity, Strength, Introspection*
Bitter	*Grandmother Moon, Purity, Clarity, Trust,*
Bonding	*Earth Mother, Shawnodese, Flicker, Elk,*
Boundaries, lack of	*Turtle clan, Snow Goose*
Boundaries, too rigid	*Cougar, Raven*
Calm	*Earth Mother, Turtle clan, Trust*
Ceremony, doubt about	*Snow Goose*
Ceremony, unfamiliar with	*Grandmother Moon, Snow Goose*
Change, desiring	*Creator, Frog clan, Butterfly clan*
Clumsy	*Butterfly clan, Deer*
Cold	*Father Sun, Wabun, Raven*
Communicating, trouble	*Butterfly clan, Wabun*
Compassion, lack of	*Creator, Earth Mother, Flicker, Wisdom*

Compulsive	*Butterfly clan*
Confidence, lack of	*Sturgeon, Trust*
Confused	*Waboose, Clarity*
Connecting heart and mind	*Wabun, Shawnodese, Wisdom*
Connecting mind and body	*Waboose, Wabun, Wisdom*
Connection with universe, lack of	*Creator*
Contentment, desiring	*Butterfly clan, Beaver*
Contracted	*Father Sun*
Control, feeling out of	*Waboose, Snow Goose, Snake*
Courage	*Creator, Turtle clan, Thunderbird clan, Sturgeon*
Creativity, increase	*Creator, Butterfly clan, Cougar, Deer*
Critical	*Wabun, Flicker, Raven, Purity*
Cynicism	*Purity, Experience*
Decisive, lack of	*Snow Goose, Sturgeon, Brown Bear*
Decisive, too	*Raven*
Defenselessness	*Snake, Elk*
Depressed	*Thunderbird clan, Wabun, Red Hawk*
Desperate	*Creator, Growth, Trust, Love*
Discipline, lacking	*Father Sun, Waboose, Mudjekeewis, Snow Goose, Strength*
Distrustful	*Shawnodese, Trust*
Don't know how to stand up for self	*Red Hawk, Sturgeon, Elk*
Doubt	*Creator, Snow Goose, Trust*
Dreams, improve	*Grandmother Moon, Deer*
Duty, no sense of	*Brown Bear*
Earth, desiring deeper connection with	*Earth Mother, Turtle clan*
Earth, feeling of hopelessness about	*Earth Mother, Turtle clan, Frog clan*
Earth, looking for solutions to the problems now on	*Creator, Earth Mother, Turtle clan, Cougar, Raven*
Earth, sadness about	*Creator, Earth Mother, Turtle clan, Butterfly clan*
Egotistical	*Thunderbird clan, Beaver, Brown Bear*

Emotional, overly	*Turtle clan, Waboose, Snow Goose*
Emotions, exploring deep	*Grandmother Moon, Frog clan, Cougar, Flicker, Snake*
Emotions repressed	*Grandmother Moon, Frog clan, Cougar, Flicker*
Energy, lack of	*Father Sun, Wabun, Thunderbird clan, Red Hawk, Deer*
Energy, need to awaken	*Creator, Wabun, Red Hawk*
Enlightenment, seeking	*Creator, Illumination*
Environmental consciousness	*Earth Mother, Cougar, Raven*
Exhaustion	*Thunderbird clan (all), Butterfly clan (all)*
Extroverted, too	*Mudjekeewis, Snake, Introspection*
Failure to learn life lessons	*Experience, Growth*
Faith, lack of	*Creator, Butterfly clan, Snow Goose*
Fearful	*Red Hawk, Sturgeon, Elk, Strength*
Fearlessness	*Thunderbird clan, Red Hawk*
Feminine, needing knowledge of	*Earth Mother, Grandmother Moon, Flicker*
Feminine, too	*Father Sun, Snow Goose*
Flamboyant, too	*Turtle clan, Snow Goose*
Following others	*Mudjekeewis, Red Hawk, Purity*
Gentleness, desiring	*Earth Mother, Grandmother Moon, Flicker, Trust, Love*
Grounded, too	*Cougar, Deer, Flicker, Raven, Snake*
Grounding, lack of	*Turtle clan, Snow Goose, Brown Bear*
Guilt	*Turtle clan (all), Shawnodese, Trust, Love*
Happiness	*Frog clan, Otter, Red Hawk, Love, Trust, Experience*
Harmony	*Beaver, Butterfly clan, Raven*
Hating men	*Father Sun, Grandmother Moon*
Hating self	*Creator, Cleansing, Wisdom, Love, Strength*
Hating women	*Earth Mother, Grandmother Moon*

Hatred	*Flicker, Raven, Love*
Heal, desire to	*Deer*
Healing, emotional	*Shawnodese*
Healing, mental	*Wabun*
Healing, physical	*Waboose*
Healing, spiritual	*Mudjekeewis*
Health, better	*Renewal*
Health, general care	*Creator*
Heartbroken	*Shawnodese*
Holding old patterns	*Cleansing*
Holding on to ideas that hurt you	*Clarity*
Humble, overly	*Thunderbird clan*
Humility, lack of	*Waboose*
Humorless	*Butterfly clan, Shawnodese, Otter*
Hysteria	*Turtle clan, Snow Goose, Brown Bear, Snake*
Idealism, desiring	*Otter, Brown Bear*
Imbalanced	*Raven*
Immature	*Mudjekeewis*
Impatient	*Earth Mother, Turtle clan (all)*
Impractical	*Brown Bear*
Impulse, fear of	*Grandmother Moon, Frog clan*
Inactive	*Thunderbird clan*
Inconsiderate	*Raven*
Indifferent	*Thunderbird clan, Butterfly clan, Cougar, Red Hawk, Deer, Elk*
Indiscriminate	*Father Sun, Turtle clan, Brown Bear*
Infertility	*Earth Mother, Grandmother Moon*
Inflexible	*Cougar, Flicker, Raven*
Inhumane	*Otter, Elk*
Initiation, desiring	*Creator, Grandmother Moon, Snow Goose*
Inner child work	*Butterfly clan, Flicker, Trust*
Insensitive	*Cougar, Flicker, Sturgeon*
Insight, lack of	*Snake, Elk*
Intensity, lack of	*Frog clan, Thunderbird clan*

Nurturing, lack of	*Earth Mother, Shawnodese, Flicker*
Old outlooks	*Renewal*
Optimism, desiring	*Red Hawk, Renewal*
Organization, lacking	*Earth Mother, Turtle clan*
Organized, overly	*Butterfly clan*
Overachieving	*Grandmother Moon, Frog clan*
Overextended	*Turtle clan, Snow Goose*
Overintellectual	*Grandmother Moon, Shawnodese, Flicker*
Paradox, understand	*Waboose*
Parenthood, preparing for	*Earth Mother, Father Sun*
Partner, seeking	*Earth Mother, Father Sun, Grandmother Moon, Frog clan, Shawnodese*
Passion, lack of	*Frog clan, Thunderbird clan, Sturgeon, Snake*
Passion, too much	*Turtle clan, Mudjekeewis*
People, disliking	*Otter, Deer*
Perseverance, lack of	*Turtle clan, Beaver*
Pessimistic	*Wabun, Red Hawk*
Physical abilities, out of touch with	*Waboose*
Physical world, lack of knowledge of	*Creator, Waboose*
Play, inability to	*Butterfly clan, Deer, Otter*
Possessive	*Elk, Trust, Love*
Power, learn about	*Thunderbird clan, Waboose*
Powerless	*Thunderbird clan, Waboose*
Pride	*Sturgeon*
Protection, desiring	*Creator, Earth Mother, Turtle clan, Thunderbird clan, Cougar*
Psychic abilities, improved	*Grandmother Moon, Waboose, Otter*
Purpose, need help with	*Mudjekeewis, Raven*
Purpose, need strength of	*Creator, Mudjkekeewis*
Radiance, lack of	*Thunderbird clan*
Reality, out of touch with own	*Creator, Turtle clan*
Rebirth	*Wabun, Waboose*

Reclusive	*Otter, Red Hawk*
Rejuvenation	*Shawnodese*
Relationship, dealing with	*Shawnodese, Trust, Love*
Relationship, difficulty in	*Shawnodese, Flicker, Trust*
Relationship, fear of	*Grandmother Moon, Elk*
Relationship, looking for	*Shawnodese*
Relationship with the Creator	*Creator, Love*
Resentment	*Brown Bear, Raven, Love*
Reserved, too	*Thunderbird clan, Butterfly clan*
Resigned	*Thunderbird clan, Wabun*
Responsibility, lacking	*Turtle clan, Snow Goose, Brown Bear*
Responsible, too	*Frog clan, Butterfly clan, Otter*
Rut, in a	*Red Hawk, Deer*
Sad	*Thunderbird clan, Otter, Red Hawk*
Scattered	*Beaver*
Seeing only ugliness	*Deer*
Self-control	*Father Sun, Snake, Snow Goose*
Self-doubt	*Waboose, Sturgeon, Snake, Elk*
Selfish	*Waboose*
Self-pity	*Thunderbird clan (all), Butterfly clan (all)*
Self-sufficiency	*Turtle clan*
Sensitivity, desiring	*Grandmother Moon, Flicker*
Sensuality, exploring	*Grandmother Moon, Sturgeon, Snake*
Sexuality, exploring	*Grandmother Moon, Sturgeon, Snake*
Sexual problems	*Grandmother Moon, Shawnodese*
Shadow side, examine	*Grandmother Moon, Flicker, Raven, Snake*
Social consciousness, lacking	*Mudjekeewis, Elk*
Soothing, desiring	*Frog clan, Raven*
Spacy	*Earth Mother, Turtle clan*
Spiritual communication, problem with	*Snake*
Spiritual values, finding	*Creator, Mudjekeewis*

Stability, lacking	*Earth Mother, Turtle clan, Snow Goose*
Stable, too	*Butterfly clan, Thunderbird clan*
Staid, too	*Butterfly clan, Otter, Flicker, Elk*
Strength, need	*Turtle clan, Mudjekeewis, Strength*
Stress, balancing	*Creator, Otter, Deer*
Stubborn	*Frog clan, Butterfly clan*
Stuck	*Grandmother Moon, Frog clan, Butterfly clan, Wabun, Snake, Growth, Experience*
Surrender	*Earth Mother, Grandmother Moon, Frog clan, Flicker, Elk*
Survival, learn about	*Turtle clan*
Tension	*Grandmother Moon, Otter, Deer, Raven*
Thin skinned	*Turtle clan, Strength*
Toxic	*Cleansing*
Tradition, resenting	*Snow Goose*
Tranquility	*Earth Mother, Snow Goose*
Transformation	*All positions*
Transformation, sudden	*Frog clan, Butterfly clan*
Truth, seeking	*Grandmother Moon, Wabun, Clarity, Wisdom, Illumination*
Unaffectionate	*Flicker, Sturgeon, Raven*
Uncertain	*Red Hawk, Sturgeon, Snake*
Uncreative	*Creator, Wabun*
Unemotional	*Frog clan, Cougar, Flicker*
Uninspiring	*Thunderbird clan*
Unity, lack of	*Creator, Purity, Love*
Universal energy, out of touch with	*Creator, Snow Goose*
Unjust	*Elk*
Unlucky	*Beaver*
Unquestioning	*Snake*
Unrooted	*Snow Goose*
Unstable	*Turtle clan*
Verbal, too	*Cougar, Snake*
Verbalizing, trouble	*Butterfly clan, Wabun*

Bibliography

Baker, Mary L. *Whales, Dolphins, and Porpoises of the World.* Garden City, N. Y.: Doubleday & Co., 1987.

Barnett, Lincoln, and Sarel Eimerl. *Wonders of Animal Life.* New York: Golden Press, 1984.

Bertin, Leon. *Larousse Encyclopedia of Animal Life.* New York: Hamlyn, 1971.

Bottley, E. P. *Rocks and Minerals.* New York: G. P. Putnam's Sons, 1969.

Branson, Oscar T. *Fetishes and Carvings of the Southwest.* Tucson, Ariz.: Treasure Chest Publications, 1976.

Burnie, David. *Bird.* New York: Alfred A. Knopf, 1988.

Chambers. *Chambers' Mineralogical Dictionary.* New York: Chemical Publishing Co., Inc., 1964.

Childerhose, R. J., and Trim Marj. *Pacific Salmon.* Seattle, Wash.: University of Washington Press, 1979.

Costello, David F. *The World of the Ant.* New York: J. B. Lippincott Co., 1968.

Dean, Loral. *Animals of North America.* Secaucus, N. J.: Chartwell Books, Inc., 1984.

Eaton, Evelyn. *I Send a Voice.* Wheaton, Ill.: Theosophical Publishing House, 1978.

Eaton, Evelyn. *The Shaman and the Medicine Wheel.* Wheaton, Ill.: Theosophical Publishing House, 1989.

Farrand, John, Jr. *Western Birds.* New York: McGraw-Hill Book Co., 1988.

Firsoff, V. A., and G. I. Firsoff. *The Rockhound's Handbook.* New York: Arco Publishing Co., 1975.

Forsyth, Adrian. *Mammals of the American North.* Ontario: Camden House Publishing Ltd., 1985.

Hamilton, W. R., A. C. Woolley, and A. R. Bishop. *The Henry Holt Guide to Minerals, Rocks and Fossils.* New York: Henry Holt and Co., Inc., 1989.

Hurlbut, Cornelius S., Jr. *Minerals and Man.* New York: Random House, 1968.

Hutchens, Alma R. *Indian Herbology of North America.* Windsor: Merco, 1968.

Kunz, George Frederick. *The Curious Lore of Precious Stones.* New York: Dover Publications, Inc., 1971.

Lopez, Barry Holstun. *Of Wolves and Men.* New York: Charles Scribner's Sons, 1978.

Medembach, Olaf, and Harry Wilk. *The Magic of Minerals.* Berlin: Springer-Verlag, 1986.

Mertens Robert. *The World of Amphibians and Reptiles.* New York: McGraw-Hill Book Co., Inc., 1960.

Nero, Robert W. *The Great Gray Owl.* Washington, D.C.: The Smithsonian Institution Press, 1980.

Newman, L. Hugh. *Ants from Close Up.* New York: Thomas Y. Crowell Co., 1967.

Perrins, Christopher, and C. J. O. Harrison. *Birds, Their Life—Their Ways—Their World.* Pleasantville, N. Y.: The Reader's Digest Association, Inc., 1979.

Ransom, Jay Ellis. *Gems and Minerals of America.* New York: Harper & Row, 1974.

Sinkankas, John. *Gemstones of North America.* New York: Van Nostrand Reinhold Co., 1959.

Skutch, Alexander F., and Arthur B. Singer. *The Life of the Hummingbird.* New York: Vineyard Books, Inc., 1973.

Sun Bear. *At Home in the Wilderness.* Happy Camp, Calif.: Naturegraph Publishers, 1968.

Sun Bear. *Buffalo Hearts.* Spokane, Wash.: Bear Tribe Publishing, 1976.

Sun Bear, Crysalis Mulligan, Peter Nufer, and Wabun. *Walk in Balance.* New York: Prentice Hall Press, 1989.

Sun Bear and Wabun. *The Medicine Wheel: Earth Astrology.* New York: Prentice Hall Press, 1980.

Sun Bear, with Wabun Wind. *Black Dawn/Bright Day.* Spokane, Wash.: Bear Tribe Publishing, 1990.

Sun Bear and Wabun, with Nimimosha. *The Bear Tribe's Self-Reliance Book.* New York: Prentice Hall Press, 1988.

Sun Bear, Wabun, and Barry Weinstock. *Sun Bear: The Path of Power.* New York: Prentice Hall Press, 1987.

Wind, Wabun. *Woman of the Dawn.* New York: Prentice Hall Press, 1989.

Wind, Wabun, and Anderson Reed. *Lightseeds.* New York: Prentice Hall Press, 1988.

Index

227

For More Information

If you would like more information about Medicine Wheel Gatherings, the Earthstone Institute, or the Bear Tribe and its programs, write

The Bear Tribe
P.O. Box 9167
Spokane, WA 99209-9167

If you would like more information about Sun Bear's schedule and activities write

Jaya Bear
P.O. Box 9167
Spokane, WA 99209-9167

If you would like more information about Wabun Wind's activities, including Medicine Wheel consultation courses, write

Wind Communications
16149 Redmond Way, Suite 308
Redmond, WA 98052

If you would like more information about workshops and activities sponsored by Crysalis Mulligan write

Crysalis Mulligan
W. 1727 Northwest Boulevard, #33
Spokane, WA 99205

Enclose a stamped, self-addressed, business-size envelope if you would like a reply. Tapes of the exercises and chants referred to in this book are available from:

Bear Tribe Publishing
P.O. Box 9167
Spokane, WA 99209-9167

About the Authors

Sun Bear, a sacred teacher of Chippewa descent, is the founder and medicine chief of the Bear Tribe, a multiracial educational society. He is a world-renowned lecturer and teacher and the author or coauthor of eight books. He is publisher of the magazine *Wildfire* and founder of the World Earth Fund.

Wabun Wind is the author or coauthor of nine books, a lecturer, ceremonialist, transpersonal practitioner, wife, and mother. She holds an M.S. from the Columbia School of Journalism and has written for a wide variety of publications. She is a contributing editor to *Wildfire* and is on the board of advisers for *Women of Power* magazine, the World Earth Fund, and the Bear Tribe. She teaches professionals how to give Medicine Wheel and Earthstone consultations.

Crysalis Mulligan is a ceremonialist, earth medicine practitioner, and healer. She is coauthor of *Walk in Balance,* an avid environmentalist, conservationist, founder of the Nurture Nature Program, mineral specialist, and sponsor of personal healing/transformation/earth medicine workshops and the Wilderness/Crystal Mining Expeditions.